S0-BCK-568

The INFORMED, Performer's DIRECTORY
OF INSTRUCTION
FOR THE
Performing Arts

Avon Books are available at special quantity discounts for bulk purchases for sales promotions, premiums, fund raising or educational use. Special books, or book excerpts, can also be created to fit specific needs.

For details write or telephone the office of the Director of Special Markets, Avon Books, Dept. FP, 1790 Broadway, New York, New York 10019, 212-399-1357. *IN CANADA:* Director of Special Sales, Avon Books of Canada, Suite 210, 2061 McCowan Rd., Scarborough, Ontario M1S 3Y6, 416-293-9404.

The INFORMED, Performer's DIRECTORY OF INSTRUCTION FOR THE Performing Arts

KAT SMITH

AVON
PUBLISHERS OF BARD, CAMELOT, DISCUS AND FLARE BOOKS

THE INFORMED PERFORMER'S DIRECTORY
OF INSTRUCTION FOR THE PERFORMING ARTS
IS AN ORIGINAL PUBLICATION OF AVON BOOKS.
THIS WORK HAS NEVER BEFORE APPEARED IN BOOK FORM.

AVON BOOKS
A DIVISION OF
THE HEARST CORPORATION
1790 BROADWAY
NEW YORK, NEW YORK 10019

COPYRIGHT © 1981 BY KAREN J. SMITH
PUBLISHED BY ARRANGEMENT WITH THE AUTHOR
LIBRARY OF CONGRESS CATALOG CARD NUMBER: 84-045880
ISBN: 0-380-89804-7

ALL RIGHTS RESERVED, WHICH INCLUDES THE RIGHT TO
REPRODUCE THIS BOOK OR PORTIONS THEREOF IN ANY FORM
WHATSOEVER EXCEPT AS PROVIDED BY THE U.S. COPYRIGHT LAW.
FOR INFORMATION ADDRESS ELLEN LEVINE LITERARY AGENCY
432 PARK AVENUE SOUTH, NEW YORK, NEW YORK 10016.

FIRST AVON PRINTING, JULY 1985

AVON TRADEMARK REG. U.S. PAT. OFF. AND IN
OTHER COUNTRIES, MARCA REGISTRADA, HECHO EN
U.S.A.

PRINTED IN THE U.S.A.

OPB 10 9 8 7 6 5 4 3 2 1

To Velma, Elwin & Arlene

CONTENTS

Explanatory Notes   ix

NEW YORK

Acting   3

Dance   57

Speech   99

Voice   119

Miscellaneous   165

Young People   193

CALIFORNIA

All Disciplines   207

REGIONAL

All Disciplines   231

Index   245

EXPLANATORY NOTES

This, the second edition of *The Informed Performer's Directory of Instruction for the Performing Arts,* is offered to the newcomer and professional performer as an objective guide to a variety of performing arts classes available in New York City, California, and around the country.

A special effort was made to cover as wide a variety of instruction as possible in all disciplines, at all levels, from all schools of thought. Tastes in educational approaches are subjective, especially in subjects related to the arts. I therefore chose to include as wide a cross section as possible to avoid making apparent any personal biases.

HOW INFORMATION WAS COMPILED

All information in this directory was obtained through written questionnaires and brochures supplied by the schools. Each school was questioned uniformly; where information is lacking, it is an omission on the part of the school. What information the school chose not to include may provide as much insight as what information was volunteered.

HOW TO READ THE LISTINGS

The listings are, for the most part, self-explanatory, but the following information may be helpful.

ADDRESS: Some private instructors teach in their homes, and addresses were omitted at their request. Whenever possible, a neighborhood is indicated in its place.

ESTABLISHED: The year the school commenced business is included as a potential indicator of the school's stability. While many young schools offer new and valid instructional alternatives, longevity in this competitive field may be considered a sign of managerial competency.

FEES: This, as well as all information in the directory, is current as of the date of publication, but subject to change at the school's discretion. These statistics are best employed as a tool for comparison; updated information should be obtained from the school.

AUDIT: Policies regarding auditing a class vary, depending upon the nature of the class and personal preference of the instructor. Many schools do allow an observer to sit in on a class in which he or she is considering enrollment. Generally, auditors do not participate in the class. Auditing is usually by special arrangement with the instructor; fees and restrictions are listed.

CANCELLATIONS: Due to the unpredictability of the typical performer's life (auditions and interviews, a changing work status, out-of-town shows, etc.), the school's cancellation policies can be of substantial importance. Information here includes refund and notification policies, penalties, make-ups, etc.

SCHOLARSHIPS: This denotes schools with private and/or federal scholarships available to students with financial need. Often programs are available where a student may offer his services (sweeping the studio, answering phones, keeping roll, etc.) in exchange for free or discounted classes.

FACILITIES: For physically demanding classes, such as dance or mime, etc., the number of dressing rooms, availability of showers, and type of floor may be of importance. The number of studios may indicate sufficient warm-up space for dancers, or potential rehearsal areas for actors. While all schools offering television and/or film courses indicated the availability of video equipment, fewer offer cue-card systems, which can be of value in some classes. Students may wish to purchase their video cassettes to submit to agents or casting directors, and schools which permit the purchase of cassettes are noted.

WAITING AREA: The availability of a waiting area where incoming students may organize and prepare is important to a smooth transition between dance classes or private vocal classes, etc.

ACCOMPANIST/ACCOMPANIMENT: Some students appreciate the presence of a professional accompanist, as they feel this frees the instructor to give full attention to his or her progress. Others prefer the privacy of working with the instructor/accompanist alone and feel this may afford more lenient cancellation policies and less expensive fees. For dance classes, the type of accompaniment is indicated (piano, drums, records, etc.).

CASSETTE: A number of voice and/or speech instructors provide prerecorded vocal-exercise cassettes, while others simply allow the student to record each lesson for the student's home practice.

CLASS SIZE: Enrollment is unlimited unless otherwise noted.

BREAKDOWN: A breakdown of students according to sex, age, and length of study is intended to offer insight into the character of the classes and/or the clientele the instructor is most experienced with. These figures are approximations.

DESCRIPTION: Each school was asked to describe its goals, the means exercised to achieve those goals, as well as whatever description would clarify for the reader the nature of the classes.

SUMMATION STATEMENT: This was given in response to a request for a summation of the teaching philosophy of the school. The summation is intended to offer some illumination of a school's personality, its preferences and prejudices.

Every attempt was made to represent fairly other major cities throughout the United States and Canada. All who responded satisfactorily to the questionnaire were included. The ratio in the Directory of New York/California instructors to regional instructors is perhaps not too disproportionate to what is, in reality, available throughout the country. This is not to say that there is not a wealth of talent and knowledge to be had outside the bicoastal capitals of this industry, as is evidenced by the "regional invasion" seen on Broadway in recent years. Many performers choose to live in areas of the country where competition is somewhat reduced and where one may hook up with a good acting company and work one's way up through the ranks. In these areas it appears practical hands-on experience is more readily available than private instruction.

A number of theatres, dance and opera companies throughout the country which do not offer performance internships do offer internships in other areas—administration, business management, stage management, technical production, dramaturgy/literary management, marketing/development. Usually these internships are unpaid positions requiring full-time commitments, although certain theatres may offer a limited number of stipends. Academic credit is usually available. Among such theatres are the Guthrie Theatre in Minneapolis, Minnesota; the Arena Theatre in Washington, D.C.; the Seattle Repertory Theatre in Seattle, Washington; the Wisdom Bridge Theatre in Chicago, Illinois; the Mark Taper Forum in Los Angeles, California; the Alliance Theatre in Atlanta, Georgia; and the Actors Theatre of Louisville in Kentucky. Those interested in such a program should write to the director of internships of the area of your choice.

Still another alternative to private instruction is university theatre/dance/voice. Outside of careers in education, most performers discover upon entering the professional arena college degrees are seldom mentioned on a professional resume. What universities do offer, however, is the opportunity for hands-on training—the chance to do shows and concerts that it may take years to earn the right to do in the professional world. Most performers find, however, that they must supplement their university training with private instruction at some point in their careers. However, there are those select universities whose programs are not only useful, but perhaps a better training ground (as well as foot-in-the-door) than many private instructors—most notably Yale and Julliard, as well as Rutgers and Carnegie-Mellon. A growing number of universities are offering educational programs in conjunction with regional theatres, such as DePaul University in Chicago, which offers accredited programs in association with the Goodman Theatre; Florida State University in Tallahassee, which works with the Asolo Theatre in Sarasota; and New York University, which has an accreditation program with Circle in the Square in New York City.

The INFORMED Performer's DIRECTORY OF INSTRUCTION FOR THE Performing Arts

NEW YORK
NEW YORK
NEW YORK
NEW YORK
NEW YORK
NEW YORK
NEW YORK
NEW YORK
NEW YORK
NEW YORK
NEW YORK

ACTING
ACTING
ACTING
ACTING
ACTING
ACTING
ACTING
ACTING
ACTING
ACTING
ACTING
ACTING
ACTING
ACTING
ACTING
ACTING
ACTING
ACTING
ACTING
ACTING
ACTING
ACTING
ACTING
ACTING
ACTING
ACTING

ACT FOR FUN

Sara Lavner, Director
Amity Arts Center
22 West 15th Street
New York, NY 10011
(212) 674-4045

PROGRAM:	Acting Technique
INSTRUCTOR:	Sara Lavner
ESTABLISHED:	1977
REGISTRATION FEE:	None
CLASS FEE:	$12 per class
SCHEDULE:	1 2-hour class per week, ongoing
AUDITING:	Permitted
AUDITING FEE:	No fee
ENTRANCE REQUIREMENTS:	Interview
CANCELLATION POLICIES:	Make-up sessions available
SCHOLARSHIPS:	Not available
NUMBER OF STUDENTS PER CLASS:	Limited to 8–10
TOTAL STUDIO ENROLLMENT:	30
STUDENT BREAKDOWN:	50% female, 50% male; 10% 18–25, 40% 26–35, 40% 36–45, 10% over 45
VIDEO EQUIPMENT:	Yes
VIDEO CASSETTES:	Students may purchase their video cassettes.
CUE-CARD SYSTEM:	No
STUDIOS:	One
DRESSING ROOMS:	Yes
BIOGRAPHY:	MS. LAVNER attended the Performing Arts High School, has a B.A. in Speech and Theatre from Brooklyn College, and is a member of SAG and AEA. She has created roles at Manhattan Theatre Club, Theatre for the New City, and at Cafe La-Mama, among others.
CLASS:	The main purpose of the class is to experience again, as openly as children, freedom with one's imagination and play via theatre games and impro-visations. All exercises are centered around "doing," or accomplishing, something in order to give a focus and lose self-consciousness.
SUMMATION STATEMENT:	"I began teaching because I realized that most adults had no outlet for the actor in themselves. As children, we all played Cowboys and Indians eas-ily. But as we became adults, there was little chance to experience that kind of freedom of imag-

ination. Therefore, this class affords the opportunity for the person who wants to learn what acting is about without the pressure of an advanced class. The class is a mixture of beginners who are doing this for a hobby and others who want to go on and act professionally. The class does perform a few times a year so that everyone can have the experience of using what they have learned in front of an audience."

ACTORS AND DIRECTORS LAB

412 West 42nd Street
New York, NY 10036
(212) 695–5429

PROGRAM:	Beginning Acting, Acting I–IV, Scene Study, Workshop, Acting Technique for the Experienced Actor, Movement
INSTRUCTORS:	John Stix, Candace Derra, Jack Garfein, Audrey Jung
ESTABLISHED:	1978
SCHEDULE:	1 2–4 hour session per week, 12 weeks, ongoing
AUDITING:	Permitted after interview
ENTRANCE REQUIREMENTS:	By interview and audition for advanced classes
CANCELLATION POLICIES:	Advance notice required, make-up available
STUDIOS:	8, and theatre
DRESSING ROOMS:	Yes
WAITING AREA:	Yes
BIOGRAPHY:	MR. STIX directed the Broadway production of *The Price* and *Family Business* Off Broadway. Helen Hayes chose him to direct *Mary Rose,* which she produced. Other Broadway shows include *What Every Woman Knows, The Wisteria Trees,* and *Too Late the Phalarope.* MR. GARFEIN's Broadway credits include *End as a Man, Girls of Summer, Shadow of a Gunman.* He produced the first major productions of *The Price* and *The American Clock,* both of which were invited to the Spoleto Festival and later opened on Broadway. MS. DERRA has appeared Off Broadway in leading roles at the Harold Clurman, Actors Studio, Shelter West, and the Mark Taper Forum. Film

CLASSES:

credits include *I Never Promised You a Rose Garden* and *He Wanted Her Back.*

Beginning Acting—The principles and application of remembered emotion through the use of the imagination and the 5 senses. We also deal with the problems of concentration, personalization, improvisation, play analysis, personal/physical characterization, etc. Experienced—This intensive 9-month program takes the actor from basic exercises through script analysis and scene study. Scene Study—This class gives actors the chance to work on specific problems through scene work. In the classroom, the actor can take the time and risks which brief rehearsal periods and the demands of the professional theatre do not allow. Movement—Students use breathing techniques and choreographed movement sequences to increase flexibility, strength, and coordination in order to evoke mood and character through a greater awareness of placement and timing.

SUMMATION STATEMENT:

"All art is personal and its value is measured by its inner content. However, without training, a truly responsive performance becomes less likely and more difficult to attain. The lab teaches the artist to observe life, and encourages him to illuminate the nature of man through behavior."

ACTORS INFORMATION PROJECT

Jay Perry, David Rosen, Directors
244 West 49th Street, 3rd floor
New York, NY 10019
(212) 245–4690

PROGRAM:	Casting Workshops, Career Support Intensives, Full-Day Workshops
ESTABLISHED:	1979
CLASS FEES:	Initial membership (valid 6 months) $150; renewal (valid 6 months) $60; classes $5–10 for members
SCHEDULE:	3-hour sessions, 10 weeks
AUDITING:	Nonmembers may audit 1 workshop.
AUDITING FEE:	No fee
ENTRANCE REQUIREMENTS:	To participate in classes, students must become a member.

SCHOLARSHIPS:	Not available
NUMBER OF STUDENTS PER CLASS:	20
STUDENT BREAKDOWN:	50% female, 50% male; 2% under 18, 40% 18–25, 40% 26–35, 10% 36–45, 8% over 45
BIOGRAPHY:	MR. PERRY is the vice-president of the Eastside Theatre Corporation and a teacher of actor/director communication at the Actors Institute. MR. ROSEN worked as an assistant and as an agent for Monty Silver, Michael Bloom, and Ann Wright.
CLASSES:	Full-Day Workshops help the actor define career goals, look at himself or herself as a business, examine how the business works, investigate marketing strategies, confront his or her presentation, and set up support systems. The Audition Workshops are designed to help the actor work on audition technique, and to find out as much as possible about who the agents and casting directors are and what they need from you to make contacts. Career Support Intensives are created to get results in commercial or theatrical areas using the power of the group to get farther, faster than you can on your own.
SUMMATION STATEMENT:	"Acting is an art; finding work is a business. You need to incorporate your creativity in the business end of your career in order to keep your whole self involved and satisfied. Actors generally like to work with other people, not alone. Working with other actors on the business is aligned with most actors' purposes."

THE ACTORS INSTITUTE

Dan Fauci, Director
5 West 19th Street, 3rd floor
New York, NY 10011
(212) 924–8888

PROGRAM:	Technique/Scene Study, Sensory Technique, Technique
INSTRUCTORS:	David Kagen, Madeline Thornton-Sherwood, Kate McGregor-Stewart
ESTABLISHED:	1977
CLASS FEE:	$50 per month

SCHEDULE:	1 4-hour session per week, ongoing
AUDITING:	Permitted
SCHOLARSHIPS:	Not available
NUMBER OF STUDENTS PER CLASS:	15–25
STUDENT BREAKDOWN:	50% female, 50% male; 2% under 18, 45% 18–25, 45% 26–35, 5% 36–45, 3% over 45; 40% under 6 months, 40% 1/2–1 year, 20% 1–2 years, 0% over 2 years
VIDEO EQUIPMENT:	Yes
STUDIOS:	4
DRESSING ROOMS:	Yes
WAITING AREA:	Yes
SUMMATION STATEMENT:	"We believe that the student is the creator of his or her own creativity and that one can generate and regenerate inspiration on the spot. Emphasis on alive, emotional stagework reaching the audience —communication outward is the key goal. We do not want students dependent on us forever—we want them out in the business, working."

ACTORS TRAINING AND ACTING THERAPY CENTER OF AMERICA

Jerome Walman
Box 31, FDR Station
New York, NY 10150
(212) 832–6659

PROGRAM:	Acting (Scene Study, Speech, Voice, Diction, Auditioning)
INSTRUCTOR:	Jerome Walman
ESTABLISHED:	1964
REGISTRATION FEE:	$25
CLASS FEES:	$150; $50 per 2-hour private session
SCHEDULE:	One 2-hour session per week, 10 weeks
AUDITING:	Permitted
AUDITING FEE:	$15
ENTRANCE REQUIREMENTS:	Open
CANCELLATION POLICIES:	24-hour notice for private; 1 make-up for group
SCHOLARSHIPS:	Partial work-exchange scholarships available.
NUMBER OF STUDENTS PER CLASS:	10
STUDENT BREAKDOWN:	50% female, 50% male; 15% under 18, 20%

	18–25, 30% 26–35, 25% 36–45, 10% over 45; 10% 1/2–1 year, 20% 1–2 years, 40% 2–3 years, 30% over 3 years
VIDEO EQUIPMENT:	Yes
STUDIOS:	2
ACCOMPANYING INSTRUMENT:	Piano
CLASS CARD:	5 classes, valid 6 months
VOCAL CASSETTES:	Provided
ACCOMPANIST:	Instructor accompanies
WAITING AREA:	No
BIOGRAPHY:	MR. WALMAN has worked with writers, performers, and directors for over 20 years. On Broadway, Off Broadway, and in film. He is the author of *Moment* and has been a psychotherapist in New York City for 20 years.
CLASS:	The class is a unique approach to the actor-singer as a whole being, starting from internal processes and establishing a coordinated whole, known as the professional performer.
SUMMATION STATEMENT:	"Acting as therapy and acting is therapy. It is impossible to have one without the other. Being a professional in both areas, we are able to integrate the whole."

STELLA ADLER CONSERVATORY OF ACTING

130 West 56th Street
New York, NY 10019
(212) 246–1195

PROGRAM:	Full-Time Program: Term 1—Technique I, Speech I, Shakespeare I, Movement I; Term 2—Technique II, Speech II, Shakespeare II, Movement II; Term 3—Script Interpretation, Scenes, Rehearsal Technique, Improvisation, Styles
REGISTRATION FEE:	$25 nonrefundable registration fee
CLASS FEES:	$275–$375 per class
SCHEDULE:	Fall and spring—15 weeks, day and evening sessions; summer—6 weeks, day and evening sessions
AUDITING:	Not permitted
ENTRANCE REQUIREMENTS:	Interview

CANCELLATION POLICIES: No refunds
SCHOLARSHIPS: Not available
SUMMATION STATEMENT: "This 2-year program leads the actor through specific stages designed to develop the innate resources that make the actor a master of his instrument. These classes will equip the actor with the technique necessary to create a character; to grasp the author's fundamental purpose; to execute, with creativity and ease, any role assigned; and to fulfill professional responsibilities."

AESTHETIC REALISM FOUNDATION, INC.

Dorothy Koppelman, Director
141 Greene Street (near Houston Street)
New York, NY 10012
(212) 777–4490

PROGRAM: Aesthetic Realism and Acting
INSTRUCTOR: Anne Fielding
ESTABLISHED: 1981
CLASS FEE: $35
SCHEDULE: 1 2-hour session every two weeks, ongoing
SCHOLARSHIPS: Available
NUMBER OF STUDENTS
  PER CLASS: Limited to 25
CLASS: The basis of this course is in the following quotes by Eli Siegel, from the Aesthetic Realism Acting Lesson: "According to Aesthetic Realism, acting shows that you don't have to be fettered to yourself. You can be other people. . . . Acting is a certain way of taking the contraries of the world. It is a way of being somebody else for the purpose of coming back home immediately. You take a trip in order to find out who you are." Scenes, improvisations, and papers are written in relation to Eli Siegel's "Is Beauty the Making One of Opposites?"; "Aesthetic Realism as Beauty: Acting"; and "We Are Emotion."

AMERICAN ACADEMY OF DRAMATIC ARTS

120 Madison Avenue
New York, NY 10016
(212) 686–9244

PROGRAM:	Acting I–V; Voice and Speech I–III; Movement I–III; Theatre History; Styles I–II; Makeup; Individual Correction and Development; Rehearsal and Performance
ESTABLISHED:	1884
REGISTRATION FEE:	$35 nonrefundable
CLASS FEE:	$2,710 per academic year
SCHEDULE:	September–May, February–August
ENTRANCE REQUIREMENTS:	By audition
SCHOLARSHIPS:	Grants, loans, and employment to assist students
NUMBER OF STUDENTS PER CLASS:	10–16
STUDIOS:	Classrooms, rehearsal halls, dance studios
DRESSING ROOMS:	Yes
WAITING AREA:	Lounge

AMERICAN MUSICAL AND DRAMATIC ACADEMY

2109 Broadway
New York, NY 10023
(212) 787–5300

PROGRAM:	Acting I–IV, Improvisation, Theatre Games, Rituals, Masks, Theatre Pieces, Technique, Textual Analysis, Scene Study, Voice and Speech I–IV, Musical Theatre Styles I–IV, Recital, Individual Voice I–IV, Dance I–IV, Jazz, Modern, Dance Styles, Dramatic Movement, Showcase
INSTRUCTORS:	Beryl Smith-Durham, Carol Kastendieck, Harry Woolever, John DeBlas, Karen Gustafson, David St. James, James Stenborg, Richard Gordon, John Lenahan, Dee Etta Rowe, Florence Bowe, Norman Carlberg, Joan Davis, Helene Guilet, Barbara Maier, Sue Starck, Helen Trezlie

ESTABLISHED:	1964
REGISTRATION FEE:	$35 nonrefundable
CLASS FEE:	$3,000 per academic year
SCHEDULE:	4 15-week terms
ENTRANCE REQUIREMENTS:	Application, interview, audition
SCHOLARSHIPS:	Work-study available
STUDIOS:	Classrooms, dance studios, voice studios, theatre
DRESSING ROOMS:	Yes
SUMMATION STATEMENT:	"AMDA offers to both beginning and professional performers integrated and intensive training for the modern theatre. AMDA is designed to bridge the gap between the artistic demands made on today's successful performer and the incompleteness of the training programs available to beginners, and is coordinated to provide equal emphasis on drama, music, and dance."

AMERICAN RENAISSANCE THEATRE

Robert Elston, Artistic Director
112 Charlton Street
New York, NY 10014
(212) 929–4718

PROGRAM:	Scene Study, Musical Comedy and Opera
INSTRUCTOR:	Robert Elston
ESTABLISHED:	1974
CLASS FEES:	$24–$28 for 4 weeks
SCHEDULE:	1 2-hour session per week
AUDITING:	Permitted
AUDITING FEE:	$3
ENTRANCE REQUIREMENTS:	Open
SCHOLARSHIPS:	Not available
NUMBER OF STUDENTS PER CLASS:	Average 10–15, limited to 20
STUDENT BREAKDOWN:	50% female, 50% male; 10% under 18, 40% 18–25, 40% 26–35, 10% 36–45; 25% under 6 months, 25% 1–2 years, 25% 2–3 years, 25% over 3 years
CLASSES:	Scene Study includes technique, monologue, improvisation. Every student works every week. Musical Comedy and Opera covers how to break down an aria, a song, and a scene for emotional content, physical acting, and musical style. The

class is designed for musical comedy and cabaret performers, and opera singers.

LESLIE HOBAN BLAKE

Chelsea Area
(212) 255–2234

PROGRAM:	Private: Scene Study; Audition Preparation—Classical, Shakespeare; Contemporary Monologues
ESTABLISHED:	1974
REGISTRATION FEE:	None
CLASS FEE:	$25
SCHEDULE:	1-hour sessions by appointment, ongoing
AUDITING:	Not permitted
ENTRANCE REQUIREMENTS:	Audition
CANCELLATION POLICIES:	With prior notice, make-up available
SCHOLARSHIPS:	Full and partial, work-exchange as member of technical crew for showcase
STUDENT BREAKDOWN:	50% female, 50% male; 5% under 18, 15% 18–25, 60% 26–35, 10% 36–45, 10% over 45; 15% under 6 months, 60% 1/2–1 year, 20% 1–2 years, 5% 2–3 years
CLASS CARD:	10-class card available, valid 1 year
BIOGRAPHY:	MS. BLAKE has been a coach for 10 years, an actress for 12 years, and a director for 3 years. She has studied at the Royal Shakespeare Company in England and appeared/directed with/for the Riverside Shakespeare Company, Bandwagon Productions, Quaigh Dramathon, Off-Off Broadway Festival, and the Alabama Shakespeare Festival. She presently directs 5 or 6 showcases and 8 or 9 readings per year through the Dramatists Guild, Women in Theatre, and New Playwrights.
CLASSES:	Every actor and every actress is an individual. Pieces are selected based on the persona of the performer (not from an audition book). The class is not acting per se, but assistance in getting working actors more work. Scripts are chosen, analyzed, and staged in a professional manner.
SUMMATION STATEMENT:	"I am a professional working with other professionals. I will not take money from someone who can-

not act—but if you have skills already, I will hone and expand them with you. Acting/coaching/directing is a collaborative venture—together we will get the next job for you. I also understand how auditions are viewed by directors. I have a *working* attitude."

BOND STREET THEATRE COALITION

Patrick Sciarratta, Artistic Director
2 Bond Street
New York, NY 10012
(212) 254–4616

PROGRAM:	Apprentice Program
INSTRUCTOR:	Patrick Sciarratta
REGISTRATION FEE:	$50 deposit applied toward total fee
CLASS FEE:	$350
SCHEDULE:	3 4-to-5-hour workshops per week, 2½ months
STUDENT BREAKDOWN:	50% female, 50% male; 10% under 18, 60% 18–25, 30% 26–35, 0% over 35; 20% under 6 months, 20% ½–1 year, 55% 1–2 years, 5% 2–3 years, 0% over 3 years
STUDIOS:	3
BIOGRAPHY:	MR. SCIARRATTA's theatre training has included study with Jerzy Grotowski and the Polish Lab Theatre, and with the Polish Mime Ballet Theatre; he also trained at the Institut for Scenkonst in Sweden; and with Colombioni, Carlo Mazzone-Clementi, and Mamako Yoneamo. He has professional faculty affiliations with many state universities and has written over 20 plays, most of which have been professionally produced.
CLASSES:	Relaxation, vigorous warm-up, basic Linklater vocal techniques, mime and juggling as focus/concentration exercises, theatre games, observation and improvisation, mask work, development of style and principles of ensemble technique as it applies to urban folk theatre.

BRITISH-AMERICAN ACTING ACADEMY

Michael Schulman, Director
28 East 10th Street
New York, NY 10003
(212) 777-3055

PROGRAM:	Full-time Program
INSTRUCTORS:	Michael Schulman, Brian Carter
ESTABLISHED:	1978
REGISTRATION FEE:	None
CLASS FEES:	September to May—$2,950; January to June—$2,450; summer (6 weeks)—$675 in New York City and London (lodging available for $550)
ENTRANCE REQUIREMENTS:	By audition, applicants 18 years of age and older
SCHOLARSHIPS:	Not available
NUMBER OF STUDENTS PER CLASS:	Limited to 18
STUDENT BREAKDOWN:	50% female, 50% male; 40% 18–25, 40% 26–35, 10% 36–45, 10% over 45
STUDIOS:	4
DRESSING ROOMS:	Yes
SHOWERS:	Yes
FLOOR:	Wood floor for dance classes
ACCOMPANYING INSTRUMENT:	Piano
BIOGRAPHY:	MR. SCHULMAN, New York director, has taught at the Strasberg Institute, The Actors Studio, LAMDA Faculty Summer Workshop. He is a professional director and playwright and the author of *Contemporary Scenes for Student Actors*. He is an assistant professor at Fordham and Rutgers universities. MR. BRIAN CARTER, London director, has worked as a professional actor and director at the Old Vic, Edinburgh Festival, ITV, BTA. He is the artistic director of the Adeline Genee Theatre and of the National Operatic and Dramatic Society.
CLASSES:	Students will be scheduled for 20 to 25 hours of classes per week, Monday through Friday, mornings or afternoons. The training is intensive and our faculty works very closely with each student. While the focus of training is on developing and refining the actor's essential craft rather than on

production, public performance projects are included in the 18-month program. In addition to classes, the exploration of the theatrical and cultural heritages of London and New York is an important part of the educational experience the program seeks to provide. The student will work in every class, and will do exercises, improvisations, monologues, and scenes. There are both group and individual exercises, and all exercises are designed to be directly applicable to scene work. Exercise work is structured in a series of progressively advancing steps, and includes sensory, emotional, and character exercises. Scenes progress from basic realities to scenes demanding advanced character and dialect work. Scene analysis, stages of rehearsal, and audition technique are covered.

SUMMATION STATEMENT: "The acting technique combines basic Stanslavski and 'method' emphases on the creation of reality with equally important development and intensification of the actor's physical and vocal expressiveness. It synthesizes the major elements of these traditions into a new method-acting technique. The goal of all programs is to develop actors who can create authentic and passionate characters and who are prepared for the entire theatrical repertory. We believe our programs are unique and fill a long-standing gap in the systematic training of the actor."

CIRCLE IN THE SQUARE THEATRE SCHOOL

E. Colin O'Leary, Director
1633 Broadway
New York, NY 10019
(212) 307-2700

PROGRAM: Professional Workshop
INSTRUCTORS: B.H. Barry (Stage Combat); Edward Berkeley (Text); Jacqueline Brookes, Barbara Colton, Terese Hayden, Peter Thompson (Acting Technique); Richard Ericson (Speech); Kenneth Frankel, Michael Kahn, Alan Langdon, Nikos Psacharo-

poulos, Maria Tucci (Scene Study); Linda Gates, Lucille Rubin (Speech and Voice); Larry Moss, Martha Schlamme (Singing Interpretation); Elizabeth Parrish (Voice); Nora Peterson, Albert Stephenson (Jazz Dance); Marjorie Phillips (Speech, Voice, Shakespeare Text); V. William Reed (Singing Technique); Mina Yakim, Moni Yakim, Randolyn Zinn (Movement); Stephen Zuckerman (Directors Lab)

ESTABLISHED:	1962
REGISTRATION FEES:	None. Audition fee—Professional Workshop $25; Summer Workshop $10
CLASS FEES:	Professional Workshop $3,750; Summer Workshop $850
SCHEDULE:	Professional Workshop—5 days per week, 28 weeks; second year by invitation; Summer Workshop—22 hours per week, 7 weeks
AUDITING:	Not permitted
ENTRANCE REQUIREMENTS:	Application, interview, audition
CANCELLATION POLICIES:	Refunds available on prorated basis prior to third week of program. Nonreturnable services fee of $350 will be deducted.
SCHOLARSHIPS:	Not available
NUMBER OF STUDENTS PER CLASS:	Limited to 18
TOTAL STUDIO ENROLLMENT:	75
STUDENT BREAKDOWN:	50% female, 50% male; 0% under 18, 80% 18–25, 20% 26–35, 0% over 35; 0% under 6 months, 0% 1/2–1 year, 100% 1–2 years
STUDIOS:	8–10
DRESSING ROOMS:	Yes
SHOWERS:	Yes
FLOOR:	Wood
ACCOMPANYING INSTRUMENT:	Piano
VOCAL CASSETTES:	Students are permitted to record vocal sessions.
ACCOMPANIST:	Provided
WAITING AREA:	Yes
CLASSES:	Classes include: Scene Study, Acting Technique, Stage Combat, Singing Interpretation, Speech and Voice, Text, Movement, Modern Dance, Jazz Dance, Styles, Directors Lab, and seminars where professional actors, directors, and playwrights relate their theatre experiences and answer students' questions.
SUMMATION STATEMENT:	"We believe strongly in an eclectic curriculum inorder to expose students to different acting styles

and to different viewpoints on those styles. Our program provides individual attention in small classes. Each program is structured and designed to develop style and technique with primary emphasis on the actor's individual capability, and to develop awareness of the subjective as well as the objective aspects of intentional communication. The Theatre School is associated with the Circle in the Square Theatre."

BOB COLLIER SUCCESS SEMINARS

Bob Collier, Director
200 West 57th Street
New York, NY 10019
(212) 582–0091/582–0092

PROGRAM:	2-Week Crash Course in Commercials; Audition Experience I–II; Commercial Improvisation; Soap Opera, Voice-Over
INSTRUCTOR:	Bob Collier
REGISTRATION FEE:	$25 for introductory qualifying lesson
CLASS FEE:	$370; Audition Experience $250
SCHEDULE:	1 or 2 1 1/2–hour sessions per week, 5 weeks
ENTRANCE REQUIREMENTS:	Qualifying lesson
CANCELLATION POLICIES:	24-hour notice
SCHOLARSHIPS:	Some working scholarships available
NUMBER OF STUDENTS PER CLASS:	3–6
VIDEO EQUIPMENT:	Color, 3/4-inch
VIDEO CASSETTES:	Students may purchase video cassettes.
CUE-CARD SYSTEM:	Yes
STUDIOS:	2
BIOGRAPHY:	MR. COLLIER has worked in television, radio, films, and theatre in every capacity, including agent, casting director, producer, and director. His more than 35 years of experience includes work with 3 networks and on thousands of television commercials.
CLASSES:	The goal of every class is to prepare performers to win auditions in television commercials, voice-overs, and soap operas. The Audition Experience course with agents and casting directors provides

SUMMATION STATEMENT:

10 on-camera private auditions with 10 leading agents and casting directors.

"We do individual, semiprivate coaching, not classes. How to do commercials, how to get them, how to be successful, motivation and self-improvement."

COMEDY PERFORMERS STUDIO
NOLA STUDIOS

250 West 54th Street
New York, NY 10019
(212) 362–3054

PROGRAM: Comedy Technique Class, Master Class, Coaching

INSTRUCTOR: Lisa Carmel
ESTABLISHED: 1978
CLASS FEE: $150
SCHEDULE: Technique: Tuesdays 8:00 PM-10:30 PM, Master: Thursdays 8:00 PM-10:30 PM, 7-week session, private coaching by appointment

AUDITING: Free
ENTRANCE REQUIREMENTS: Interview
CANCELLATION POLICY: Class can be made up if student calls within 2 hours of class.

SCHOLARSHIPS: Work-exchange available
NUMBER OF STUDENTS
  PER CLASS: 10–15
BIOGRAPHY: MS. CARMEL is a professional comedy writer, director and performer. She has appeared in films and has television credits in New York and in London. She has studied with Marilyn Rosen of the Actor's Studio, and with David Shepard, founder of Second City in Chicago.

CLASSES: Comedy Technique Class consists of explorations of different methods of achieving peak comedic performance, with attention to improvisation, comedy timing, delivery, material, stage performance, auditioning and character study. Emphasis is on building stand-up routines, comedy monologues for stage, television or commercial work, using student's own personal and individual style. Masterclass is a continuation of Technique Class and for performers in nightclubs, television or commerials. Attention is given to the finer points in performance, material enhancement and career placement. Well-known comics will be invited to answer questions. The use of video is also incorporated so performers can see themselves perform. Promising students will be given a chance to perform in top comedy clubs and be submitted to casting directors for jobs.

SUMMATION STATEMENT: The Comedy Performers Studio has received extensive coverage on "PM Magazine," "The Today Show," and was the subject of an NBC special on comedy. Workshops were filmed for public television in Europe. Comedy Performers Studio accepts people with strong commitment to the art of comedy and a willingness to achieve goals in all fields of media. Students are provided with individualized directions according to specific needs.

CONFRONTATIONS ON CASTING

Trent Gough, Director
353 West 54th Street
New York, NY 10019
(212) 245–6757

PROGRAM:	Casting Seminars, Career Development
ESTABLISHED:	1973
REGISTRATION FEE:	None
CLASS FEE:	$115
SCHEDULE:	One $2^{1}/_{4}$-hour session per week, 12 weeks
AUDITING:	No audit
ENTRANCE REQUIREMENTS:	By interview
CANCELLATION POLICIES:	No refunds
SCHOLARSHIPS:	Not available
REQUIRED MATERIALS:	14 nonreturnable picture/resumes
NUMBER OF STUDENTS PER CLASS:	50
TOTAL STUDIO ENROLLMENT:	150
STUDENT BREAKDOWN:	55% female, 45% male; 0% under 18, 40% 18–25, 40% 26–35, 15% 36–45, 5% over 45; 40% under 6 months, 30% $^{1}/_{2}$–1 year, 15% 1–2 years, 12% 2–3 years, 3% over 3 years
VIDEO EQUIPMENT:	Yes

VIDEO CASSETTES:	Students may not purchase video cassettes.
CUE-CARD SYSTEM:	No
STUDIOS:	1
CLASSES:	Each week a different director, casting director, or agent will answer questions, interview and audition group members on color video, and give honest feedback as to how they assess the talent of members. A book of picture/resumes will be presented to each guest. They will read members in new or recent plays, films, television pilots, and commericals; and will evaluate monologues and audition scenes.

JESSICA DRAKE

Upper West Side
(212) 724-3719

PROGRAM:	Private Coaching: Audition Techniques, Basic Shakespeare
INSTRUCTOR:	Jessica Drake
ESTABLISHED:	1980
REGISTRATION FEE:	None
CLASS FEE:	$20–$25 per class
SCHEDULE:	1-hour sessions
AUDITING:	Not permitted
ENTRANCE REQUIREMENTS:	Open; Shakespeare requires "working understanding of the English language."
CANCELLATION POLICIES:	24-hour notice required to reschedule; no refunds
SCHOLARSHIPS:	Not available
TOTAL STUDIO ENROLLMENT:	21
STUDENT BREAKDOWN:	75% female, 25% male; 10% 18–25, 40% 26–35, 30% 36–45, 20% over 45; 100% under 6 months
BIOGRAPHY:	MS. DRAKE has been around show business all her life. In addition to her professional credits she has had 7 years of formal training, including a degree from the Julliard School of Drama. She has worked with Livui Ciulei and Des McAnuff, and at Joseph Papp's Public Theatre; she has also appeared with the Lincoln Center Touring Company in New York City. Her many regional credits include *Sister Mary Ignatius Explains It All for You* in Los Angeles. Television audiences have seen her in "St. Elsewhere," "The Edge of Night," and commercials. She has taught auditioning, speech, di-

CLASSES:

alects, and Shakespeare privately for four years both in New York and Los Angeles.

Audition Techniques is designed to help actors with each phase of preparation. "I help them find unique material that works well for them; stage that material; and tackle any other problems they may have with auditioning. I work in 4 sessions. The first 2 are devoted to material selection and the second 2 to staging that material." The goal of the class is to help you—on a one-session-at-a-time basis—present material that will get you the kind of roles you want. Basic Shakespeare is designed to give the novice a working understanding of Shakespearean texts. Beginning with basic structure (iambic pentameter), and concluding with a fully applied ability to act the text, the actor learns to understand and interpret the directions Shakespeare has given through the structure of his verse. Work begins with sonnets and simple passages and goes on to soliloquies. This class is one-on-one and can be adapted to meet individual needs.

SUMMATION STATEMENT:

"I want to pass along what I have learned about auditioning over the years as a result of having done them under so many different circumstances. Auditioning is a skill—the most important one there is, since you have to audition to get a job. Too many actors dread this experience, when with the proper preparation, it can be an enjoyable part of an actor's job. I work on a one-to-one basis because how each person successfully auditions is a very individual thing. I want to be able to tailor my techniques to your needs. You can be confident, relaxed, and ready in an audition."

DRAMA TREE INC.

Anthony Mannino, Director
215 Park Avenue South
New York, NY 10003
(212) 228–3932

PROGRAM:	Movement, Technique I–VI
INSTRUCTORS:	Anthony Mannino, Andrea Bernard, Barbara Clark
ESTABLISHED:	1959

AUDITING:	Permitted
AUDITING FEE:	No fee
ENTRANCE REQUIREMENTS:	Open
NUMBER OF STUDENTS PER CLASS:	10
STUDENT BREAKDOWN:	60% female, 40% male; 0% under 18, 60% 18–25, 35% 26–35, 2% 36–45, 3% over 45
STUDIOS:	2
BIOGRAPHY:	MR. MANNINO has studied with Sanford Meisner, Lee Strasberg, and Stella Adler. Broadway and Off-Broadway credits include *The Playboy of Newark,* and *Yours A. Lincoln* with Vincent Price. He appeared in the films *Those Lips, Those Eyes* and *Tattoo,* and on television in "All My Children" and "Saturday Night Live."
CLASSES:	Technique I—All dramatic elements are introduced in the first 13 weeks. Exercises and scene-size improvisations. Technique II—Acting is reacting to objects. The psycho-physical work of exploring the sensory apparatus, freeing it for application to acting. Technique III—Knowledge acquired in I and II are applied to scenes—rehearsal technique and script analysis. Technique IV—Transposing the intellectual understanding of a character into the actual execution of the role. Technique V—Introduce 8 additional imaginative techniques for furthering character interpretation. Technique VI—Scene study culminates in scene showcases by graduating students. Movement—Class goal is to improve the basic postural patterns of the student; to bring muscles which are overrelaxed into action; and to relax overtense muscles.
SUMMATION STATEMENT:	"I have sought to discover the most effective methods of teaching technique, developing the fullest utilization of the actor's 'self' toward creative expression."

ENSEMBLE STUDIO THEATRE INSTITUTE FOR PROFESSIONAL TRAINING

Annette Holloway, Director
12 West End Avenue
New York, NY 10023
(212) 581–9409

PROGRAM:	Audition Preparation, Play Analysis, Scene Study, Technique, Acting for Directors and Playwrights
INSTRUCTORS:	Gina Barnett (Audition Technique, Acting for Directors and Playwrights), Bill Cwikowski (Scene Study), Deborah Hedwall (Advanced Scene Study), Curt Dempster (Advanced Acting), Jane Hoffman (Audition Technique), Elinor Renfield (Script Analysis), Melodie Somers (Acting Technique)
ESTABLISHED:	1978
REGISTRATION FEE:	None
CLASS FEES:	$200–$300
SCHEDULE:	1 or 2 3-to-6-hour classes per week, 9 weeks
AUDITING:	Not permitted
ENTRANCE REQUIREMENTS:	Application, interview
CANCELLATION POLICIES:	Refunds given for paid professional work in the field.
SCHOLARSHIPS:	Work-exchange available
NUMBER OF STUDENTS PER CLASS:	Limited to 10–15
TOTAL STUDIO ENROLLMENT:	80–100
STUDENT BREAKDOWN:	60% female, 40% male; 0% under 18, 40% 18–25, 50% 26–35, 10% 36–45, 0% over 45; 50% under 6 months, 25% 1/2–1 year, 20% 1–2 years, 5% 2–3 years, 0% over 3 years
VIDEO EQUIPMENT:	No
STUDIOS:	2
DRESSING ROOMS:	1
WAITING AREA:	Yes
BIOGRAPHY:	MS. HEDWALL has appeared off Broadway in *Extremities,* at the Manhattan Theatre Club, and at Circle Repertory. On Broadway she has been seen in *Equus* and *Soloman's Child.* MS. HOFFMAN created the role of Momee in Albee's *The American Dream* and *The Sandbox* and has appeared at numerous New York City theatres, including the

Phoenix and the Public Theatre. Her film credits include *Up the Sandbox, Tattoo,* and *Day of the Locust.* MR. DEMPSTER founded EST in 1971. As a director, he has staged new plays by Joyce Carol Oates, Tennessee Williams and Frank D. Gilroy. As a playwright, his works include *Déjà Vu* and *Mimosa Pudica,* which was selected for the *1978–79 Best Short Plays.* As an actor, he has appeared in roles on and off Broadway. MS. BARNETT has been an active member of EST since 1978. She has acted in several productions at EST as well as at a number of other Off-Broadway and regional theatres. MR. CWIKOWSKI appeared this year in *Little Victories* at the American Place Theatre, in *The Dolphin Position* in EST's Marathon '83, and in the Off-Broadway production of Shel Silverstein's *Wild Life.* MS. RENFIELD's recent directorial credits include *Open Admissions, Buck, Chucky's Hunch, Scenes From Everyday Life,* and *Shay.* MS. SOMERS recently appeared in *Baby with the Bathwater* and *Beyond Therapy.* She has performed at the Actor's Theatre of Louisville's New Play Festival; and at EST in new plays by David Mamet, Frank D. Gilroy, John Ford Noonan, and Albert Innaurato.

CLASSES:

Acting for Directors and Playwrights is a course to familiarize directors and playwrights with the many processes actors use to personalize and create their characterizations. The First Steps is a nuts-and-bolts approach to scene study and monologue coaching, working in a constructed, realistic situation while exploring the basic techniques of acting. Advanced Scene Study is to further explore those acquired skills concerning the ability to live truthfully under imaginary circumstances. Advanced Acting is a highly individual course which stresses each actor's own unique potential. Audition Technique works with both prepared material and cold readings, exploring how to make personal choices and evaluate scripts quickly. In Basic Scene Study students receive specific feedback regarding understanding texts and creating characters, while exploring techniques used to bring a scene to performance level. Script Analysis focuses on texts and the analysis of acting and event—how to approach scene work conceptually so that your interpretation is an extension of your vision. Acting

SUMMATION STATEMENT:

Technique, intermediate and advanced levels, is for students committed to deepening their inner connection to their work and to increasing artistic self-awareness through a specific process based on prepared improvisations.

"EST's Institute for Professional Training was established as a training ground for the development of new talent and as a place where members of the theatre can teach and work at their crafts."

WILLIAM ESPER STUDIO, INC.

William Esper, Director
723 Seventh Avenue
New York, NY 10019
(212) 354-0421

PROGRAM:	Acting Technique
INSTRUCTORS:	William Esper, Suzanne Oberjat, Maggie Flanigan, Joel Rooks
ESTABLISHED:	1959
REGISTRATION FEE:	None
CLASS FEES:	Mr. Esper's classes $135; Associate teachers $110 per month
SCHEDULE:	2 3-hour classes per week
AUDITING:	Not permitted
ENTRANCE REQUIREMENTS:	Personal interview with Mr. Esper (sometimes by audition)
SCHOLARSHIPS:	Not available
NUMBER OF STUDENTS PER CLASS:	Limited to 22
TOTAL STUDIO ENROLLMENT:	150
STUDENT BREAKDOWN:	50% female, 50% male; 0% under 18, 20% 18–25, 50% 26–35, 25% 36–45, 5% over 45; 2% under 6 months, 0% $1/2$–1 year, 98% 1–2 years, 0% over 2 years
STUDIOS:	2
WAITING AREA:	Yes
BIOGRAPHY:	MR. ESPER is a graduate of the Neighborhood Playhouse and was trained there as an actor, director, and teacher by Sanford Meisner. He served 12 years on the staff of the Neighborhood Playhouse and as associate director of the Acting Department from 1972 to 1976. In 1975-76 he was

director of the company workshop for Circle Repertory Company. Mr. Esper has been head of the Professional Actor Training Program at Rutgers University since 1976 and head of his own studio in New York for the past 16 years. MS. OBERJAT was trained as an actress by Sanford Meisner and William Esper and is a graduate of the Neighborhood Playhouse. She has been seen with many Off-Broadway, regional, and stock-touring companies. MS. FLANIGAN trained as an actress and teacher with William Esper. MR. ROOKS trained as an actor and teacher with William Esper and is active as an actor Off-Broadway and in regional theatres, including Yale Rep and the Annenberg Center, as well as in television and film.

CLASS:

First-year work develops a truthful acting instrument. Students proceed through a carefully worked out system of improvisational exercises and scenes all designed to develop a creative, truthful, sensitized, and responsive actor. The work develops a sense of truth, awareness, imagination, and emotional responsiveness in order to attain the virtuosity necessary for a first-rate professional actor. Second-year work undertakes work in interpretation and character work.

SUMMATION STATEMENT:

"Acceptance is limited to those actors who are truly dedicated to the pursuit of excellence in their craft and are willing to strive for the demanding standards which we set for all aspects of the student's work. Teaching approach is based on Mr. Esper's 15-year association as a teacher with Sanford Meisner and comes out of the best American Stanislavski tradition. We strive to develop truthfully alive and professionally competent actors."

EXPRESSIONS

Bernice Loren, Director
350 West 55th Street
New York, NY 10019
(212) 586–8604

PROGRAM: The Performing Art: Acting, Voice, and Dance Approached as a Unit
INSTRUCTOR: Bernice Loren

ESTABLISHED:	1973
REGISTRATION FEE:	$25
CLASS FEE:	$165 per term
SCHEDULE:	A minimum of 1 3½-hour session per week, 12 weeks
AUDITING:	Not permitted
ENTRANCE REQUIREMENTS:	Interview
CANCELLATION POLICIES:	Prorated refunds
SCHOLARSHIPS:	Not available
NUMBER OF STUDENTS PER CLASS:	Limited to 4
STUDIOS:	1
DRESSING ROOMS:	1
FLOOR:	Wood, Fabulon finish
ACCOMPANYING INSTRUMENT:	Tapes, piano
ACCOMPANIST:	Most work is a cappella.
WAITING AREA:	No
BIOGRAPHY:	MS. LOREN has worked as an actress and director in Off-Broadway, resident, stock, and community theatres. She is a teacher at City College and the author of a text on voice and speech. She has a background in the work of Stanislavski; epic theatre with Erwin Piscator; and she has observed, or performed under the direction of, numerous foreign directors at work. She has an extensive background in singing, dialects, dance, and health systems, and is cofounder and director of 2 theatres.
CLASS:	All students work during every class, building a strong foundation in this unified approach and developing solid skills that all flow from a consistent central source of expression, technique, and creativity. Basic principles and methods common to acting, voice, and dance are established and applied to each discipline, blending each with the other and with a thorough approach to characterization—all of which is applicable to work in total theatre and in the specialties. Once the foundation and principles are established, they are applied to performing material—scripts, songs, dance, etc. Among the basic dealt with are relaxation, breathing, concentration, establishment of a psychophysical center, motivation, sensory awareness and recall, rhythm, inner truth, connection with intuitive sources.
SUMMATION STATEMENT:	"Expressions was founded with the purpose of contributing to the improvement of the arts through

a training program and, ultimately, with the estab-
lishment of a theatre company. The program was
based on the perception that many common principles apply to all the arts and that each can
strengthen and reinforce the others. The performing program is particularly concerned with eliminating the inconsistencies and contradictions
students often encounter when studying acting,
voice and speech, and dance as separate spe-
cialties; and with developing artists whose perfor-
mances are balanced, integrated, strong, and true
in every area, with no break in the flow of character, from acting through voice through movement."

THE FOCUS IS YOU: AUDITIONING AND PERFORMING WORKSHOP

Midtown
(212) 757–1510

PROGRAM:	Audition
INSTRUCTOR:	Carol L. Nadell
ESTABLISHED:	1979
REGISTRATION FEE:	None
CLASS FEE:	$185 per term
SCHEDULE:	1 2-hour session per week, 6 weeks
AUDITING:	Permitted
AUDITING FEE:	None
ENTRANCE REQUIREMENTS:	Open
SCHOLARSHIPS:	Not available
NUMBER OF STUDENTS PER CLASS:	Limited to 8
STUDENT BREAKDOWN:	65% female, 35% male; 35% 18–25, 45% 26–35, 15% 36–45, 5% over 45
VIDEO EQUIPMENT:	3/4-inch color video system
CUE-CARD SYSTEM:	No
BIOGRAPHY:	MS. NADELL is a working actress who has appeared on Broadway and can be seen on television, in films, and in numerous commercials. She is a member of the faculty of the AADA and Western Connecticut State College and has taught at Princeton. She is also a casting consultant for corporate television.

CLASS:

"The workshop is in-depth and nonpressured, designed to build awareness, technique, and confidence through personal attention and guidance. Each week a different aspect of the business will be covered, giving the participants a feeling of what it is really like to audition for daytime drama, radio and television commercials, industrial television and film production, as well as for the stage."

MIRIAM FOND

Midtown Manhatten
(212) 586–7983

PROGRAM:	Musical Theatre Performance
ESTABLISHED:	1979
REGISTRATION FEE:	None
CLASS FEES:	$15 per class; $50 for 5 classes; $75 for 10 classes
SCHEDULE:	1 2-hour class per week, ongoing
AUDITING:	Permitted
AUDITING FEE:	None
ENTRANCE REQUIREMENTS:	Interview
CANCELLATION POLICIES:	No refunds, excepting emergencies or out-of-town employment
SCHOLARSHIPS:	Not available
REQUIRED MATERIALS:	Prepared songs or scenes
NUMBER OF STUDENTS PER CLASS:	3–8, unlimited
TOTAL STUDIO ENROLLMENT:	10
STUDENT BREAKDOWN:	50% female, 50% male; 0% under 18, 20% 18–25, 80% 26–35, 0% over 35; 5% under 6 months, 5% 1/2–1 years, 20% 1–2 years, 20% 2–3 years, 50% over 3 years
STUDIOS:	1
ACCOMPANYING INSTRUMENT:	Piano
CLASS CARD:	5–10 classes, valid 5–10 weeks
VOCAL CASSETTES:	Students may record sessions.
ACCOMPANIST:	Provided
BIOGRAPHY:	MS. FOND is a professional director and choreographer who has directed over 75 productions in New York City and throughout the United States and Canada.
CLASS:	The class is to help each student with his or her particular needs, Choice of audition material,

preparation of such material, scene study, coaching for specific roles, and even work for a nightclub act.

SUMMATION STATEMENT:

"My approach is totally pragmatic. Each person is different and each has different needs. There is a wide range of experience levels in the class and each person is helped according to his or her particular skills, weaknesses, and interests. All levels work together and learn from one another."

GENE FRANKEL
THEATRE WORKSHOP INC.

36 West 62nd Street
New York, NY 11201
(212) 522–5569/724–7400

PROGRAM:	Technique I–IV, Master Class, Musical Theatre, Theatre to Film and Television
INSTRUCTORS:	James Brick, Sanford Morris, Gene Frankel, Fred Silver, Meg Mundy
ESTABLISHED:	1946
REGISTRATION FEE:	None
CLASS FEES:	$150–$200
SCHEDULE:	1 3-hour session per week, 10 weeks
AUDITING:	Permitted following interview
AUDITING FEE:	No fee
ENTRANCE REQUIREMENTS:	Interview and audition
SCHOLARSHIPS:	Limited number available
NUMBER OF STUDENTS PER CLASS:	Limited to 15
STUDIOS:	2; stage
DRESSING ROOMS:	Yes
WAITING AREA:	Yes
BIOGRAPHY:	MR. BRICK has acted, taught, and directed for many years at a number of theatres and universities. MR. MORRIS is an actor, teacher, and director. MR. FRANKEL's Broadway and Off-Broadway credits include *Indians, Lost in the Stars,* and *Cry of Players.* His awards include 3 Obies, the Vernon Rice Award, the Lola D'Annunzio Award and the Burns Mantle Award. MS. MUNDY is a contract player for "The Doctors" and has worked with Basil Rathbone, Robert Redford, and Albert Marre.

CLASSES:

Technique I—Teaches the techniques to bring yourself, your imagination, and your own experience to your acting work; sense memory, improvisation, and other creative tools. Technique II—Explores the technique for the intellectual and emotional preparation of a role through exercises and beginning scene study. Technique III—Further develops the technique for preparation of a role, with emphasis on how to make right choices to meet ongoing working objectives. Technique IV—Scene study for the more experienced actor, covering character analysis and audition techniques. Master Class—Career advancement course for the professional. Theatre to Film and Television is for actors that are ready to make the transition from theatre to film and television. It includes how to apply acting skills on camera; create a character from a scene; and how to read (soap) scripts.

GERRY GOODMAN

318 East 11th Street
New York, NY 10003
(212) 730–1188

PROGRAM:	Coaching for Shakespeare, Private
REGISTRATION FEE:	None
CLASS FEE:	$25 per class
SCHEDULE:	1-hour sessions, ongoing
AUDITING:	Not permitted
ENTRANCE REQUIREMENTS:	Telephone interview
CANCELLATION POLICIES:	24-hours notice or full fee billed
SCHOLARSHIPS:	Not available
BIOGRAPHY:	MR. GOODMAN is an actor who has lived in New York for 13 years. He trained at Shakespeare & Company, the Actors Institute, and at the State University at Purchase, where he received his B.F.A. in 1977.
CLASS:	Classes break down into two kinds of students: those who meet with Mr. Goodman on an ongoing once-a-week basis, and those who have an upcoming classical audition and want a single coaching session. The work with the former is more detailed, slower, more thorough; while work with the

latter is to give final shape to a piece that's already been worked on.

SUMMATION STATEMENT: "My basic philosophy is that the emotional life of the actor can only be revealed through the clarity of his or her thought. I work with students to ensure that they experience as fully as possible the actual words of the text they are using, so that ultimately they "own" them, and speak them anew as if they were not written by someone else. This allows the actor then to be fully present in the speech, and his or her inner life will naturally and appropriately come forth."

MAX GARTENBERG STUDIO

218 West 47th Street, 3rd floor
New York, NY 10036
(212) 249–1516

PROGRAM:	Emotions for Theatre; Scene Study/Play Analysis
INSTRUCTOR:	Max Gartenberg
ESTABLISHED:	1960
REGISTRATION FEE:	None
CLASS FEE:	$720 per term
SCHEDULE:	1 4-to-6-hour class per week, 36 weeks
AUDITING:	Not permitted
ENTRANCE REQUIREMENTS:	Interview; minimum age 20, some training preferred
CANCELLATION POLICIES:	No refunds, no make-up sessions
SCHOLARSHIPS:	Not available
NUMBER OF STUDENTS PER CLASS:	20
TOTAL STUDIO ENROLLMENT:	60
STUDENT BREAKDOWN:	65% female, 35% male; 0% under 18, 20% 18–25, 70% 26–35, 10% 36–45, 0% over 45; 10% under 6 months, 15% $1/2$–1 year, 20% 1–2 years, 30% 2–3 years, 25% over 3 years
STUDIOS:	2
WAITING AREA:	Yes
BIOGRAPHY:	MR. GARTENBERG has been teaching and directing since 1960, and is an associate of Mary Tarcai. He also coaches privately.
CLASSES:	Emotions for Theatre is structured so that the student will learn how to make appropriate use of

emotions; apply them to written dialogue; and provide emotional energy to scripted material. Scene Study is designed so that the students will take scripted material and learn how to break it down; continue to stretch themselves and make the fullest use of themselves and their abilities.

SUMMATION STATEMENT: "We work for the individual performer to find his or her own core of truth before we begin to find the character's. Learning to trust oneself and being able to take risks is part of this process."

HB STUDIO

Muriel Burns, Director
120 Bank Street
New York, NY 10014
(212) 675–2370

PROGRAM:	Classics, Comedy, Experimental, How To Do Homework, Improvisations, Monologues, Musical Comedy, Musical Performance, Opera, Play Analysis, Play Laboratory, Poetry, Scene Study, Shakespeare, Technique, Theatre Games, Movement
INSTRUCTORS:	Herbert Berghof, Uta Hagan, Walt Witcover, Aaron Frankel, Naomi Riordan, Stephen Strimpell, Carol Rosenfeld, Hal Holden, Edward Morehouse, Dorothy Dorff, Katherine Sergava, Joan Matthiessen, Elizabeth Dillon, Salem Ludwig, Michael Beckett, William Hickey, Rochelle Oliver, Sandy Dennis, Richard Morse, William Packard, Frank Geraci, Jess Osuna, Constance Mayer, Lloyd Williamson
ESTABLISHED:	1945
REGISTRATION FEE:	$7.50
CLASS FEES:	$95 (average)
SCHEDULE:	$1^1/_2$–$2^1/_2$ hours per week, 19 weeks, ongoing
AUDITING:	Permitted
AUDITING FEE:	$1.50 for first audit; $4 for subsequent audit of same class
ENTRANCE REQUIREMENTS:	Open (for most classes)
CANCELLATION POLICIES:	No refunds given after term has started and no credit given for classes missed
SCHOLARSHIPS:	Work-exchange available
NUMBER OF STUDENTS PER CLASS:	15–35

TOTAL STUDIO ENROLLMENT: Over 3,000
STUDENT BREAKDOWN: 60% female, 40% male; 5% under 18, 45% 18–25, 20% 26–35, 20% 36–45, 10% over 45; 5% under 6 months, 10% $1/2$–1 year, 25% 1–2 years, 40% 2–3 years, 20% over 3 years
VIDEO EQUIPMENT: Yes
VIDEO CASSETTES: Students may purchase video cassettes.
CUE-CARD SYSTEM: Yes
STUDIOS: 5
DRESSING ROOMS: 2
SHOWERS: None
FLOOR: Dance
ACCOMPANYING
 INSTRUMENT: Piano
VOCAL CASSETTES: No
ACCOMPANIST: Yes
WAITING AREA: Yes
SUMMATION STATEMENT: "The HB Studio began in 1945 and aims for a meaningful dramatic expression of the times and country in which we live. To help establish a theatre of experimentation based on classic tradition, the Studio is dedicated to the development of individual artists who may actively contribute to a theatre of national character. Conceived as an artistic and working home, it offers an outlet for practice and growth for the professional theatre artist, and an opportunity for the young to establish roots in their intended crafts. The Studio's guiding principle is creative freedom, which has as its logical consequence responsibility to a noble art."

HUDSON GUILD THEATRE SCHOOL

David Kerry Heefner, Producing Director
441 West 26th Street
New York, NY 10001
(212) 760–9836

PROGRAM: Acting Technique
INSTRUCTOR: David Kerry Heefner, assisted by Evanne Christian
ESTABLISHED: 1982
REGISTRATION FEE: None
CLASS FEE: $250 per term

SCHEDULE:	1 3-hour session per week, 10 weeks (offered twice per year)
AUDITING:	Not permitted
ENTRANCE REQUIREMENTS:	Picture and resume submitted; interview
CANCELLATION POLICIES:	No refunds after the fifth week of class. Make-up sessions may be possible during the next class term.
SCHOLARSHIPS:	Not available
NUMBER OF STUDENTS PER CLASS:	Limited to 25
TOTAL STUDIO ENROLLMENT:	50
STUDENT BREAKDOWN:	50% female, 50% male; 30% 18–25, 65% 26–35, 5% 36–45
STUDIOS:	2
DRESSING ROOMS:	2
BIOGRAPHY:	MR. HEEFNER is the producing director of Hudson Guild Theatre which has presented the New York premieres of *On Golden Pond; Da; Come Back to the Five and Dime, Jimmy Dean.* MS. CHRISTIAN is the casting and literary assistant at the Hudson Guild Theatre.
CLASS:	This is a workshop structured for the professional actor. The goal of the workshop is to improve the individual actor's technique by solving individual problems, working on script interpretation, character analysis, cold readings, etc.
SUMMATION STATEMENT:	"This workshop offers actors a chance to practice their craft in a professional theatre, under the guidance of a professional director/producer, in a class of carefully selected working professional actors."

DENNIS MOORE

344 West 72nd Street
New York, NY 10023
(212) 496–7917

PROGRAM:	Scene Study/Technique, Script Analysis
INSTRUCTOR:	Dennis Moore
ESTABLISHED:	1977
REGISTRATION FEE:	None
CLASS FEES:	Scene Study/Technique—$250; Script Analysis—$50
SCHEDULE:	Scene Study/Technique—2 2-hour sessions per

AUDITING:

week, 10 weeks, ongoing; Script Analysis—1 3-hour session per week, two weeks

Scene Study, yes; Script Analysis, no

AUDITING FEE: $15

ENTRANCE REQUIREMENTS: Interview (and audit for Scene Study/Technique)

CANCELLATION POLICIES: Make-up sessions available

SCHOLARSHIPS: Limited number available

NUMBER OF STUDENTS
  PER CLASS: Limited to 12–15

TOTAL STUDIO ENROLLMENT: 60

STUDENT BREAKDOWN: 50% female, 50% male; 0% under 18, 20% 18–25, 70% 26–35, 5% 36–45, 5% over 45; 10% under 6 months, 15% $1/2$–1 year, 30% 1–2 years, 30% 2–3 years, 15% over 3 years

STUDIOS: 1

DRESSING ROOMS: 1

CLASS CARD: Yes, 20 classes per card, valid 10 weeks

BIOGRAPHY: MR. MOORE was a faculty member of the American Academy of Dramatic Arts for 5 years. He taught all levels of acting and directed more than 30 student productions. He was also director of the Academy's Adult Education Division. Previously Mr. Moore has taught acting for Gene Frankel. He has acted as artistic director of Michael Moriarty's Potter's Field Theatre Company and directed Mr. Moriarty in the Public Theatre's production of *Phedra*. He was a resident director at the WPA Theatre for several seasons and has directed at LaMama, ETC. He has been the director of the National Academy of Television Arts and Sciences Acting Workshop and recently directed the Off-Broadway production of *Dog Play,* starring Lonny Price and Josh Mostel.

CLASSES: Scene Study/Technique permits an actor to access emotion and spontaneity directly, without elaborate external preparation. Incorporating some of the ideas of Michael Chekov, Kristen Linklater, and the Alexander technique, blended with his own method, Mr. Moore uses suggestions of creative imagery and fantasy in an attempt to stimulate mind-body self-awareness as an aid to relieving tension. This technique, integrated with more or less traditional physical exercises and an intense scene study section, is designed to allow an actor to find his or her own personal formula for approaching a role. Script Analysis is a lecture and discussion class designed to help actors break down a script in order to draw out the playwright's intentions. Rather than a "how-to" approach, which frequently leads to a results-oriented interpretation, the class is designed to lead actors to explore the "why" in character development and interrelations. Working from the literal and subconcious levels, this method attempts to find a natural "line-thru" for the development of a character or situation.

SUMMATION STATEMENT: "The object of the classes is to prepare actors to encounter roles with freedom and objectivity, whether for stage or film or television. It allows the actor to reveal his or her own mental physical potential and to develop the confidence to freely use that potential in creating and playing a role. Classes are restricted to promising newcomers and established professionals; and take a no-nonsense approach to revealing the core of a character or a script."

GEORGE MORRISON STUDIO

George Morrison, Director
212 West 29th Street
New York, NY 10001
(212) 594–2614

PROGRAM:	Scene Study, Theatre Games
INSTRUCTORS:	George Morrison, David Cohen
ESTABLISHED:	1956
REGISTRATION FEE:	$15
CLASS FEES:	$80–$95 per month
SCHEDULE:	1 4½-hour class per week, 50 weeks a year, ongoing
AUDITING:	Not permitted
ENTRANCE REQUIREMENTS:	Interview
CANCELLATION POLICIES:	Students may drop out for 4-week periods at no charge.
SCHOLARSHIPS:	Not available
NUMBER OF STUDENTS PER CLASS:	Limited to 24
TOTAL STUDIO ENROLLMENT:	24
STUDENT BREAKDOWN:	45% female, 55% male; 35% 18–25, 50% 26–35, 10% 36–45, 5% over 45; 10% under 6 months,

20% 1/2–1 year, 40% 1–2 years, 20% 2–3 years, 10% over 3 years

BIOGRAPHY: MR. MORRISON is the senior faculty member of the Professional Actor Training Program at the State University of New York at Purchase. He attended Yale Drama School and studied with Strasberg, Alvina Krause, John Grinder, Jean Huston. He trained Gene Hackman, Barbara Harris, and Ron Liebman. He has directed on and off Broadway and for network television.

CLASS: The first half of Scene Study is devoted to exercises including sensory work, the second half to prepared scenes.

SUMMATION STATEMENT: "The work is based on a respect for the individual student, and a belief that the hard work of training can be a joyful experience. The approach utilizes the latest information on right and left hemispheres, learning through multi-sensory involvement, and states of consciousness."

MOSCOW DIRECTORS' THEATRE OF NEW YORK

Marat Yusim, Director
242 West 76th Street #6F
New York, NY 10023
(212) 724–9957

PROGRAM: Acting Technique
INSTRUCTOR: Marat Yusim
ESTABLISHED: 1979
REGISTRATION FEE: None
CLASS FEE: $450 per term
SCHEDULE: 3 3-hour sessions per week, 3-month term
AUDITING: Not permitted
ENTRANCE REQUIREMENTS: Interview
SCHOLARSHIPS: Limited work-study positions available
NUMBER OF STUDENTS
  PER CLASS: 10–15
STUDENT BREAKDOWN: 60% female, 40% male; 80% 18–25, 20% 26–35; 10% under 6 months, 10% 1/2–1 year, 40% 1–2 years, 40% 2–3 years
BIOGRAPHY: MR. YUSIM is a 20-year veteran of the theatre and has presented the work of Shakespeare, Moliere,

Gorky, Chekhov, and many others throughout Russia. Before his arrival in the United States, Mr. Yusim directed over 60 productions in his homeland. He has taught at the Sonia Moore Studio and the Actor/Directors Lab and is currently on the staff of the High School of the Performing Arts. His most recent film credit is Michael Cimino's *Heaven's Gate.* Founder of the Moscow Directors' Theatre, Mr. Yusim directed its inaugural season of plays—*Princess Turandot* and *The Game of Love and Chance.*

CLASS: Term I is devoted to gaining the basics of artistic technique by exercises, including improvisation and études, logic and consecutiveness of an action as influences on emotional memory. Term II deals with the study of logic, consecutiveness and organic action while reaching for a given goal, all within given circumstances—to repeat without repeating; to really think on stage; not to pretend; and to act clearly and strongly without approximations. Verbal interaction, listening and reacting, united verbal and physical action, uses of tempo and rhythm, mise-en-scène, and characterization are covered. Term III focuses on self-preparation, acting from oneself, study of character creation. The student is taught to work independently with the author's theme and idea, events, main conflict, action/counteractions, main objectives; and to master the logic of the character's thoughts, actions, and an unbroken chain of interaction.

DOUG MOSTON

21st Street, off 5th Avenue
(212) 674–1166

PROGRAM:	Acting Technique
ESTABLISHED:	1979
REGISTRATION FEE:	None
CLASS FEE:	$75 per month
SCHEDULE:	1 3-hour class per week, 11 months per year, ongoing
AUDITING:	Permitted
AUDITING FEE:	No fee
ENTRANCE REQUIREMENTS:	Interview

CANCELLATION POLICIES:	Make-ups, private coaching
SCHOLARSHIPS:	Not available
NUMBER OF STUDENTS PER CLASS:	Limited to 10
STUDENT BREAKDOWN:	65% female, 35% male; 20% 18–25, 60% 26–35, 20% 36–45; 20% 1–2 years, 60% 2–3 years, 20% over three years
STUDIOS:	1
DRESSING ROOMS:	1
SHOWERS:	1
FLOOR:	Wood
ACCOMPANYING INSTRUMENT:	Piano
BIOGRAPHY:	MR. MOSTON studied and worked in New York for 15 years. He has appeared in theatre, soap operas, and in film. He studied for 1 year at the Actor's Studio.
CLASS:	The class begins with relaxation techniques dealing with any existing tension/anxiety experienced by the actor. These are followed by exercises in craft: making choices, preparation, relationship, objectives, vulnerability, etc. Next come detailed sense memory work and individual work on the instrument (feeling and expressing emotions), alternated with character and customized exercises dealing with individual acting problems. Next, scenes and monologues are presented for critique.
SUMMATION STATEMENT:	"I believe that actors must possess the ability to challenge themselves. Therein lies the real drama. By dealing with this principle, you will gain an incredibly profound insight into the character and be amazingly compelling onstage. Your essence is your uniqueness. My work is designed to help you express that uniqueness every single time you step onstage or in front of a camera. The atmosphere of the class will support you in taking risks and in feeling permitted to work. Our work is exciting. When you learn it and use it, your work will be exciting too."

NEIGHBORHOOD PLAYHOUSE SCHOOL OF THE THEATRE

Lydia S. Saunders, Administrative Director
340 East 54th Street
New York, NY 10022
(212) 688–3770

PROGRAM:	Acting, Movement, Speech and Voice, Fencing, Makeup, Lectures, Stage Techniques, Performances
INSTRUCTORS:	Sanford Meisner, William Alderson, Greg Zittel, Phillip Gushee, Richard Pinter, Barbara Cole, Gary Gendell, Lida-Virginia Parker, Beverly Wideman, Joseph Daly, Carmen Gebbia, Kevin Keenan, Ron Shetler, Skip Kennon
ESTABLISHED:	1928
REGISTRATION FEE:	$550
CLASS FEE:	$2,950 per academic year
SCHEDULE:	September–May, full time
ENTRANCE REQUIREMENTS:	Interview and audition; audition fee—New York $25, regional $35
STUDIOS:	5-story building with classrooms, dance studio, auditorium, production annex, library
SUMMATION STATEMENT:	"We offer a stern apprenticeship of 2 years under teachers each of whom is an artist in his field and therefore an exacting taskmaster. Come here only if you are willing to work with the intensity necessary to meet the standards which these teachers will hold for you."

PROFESSIONAL ACTING

Mailing Address: 10 Bethune Street #3C
New York, NY 10014
(212) 242–4492

PROGRAM:	Acting Technique, Scene Study
INSTRUCTOR:	Greg Zittel
REGISTRATION FEE:	None
CLASS FEE:	$100 per month
SCHEDULE:	2 3-hour classes per week, ongoing
AUDITING:	Not permitted

SCHOLARSHIPS: Limited work-study scholarships available
REQUIRED MATERIALS: None
NUMBER OF STUDENTS
  PER CLASS: Limited to 15
TOTAL STUDIO ENROLLMENT: 55
STUDENT BREAKDOWN: 50% female, 50% male; 30% 18–25, 60% 26–35,
                                  10% 36–45; 50% under 6 months, 40% 2–3 years,
                                  10% over three years
BIOGRAPHY: MR. ZITTEL is a veteran actor and teacher.
CLASSES: Each student works in each class on basic training
                                  exercises which progress in difficulty and which
                                  parallel scenes appropriate to the student's devel-
                                  opment. The goals are to bring the actor into con-
                                  tact with his fellow actor, learning to bring through
                                  motivated response an imaginative sense of him-
                                  self to his acting in improvisations or scenes. The
                                  class helps to develop habits that can be practi-
                                  cally applied to a role when the student leaves the
                                  class and enters the profession on the stage, in
                                  film or television.
SUMMATION STATEMENT: "The teaching philosophy in acting as developed
                                  by Sanford Meisner and practiced by the teachers
                                  at the Neighborhood Playhouse, both at the school
                                  and privately, continues to offer leadership in the
                                  development of actors. Thorough training of the
                                  actors in the use of their imaginations develops a
                                  fuller sense of the human experience: a sense of
                                  the actor in conjunction with the poetic reality of the
                                  author."

PROFESSIONAL ACTING WORKSHOP

Ira Zuckerman, Director
215 West 29th Street
New York, NY 10001
(212) 736–0139

PROGRAM: Acting (Class), Private Coaching
INSTRUCTOR: Ira Zuckerman
ESTABLISHED: 1977
REGISTRATION FEE: $10
CLASS FEE: $80 per month; coaching $25 per hour
SCHEDULE: 1 session per week
AUDITING: Permitted after interview

ENTRANCE REQUIREMENTS:	Applicants 18 years of age will be interviewed
CANCELLATION POLICIES:	24-hour notice per class
SCHOLARSHIPS:	Not available
NUMBER OF STUDENTS PER CLASS:	Limited to 15
STUDENT BREAKDOWN:	55% female, 45% male; 0% under 18, 55% 18–25, 45% 26–35, 0% over 35; 0% under 6 months, 50% $1/2$–1 year, 50% 1–2 years, 0% over 2 years
BIOGRAPHY:	MR. ZUCKERMAN's directing credits in regional theatre include *Twelfth Night* at the Barter Theatre, and *The Hostage* at the Tranquility Square Playhouse. Off Broadway he staged the first American production of Pinter's *A Slight Ache* and he was a directing member of the Open Theatre. His film credits include director of the Canadian feature *Threshold* and assistant to Francis Ford Coppola on *The Godfather.* He is a member of SSD&C, and has taught at the Hartford Conservatory, Boston University, and in New York City at the Clark Center, High School of the Performing Arts, AADA, and Marymount Manhattan College.
CLASSES:	The workshop combines scene study, acting technique, and improvisation for stage and film and has both beginning and advanced sections. The training at the workshop includes developing an acting craft through conscious approach to scene study and monologues, script analysis; expanding expression of performer's physical and vocal abilities, improvisational skills, and rehearsal and auditioning techniques.
SUMMATION STATEMENT:	"I train my students to meet the demands of skill and discipline that today's performer must possess to have a career in the theatre and be a creative artist."

THE PROFESSIONAL WORKSHOP

Ed Kovens, Director
112 West 21st Street
New York, NY 10014
(212) 929–3125

PROGRAM:	Technique and Scene Study
INSTRUCTOR:	Ed Kovens
ESTABLISHED:	1974

REGISTRATION FEE:	None
CLASS FEE:	$100 per month
SCHEDULE:	1 or 2 4-hour classes per week, ongoing
AUDITING:	Permitted
AUDITING FEE:	None
ENTRANCE REQUIREMENTS:	Interview. Students must be at least 18 years of age with some previous training.
CANCELLATION POLICIES:	No cancellation penalties; refunds and make-ups available
SCHOLARSHIPS:	None
REQUIRED MATERIALS:	None
NUMBER OF STUDENTS PER CLASS:	12–20, limited
TOTAL STUDIO ENROLLMENT:	36–60
STUDENT BREAKDOWN:	50% female, 50% male; 25% 18–25, 50% 26–35, 20% 36–45, 5% over 45; 25% under 6 months, 10% 1/2–1 year, 15% 1–2 years, 15% 2–3 years, 35% over three years
STUDIOS:	1
DRESSING ROOMS:	2
SHOWERS:	Yes
CLASS CARD:	No
BIOGRAPHY:	MR. KOVENS has been a teacher and coach since 1965. He is a director of plays, musicals, and club acts; a member of SSD&C, AEA, SAG, AFTRA; and has been an actor since 1953.
CLASS:	The technique is method-oriented for the professional actor and covers sensory exercises and scene study. Audition material, cold readings, commercials, improvisations and song work are also covered.
SUMMATION STATEMENT:	"This is not a class for those who do not wish to be professional actors. The emphasis is on getting work and keeping the job once you've got it; discovering what is individual about each actor; and quickly and fully developing it."

WARREN ROBERTSON THEATRE WORKSHOP

Janet M. Doeden
303 East 44th Street
New York, NY 10017
(212) 687-6430

PROGRAM:	Acting, Musical Comedy, Musical Theatre, Classical and Modern Monologue
INSTRUCTORS:	Warren Robertson, Clifford David, Larry Moss, Nancy Gabor, Ken Fischer, Jacqueline Knapp, Carmel Ross
ESTABLISHED:	1976
REGISTRATION FEE:	$20
CLASS FEES:	$60–$100 per month
SCHEDULE:	1 2½-to-4-hour class per week, ongoing
AUDITING:	Permitted
AUDITING FEE:	$20
ENTRANCE REQUIREMENTS:	Interview
CANCELLATION POLICIES:	No refunds
SCHOLARSHIPS:	Work-study available; terms negotiable
REQUIRED MATERIALS:	None
NUMBER OF STUDENTS PER CLASS:	5+
TOTAL STUDIO ENROLLMENT:	300
STUDENT BREAKDOWN:	50% female, 50% male; 6% under 18, 35% 18–25, 50% 25–35; 6% 36–45; 3% over 45; 10% under 6 months, 90% ½–1 year
STUDIOS:	3
DRESSING ROOMS:	2
ACCOMPANYING INSTRUMENT:	2 pianos
BIOGRAPHY:	MR. ROBERTSON has been training actors for the past 19 years. The *Yale Theatre Review* and *New York Times Magazine* have noted him one of the most prominent drama teachers of our time. He is the artistic director of the Actors Repertory Theatre. MR. DAVID has starred in several Broadway plays, appeared in many film and television productions, and is a member of The Actors Studio. MR. MOSS is an actor with many Broadway, Off-Broadway, and television credits. He has taught at the Workshop since its inception. MS. GABOR has been teaching acting in New York City for 15 years; has directed at LaMama, the Open Theatre, Soho

Theatre, and on European tours. MR. FISCHER is a certified movement analyst and has taught at the Yale Drama School, the O'Neill Center, and at Southern Methodist University. MS. KNAPP has been actively involved as an actress in the theatre for the last 10 years and as a member of The Actors Studio for the past 5. MS. ROSS has an M.A. honors degree from the University of Oxford and is a graduate of the Royal Academy of Dramatic Art. A voice and drama coach to St. George's Shakespeare Theatre in London, she also assisted her late husband, David Ross, in a series of award-winning classical productions in New York.

CLASSES: Ms. Gabor's class is composed of exercise, improvisation, and scene study. Emphasis is on ensemble work, stage technique, relaxation, and body awareness. Mr. Fischer's class stresses basic acting skills, individual attention to free personal energy, and to expand emotional power and range. Ms. Knapp's class focuses on the actor's instrument—developing awareness and integration of, and respect for, the body, mind, and emotions. Musical Comedy is designed to help musical artists break down the components of a song and learn to perform it for the theatre. Musical Theatre is especially designed to help the actor-singer rid himself or herself of fear during auditions and to bring him or her to performance levels mandatory in the professional musical theatre. The class also stresses individual creative interpretation of musical works. Monologues has been planned to assist students in selecting audition material with which they can personally empathize and which will reflect the state of their work to best advantage; and to help students study monologues as instruments through which they will be free to experiment in the area of their own emotional range and vocal technique.

SUMMATION STATEMENT: "WRTW was founded in 1976 to create an environment for the art of acting: to integrate voice, body, emotion, and intellect into a heightened whole in which the actor may develop technique without sacrificing individuality.

DYLAN ROSS ACTING ACADEMY

408 West 48th Street
New York, NY 10036
(212) 757–0716/869–2920

PROGRAM:	Private Coaching
ESTABLISHED:	1958
REGISTRATION FEE:	None
CLASS FEE:	$30–$75 per session
SCHEDULE:	2-to-3-hour sessions, ongoing
AUDITING:	First class free
BIOGRAPHY:	MR. ROSS has been involved in theatre professionally for over 39 years. His film credits include *King Kong, Marathon Man, King of the Gypsies,* and *Hair.* He has taught acting at Princeton, North Carolina State, Colby-Sawyer, Cornell, and the Berkshire Center for the Performing Arts. He was co-worker in Hollywood with Michael Chekov and teaches his system.
CLASSES:	"I do not 'teach acting.' Each session is geared to elimination or redirection of the problems. Great stress is put on the practical and not the theoretical aspects. I work with beginner and advanced students. The major goal is for the actor to be able to rehearse under professional conditions, regardless of the medium."

CLIFFORD E. SEIDMAN

Astor Place Area
(212) 677–8575

PROGRAM:	Private Movement for the Actor
REGISTRATION FEE:	None
CLASS FEES:	$30 per class; 5 classes—$120, payable at first class
SCHEDULE:	1-hour sessions
ENTRANCE REQUIREMENTS:	Open
SCHOLARSHIPS:	Not available
BIOGRAPHY:	MR. SEIDMAN is an actor with an M.F.A. in acting from New York University's School of the Arts. He is a former member of the Working Theatre, where

he was trained as a teacher by Kristin Linklater, Peter Kass, and Joseph Chaikin. He has taught at American University, the University of Oklahoma, the State University of New York—Fedonia, and at the National Theatre of Spain in Madrid.

CLASS: "I deal with the student's specific tension areas and give him or her a set of exercises to follow to achieve alignment, flexibility, and spontaneity."

LEE STRASBERG THEATRE INSTITUTE

Anna Strasberg, Artistic Coordinator
115 East 15th Street
New York, NY 10003
(212) 533–5500

PROGRAM: Acting, Sense Memory, Improvisation, Film and Television Acting/Directing, Auditions, Commercials, Dance, Directing, Musical Comedy, Play Production, Rhythm/Movement, Seminar, Singing, Tai Chi Chu'an, Theatre History, Voice

ESTABLISHED: 1969

REGISTRATION FEE: None

SCHEDULE: 22 hours per week, 36 weeks

ENTRANCE REQUIREMENTS: Interview

SUMMATION STATEMENT: "The Lee Strasberg Theatre Institute offers the actor an opportunity to gain firsthand knowledge of the fundamental concepts of the Strasberg work. We believe that to train an actor properly takes from 3–4 years of daily work. No matter how much feeling an actor may have and no matter how aware intellectually the actor may be, the ability to express and to do onstage what is required can only be accomplished by systematic work on every facet of his instrument."

TOTAL ARTISTS WORKSHOP

The Little Theatre
100 Riverside Drive
New York, NY 10024
(212) 242–6036

INSTRUCTOR:	Melba LaRose
ESTABLISHED:	1978
REGISTRATION FEE:	None
CLASS FEE:	$80 per month
SCHEDULE:	2 2½-hour classes per week, ongoing
AUDITING:	Permitted
AUDITING FEE:	$5
ENTRANCE REQUIREMENTS:	Interview
CANCELLATION POLICIES:	No refunds
SCHOLARSHIPS:	Partial or full work-exchange scholarships available
NUMBER OF STUDENTS PER CLASS:	Limited to 6
STUDENT BREAKDOWN:	50% female, 50% male; 0% under 18, 25% 18–25, 25% 26–35, 25% 36–45, 25% over 45; 0% under 1 year, 25% 1–2 years, 75% 2–3 years, 0% over 3 years
BIOGRAPHY:	MS. LAROSE, who is an actress, playwright, director, and poet, is a veteran of New York theatre, film, and television, and a long-time member of Lonny Chapman's Group Repertory Theatre. She is currently a member of the Playwrights Unit of American Theatre of Actors, and the Commotion-Poets & Co. In 1982, in order to extend the results of her workshops, she created Artists Unlimited, a theatrical production company. AU produced *City-scapes 3* and *Jump Down, Spin Around.* In 1983 ATA produced Ms. LaRose's *Who's There?* All three productions were developed from the TAW.
CLASS:	"We begin with monologues and technique exercises in order to find one's sense of truth in behavior. When this is achieved, scene work is encouraged to extend the experience of speaking words as if they are your own (living truthfully under imaginary circumstances). Technique exercises are assigned as it is discovered what is needed to free up the actor's instrument. Some of these are physical, some emotional (or sense memory), some simple object work. There is no set regimen; instruction is

SUMMATION STATEMENT:

extremely individualized and supportive. In the latter part of each session, students are given original scenes and poems for experience in cold reading. These may be developed further as prepared readings, scenes, and productions."

"An artist is composed of many things. I encourage students to create their own monologues. I find that in writing his or her own monologue, the actor becomes connected organically with the dialogue and can then extend that experience to characters created by others. In the process, maybe also discovering that he or she can write for the theatre at large."

CLYDE VINSON STUDIOS

612–616 Eighth Avenue, 3rd floor (between 39th and 40th Streets)
New York, NY 10001
(212) 924–6360

PROGRAM:	Acting, Acting from the Body, Text Analysis
INSTRUCTORS:	Clyde Vinson, Steve Ivcich
REGISTRATION FEE:	First payment of $150 due 1 week before term begins
CLASS FEES:	Acting—$300; Acting from the Body—$150; Text Analysis—$120
SCHEDULE:	Acting—1 4-hour session per week, 12 weeks; Body—2 6-hour sessions per week, 2 weeks; Text—1 3-hour session per week, 10 weeks
ENTRANCE REQUIREMENTS:	Interview
NUMBER OF STUDENTS PER CLASS:	Limited to 14–16
BIOGRAPHY:	MR. VINSON has taught for more than 25 years, in universities and privately in New York. He received his Ph.D. from Northwestern University and spent 2 years with the Working Theatre in New York City, a foundation-sponsored training program in voice, movement, and acting founded by Kristin Linklater, Joseph Chaikin, and Peter Kass. He did two years of Alexander technique, is conversant with Rolfing, and has done workshops with Charlotte Selver, Eric Morris, Bob Chapra, and Moshe Feldenkrais. For the past year he has been studying at the Psychosynthesis Institute of New York and believes that work has profound implications for

the actor. He has directed both in universities and professionally. Apart from the studio-work in mid-town and work with leading actors in McCann-Nugent productions, his greatest alliance is with the Circle Repertory Company. MR. IVCICH is a graduate of Northwestern University and has studied with Etienne Decroux at the École du Mime in Paris. He has a great deal of experience as a performer, director, and teacher. He has done a superb job of translating the body work andmask work of the mime to meet the needs of the actor.

CLASSES:

Acting—The work may be roughly divided into four phases or steps: (1) Basic Being and Personalization—Individual process work to get to a state that is affectable (2) Basic Techniques—Games and other exercises to create the who, where, what of a scene (3) Interaction and Relationship—Exercises to develop genuine listening and response; to create relationships that the actor and audience can believe, and (4) Intention and Obligations—Exercises to help the actor find the intention in a scene and make choices in fulfilling it. Each term focuses on one of the above and all work is channelled into scene and monologue work. Focus of subsequent terms will be on Mask, Styles, or Shakespeare. Acting from the Body—The 3 areas of work covered are (1) an exploration of the actor's physical self (2) synthesis of the physical elements of "presence" onstage (3) the development of personal comfort in performance. Through a series of solo, duet, and group exercises, the actor is guided to a resolution of physical problems. Each exercise deals with a specific aspect of the actor's circumstance as he stands before the audience. Each builds on its predecessor and adds a single new piece of information. Text Analysis—Intent is to help the actor know how to read and interpret the script. Purpose is to help the actor know the playwright's vision of the world and the statement he or she is making about the world. Ten plays are studied, first looking at it from the director's point of view, and then from the actor's.

SUMMATION STATEMENT:

"The goal of all this work is to unify and integrate the body, voice, thought, and emotion so that the actor is centered and in touch with all parts of the self, with no split between thought and feeling and the expression of it—so that the body and voice do not mask thought and feeling but reveal it."

TAMARA WILCOX

484 West 43rd Street #40S
New York, NY 10036
(212) 244–4666

PROGRAM:	Improvisation
INSTRUCTORS:	Tamara Wilcox, Christopher Smith
ESTABLISHED:	1976
REGISTRATION FEE:	None
CLASS FEE:	$100 per month
SCHEDULE:	2 2 1/2-hour classes per week, 16 weeks, not ongoing
AUDITING:	Permitted
AUDITING FEE:	No fee
ENTRANCE REQUIREMENTS:	Interview
CANCELLATION POLICIES:	2-week cancellation notice
SCHOLARSHIPS:	Limited number available
NUMBER OF STUDENTS PER CLASS:	Limited to 15
STUDENT BREAKDOWN:	40% female, 60% male; 80% 18–25, 20% 25–35
STUDIOS:	1
ACCOMPANYING INSTRUMENT:	Piano
ACCOMPANIST:	Provided
BIOGRAPHY:	MS. WILCOX was a member of The Committee as well as a television and film actress; she had a featured role in the film *M*A*S*H*. She is creative director of On Target, a film production company; a writer for film and television; and author of children's books. She was a CAPS grant recipient and was recently voted Best Director by the National Academy of Cabaret and Concert Artists for her direction of *Interplay*. MR. SMITH, a member of Interplay, is a graduate of Kenyon College, where he originated the role of Freeman Gunn in Michael Christofer's *CC Pyle and the Bunion Derby*, directed by Paul Newman. He also appeared in the tenth anniversary *Godspell*, directed by its author, John-Michael Tabelak; his one-man show *Groucho* has toured the United States and England. He is a writer for film and stage.

CLASS:	The class teaches improvisational techniques which the actor may use as tools to develop traditional acting roles or to perform improvisationally to help the performer free his or her imagination, create new ideas, and communicate spontaneously with other performers and with the audience.
SUMMATION STATEMENT:	"Each artist has a special artistic viewpoint that should be supported and directed by giving him or her the applicable techniques needed to reach particular goals."

WEIST-BARRON SCHOOL OF TELEVISION

Bob Barron, Dwight Weist, Co-directors
35 West 45th Street, 6th floor
New York, NY 10036
(212) 840–7025

INSTRUCTOR:	Dwight Weist, Frank Spencer, Jerry Coyle, Kate Carr, John Bogden, MaryJo Slater, Ed Ferron, Nancy Andrews, Annamarie Kostura, Laura Gleason, Jim Kramer, Marc Brown, Vivian Taylor, Dino Narizanno
ESTABLISHED:	1957
CLASS FEE:	$300–325
SCHEDULE:	Soaps—six 4-hour sessions; Voice-over and Character Voices—two 2-hour sessions/week, 5 weeks; Advanced Commercials—two 2-hour sessions/week, 5 weeks
ENTRANCE REQUIREMENTS:	Audition for all classes but commercials
CANCELLATION POLICIES:	Full refund up to one week before term starts; $50 fee for cancellations within the week before term starts; no refunds after start of classes
SCHOLARSHIPS:	Limited scholarship opportunities announced twice yearly in *Backstage*
FACILITIES:	Color Video; cue cards and teleprompter; 6 studios; students may purchase video sessions on request
NUMBER OF STUDENTS PER CLASS:	Limited to 12
BIOGRAPHY:	All instructors in commercial classes are working performers with many commercials to their credit. An aggregate number of commercials performed by all would be over 1,000. Only teachers who

enjoy teaching and take a serious, personal interest in all their students are hired.

CLASSES: Soap Opera; Commercials; Advanced Commercials; Character Voices; Voice-over; Children's and Teens' Division; Newscasting Division

SUMMATION STATEMENT: "The goal of the class is to bring each student up to competition level. Expert training by professionals, directors and casting directors. In soap classes, two camera monitors to simulate actual soap conditions. Individual consultation and many hours of on-camera work with playback and critique are offered.

DANCE
DANCE
DANCE
DANCE
DANCE
DANCE
DANCE
DANCE
DANCE
DANCE
DANCE
DANCE
DANCE
DANCE
DANCE
DANCE
DANCE
DANCE
DANCE
DANCE
DANCE
DANCE
DANCE
DANCE

ACTORS AND DIRECTORS LAB

412 West 42nd Street
New York, NY 10036
(212) 695–5429

PROGRAM:	Ballet; Jazz—Beginning, Intermediate; Tap—Beginning, Advanced
INSTRUCTORS:	Erika Goodman, B.J. Hanford
ESTABLISHED:	1978
CLASS FEE:	$150
SCHEDULE:	12-week term
STUDIOS:	8; and theatre
DRESSING ROOMS:	Yes
WAITING AREA:	Yes
BIOGRAPHY:	MS. GOODMAN studied dance at the Philadelphia Dance Academy; the School of American Ballet; and at the American Ballet Center. She performed with the Pennsylvania Ballet, the Boston Ballet, and was a principal dancer in the Joffrey Ballet. As an actress, she appeared in *Marat Sade* and *Bread and Roses*. MS. HANFORD performed in Boston with modern dance companies and ballet companies. She has worked with Broadway choreographers Ron Fields, Michael Bennett, and Onna White. She danced in the original production of *Cabaret* and with the national tours of *Promises, Promises; Applause;* and *Mame*.
CLASSES:	Ballet concentrates on ballet technique with the actor's particular needs in mind. Emphasis is on placement and line to facilitate the actor's experiencing freedom and comfort in movement, which leads to a complete expressiveness, complementing the actor's other skills. The class also covers period dancing. Jazz offers standing stretches, isolations, floor stretches, limbering exercises, and barre work to increase strength and coordination. Center work combines the style, rhythmical transitions, and intricate coordinations of current Broadway choreographers and the lyrical jazz styles of the 1930s, 1940s and 1950s. Tap is designed to introduce the actor to basic tap steps and combinations. Advanced classes focus on styles, especially those from musicals of the 1940s.
SUMMATION STATEMENT:	"All art is personal and its value is measured by its inner content. However, without training, a truly

responsive performance becomes less likely and more difficult to attain. The lab teaches the artist to observe life, and encourages him or her to illuminate the nature of man through behavior."

AESTHETIC REALISM FOUNDATION, INC.

141 Greene Street (near Houston Street)
New York, NY 10012
(212) 777–4490

PROGRAM:	Dance—Ballet, Jazz, Modern, Primitive
INSTRUCTOR:	Margot Carpenter
ESTABLISHED:	1980
CLASS FEE:	$35
SCHEDULE:	1 1³/₄-hour session every two weeks, 16 weeks
AUDITING:	Permitted
AUDITING FEE:	$5
SCHOLARSHIPS:	Not available
NUMBER OF STUDENTS PER CLASS:	15–20
STUDENT BREAKDOWN:	75% female, 25% male; 25% under 18, 30% 18–25, 30% 26–35, 15% 36–45
STUDIOS:	1
DRESSING ROOMS:	2
SHOWERS:	No
FLOOR:	Wood
BIOGRAPHY:	MS. CARPENTER has been an Aesthetic Realism Counselor since 1972, and has a background in dance and theatre, which includes stage and film work. She was a soloist with the Miami Ballet for 5 years.
CLASS:	The purpose of the class is to see, as the Aesthetic Realism of Eli Siegel teaches, that the permanent opposites of reality are as one in dance and have opposites of more than one in ourselves. This is done by learning all types of dance, including ballet, jazz, modern, and primitive.

ALVIN AILEY AMERICAN DANCE CENTER

1515 Broadway
New York, NY 10036
(212) 997–1980

PROGRAM:	Ballet I–III, Special Exercise, Jazz I–III, Modern I–III, Composition, Dance History, Dunham Technique I–II, Horton I–IA, Partnering, Pointe, Repertory Ensemble
INSTRUCTORS:	Deloras Brown, Robert Christopher, Barbara Cole, Michael Maule, Michael Vernon, Walter Raines, Wendy Amos, Christine Dhimos, Jean Paul Mustone, Jeff Ferguson, Miguel Godreau, Jose Meier, Beau Parker, Anna Marie Forsythe, Penny Frank, Denise Jefferson, Pearl Lang, Debbie Lukitsch, Diane Hunt Maroney, Ross Parkes, Marjorie Perces
REGISTRATION FEE:	$10 (includes one free class)
CLASS FEES:	Single class $5, 10-class card $45, 20-class card $75. Professional rates: 10-class card $35
SCHEDULE:	1½-hour sessions, 7 days per week, ongoing
AUDITING:	No audit
ENTRANCE REQUIREMENTS:	Open
CANCELLATION POLICIES:	No transfers, refunds, or extensions
SCHOLARSHIPS:	Available for full- and part-time study, audition required

AMERICAN BALLET THEATRE SCHOOL

Leon Danielian, Director
3 West 61st Street
New York, NY 10023
(212) 586–3355

PROGRAM:	Ballet
INSTRUCTORS:	Nansi Clement, Leon Danielian, Michael Maule, Olga Merinowa, Valentina Pereyaslavec, Patricia Wilde
ESTABLISHED:	1952
REGISTRATION FEE:	None

CLASS FEE: $5 per class; professional rate: $4 per class
ENTRANCE REQUIREMENTS: Open
SCHOLARSHIPS: Available for students ages 13–18
NUMBER OF STUDENTS
  PER CLASS: 30
TOTAL STUDIO ENROLLMENT: 1,500
STUDIOS: 6
DRESSING ROOMS: Yes
SHOWERS: Yes

AMERICAN DANCE MACHINE TRAINING FACILITY

4 East 75th Street, 3rd floor
New York, NY 10021
(212) 879–5750

PROGRAM: Theatre Dance, Repertory Dance Theatre, Jazz, Ballet
INSTRUCTORS: Nancy Chismar, Nenette Charisse, Phyllis Goldman, Buzz Miller, Lee Theodore
ESTABLISHED: 1977
REGISTRATION FEE: $5
CLASS FEE: $4 per class; $35 for 10 classes
ENTRANCE REQUIREMENTS: Open
SCHOLARSHIPS: Work-scholarships available
NUMBER OF STUDENTS
  PER CLASS: 20
TOTAL STUDIO ENROLLMENT: 250
STUDENT BREAKDOWN: 65% female, 35% male; 25% under 18, 40% 18–25, 10% 26–35, 25% 36–45, 0% over 45; 15% under 6 months, 25% $1/2$–1 year, 35% 1–2 years, 15% 2–3 years, 5% over 3 years
STUDIOS: 4
DRESSING ROOMS: Yes
SHOWERS: Yes
ACCOMPANYING
  INSTRUMENT: Percussion, Piano
CLASS CARD: Yes

MARY ANTHONY DANCE STUDIO

Mary Anthony, Ross Parkes, Daniel Maloney, Directors
736 Broadway
New York, NY 10003
(212) 674–8191

PROGRAM:	Ballet
INSTRUCTORS:	Pamela Critelli and company members
ESTABLISHED:	1954
REGISTRATION FEE:	None
CLASS FEES:	Single class $5; 4-class card $18; 8-class card $34; 12-class card $48; 16-class card $60; 20-class card $70 (all valid one month). Professional rates: single class $4; 5-class card $18.75; 10-class card $35; 15-class card $48.75; 20-class card $60 (all valid six months)
SCHEDULE:	1³/₄-hour sessions, ongoing
ENTRANCE REQUIREMENTS:	Open
SCHOLARSHIPS:	Available, audition required
NUMBER OF STUDENTS PER CLASS:	15–25
STUDENT BREAKDOWN:	75% female, 25% male; 25% under 18, 50% 18–25, 25% 26–35, 0% over 35
STUDIOS:	1
DRESSING ROOMS:	Yes
FLOOR:	Wood
ACCOMPANYING INSTRUMENT:	Piano and/or drum
CLASS CARD:	Yes, see fees above
WAITING AREA:	Yes
SUMMATION STATEMENT:	"Classes are for those who intend to go on in dance or for those willing to increase their commitment."

BALLET ACADEMY EAST

Julia R. Dubno, Director
340 West 79th Street, 2nd floor
New York, NY 10021
(212) 861–5204

PROGRAM:	Ballet, Jazz—Adult and Children
INSTRUCTORS:	Julia R. Dubno, Ian Guthrie, Frances Patrelle

ESTABLISHED:	1979
REGISTRATION FEE:	None
CLASS FEES:	8 classes $48, 15 classes $82, 30 classes $155
SCHEDULE:	1-hour sessions, ongoing
ENTRANCE REQUIREMENTS:	Open
CANCELLATION POLICIES:	Missed classes can be made up.
SCHOLARSHIPS:	Available for children only, by audition
NUMBER OF STUDENTS PER CLASS:	Limited to 15
STUDENT BREAKDOWN:	95% female, 5% male; 50% under 18, 25% 18–25, 21% 26–35, 5% 36–45, 1% over 45; 20% under 6 months, 20% 1/2–1year, 30% 1–2 years, 30% 2–3 years, 20% over 3 years
STUDIOS:	1
DRESSING ROOMS:	2
FLOOR:	Marley
ACCOMPANYING INSTRUMENT:	Piano, records
CLASS CARD:	Yes, see fees above
WAITING AREA:	Yes
BIOGRAPHY:	JULIA DUBNO has danced professionally with the Julliard Dance Ensemble and with various concert groups. She received her training at the Julliard School, the Fokine Ballet School, and with such teachers as Francis Patrelle, Oleg Sabline, and Igor Schwezoff.
SUMMATION STATEMENT:	"Our training is based on the traditional methods of the Imperial Russian Ballet School, combined with modern ballet as we know it today. We emphasize individual attention and offer each class as a pleasant and enriching experience for the student."

BALLET HISPANICO SCHOOL OF DANCE

Tina Ramirez, Director
167 West 89th Street
New York, NY 10024
(212) 362–6710

PROGRAM:	Ballet, Modern, Dunham Technique, Gymnastic Dance, Spanish Dance
INSTRUCTORS:	Virginia Cesbron, Coco Ramirez, Bertram Ross,

	Toby Towson, Pearl Reynolds, Alba Calzada, Sandra Rivera
ESTABLISHED:	1970
SCHEDULE:	1-to-1½-hour sessions, ongoing
AUDITING:	Not permitted
ENTRANCE REQUIREMENTS:	Open
CANCELLATION POLICIES:	Two-week written notice
SCHOLARSHIPS:	Limited number available
NUMBER OF STUDENTS PER CLASS:	17
STUDENT BREAKDOWN:	95% female, 5% male; 78% under 18, 15% 18–25, 7% 26–35, 0% over 35
VIDEO EQUIPMENT:	Yes
STUDIOS:	2
DRESSING ROOMS:	2
FLOOR:	Wood on wood
ACCOMPANYING INSTRUMENT:	Piano or drums
CLASS CARD:	Yes, valid 5 weeks
WAITING AREA:	Yes

PHIL BLACK DANCE STUDIO

1630 Broadway
New York, NY 10010
(212) 247–2675

PROGRAM:	Jazz, Ballet, Tap
INSTRUCTORS:	Phil Black, Robin Black, Dennis Dennehy, Jean Giardano
ESTABLISHED:	1961
REGISTRATION FEE:	None
CLASS FEE:	$3.50 per class
ENTRANCE REQUIREMENTS:	Open
SCHOLARSHIPS:	Not available
NUMBER OF STUDENTS PER CLASS:	20
TOTAL STUDIO ENROLLMENT:	400
STUDENT BREAKDOWN:	25% under 18, 40% 18–25, 20% 26–35, 10% 36–45, 5% over 45; 30% under 6 months, 25% ½–1 year, 25% 1–2 years, 0% 2–3 years, 20% over 3 years
STUDIOS:	2
DRESSING ROOMS:	Yes
SHOWERS:	No

ACCOMPANYING
   INSTRUMENT: Records, drums
CLASS CARD: Yes

BEVERLY BOROUGH

Showcase Studios
950 Eighth Avenue
New York, NY 10019
(212) 864-1586

PROGRAM:	Modern—Beginner-Intermediate, Intermediate
ESTABLISHED:	1976
REGISTRATION FEE:	None
CLASS FEE:	$3 per class
SCHEDULE:	2-hour sessions, ongoing
AUDITING:	Permitted
AUDITING FEE:	No fee
ENTRANCE REQUIREMENTS:	Open
SCHOLARSHIPS:	Available at instructor's discretion
NUMBER OF STUDENTS PER CLASS:	10–12
STUDENT BREAKDOWN:	50% female, 50% male; 0% under 18, 45% 18–25, 40% 26–35, 15% 36–45, 0% over 45
STUDIOS:	5
DRESSING ROOMS:	Yes
SHOWERS:	None
FLOOR:	Wood
ACCOMPANYING INSTRUMENT:	Piano, drum, or tape
BIOGRAPHY:	MS. BOROUGH studied dance extensively with the National Ballet in Washington, D.C. She has danced with the Potatoes Only Company in Tampa and has been a free-lance choreographer in Chicago, San Francisco, and Wisconsin.
CLASSES:	Classes are geared toward actors and singers with a feeling of relaxation minus competitiveness. Horton, Limon, and Graham techniques, some ballet, centering, relaxation, combinations, and work across the floor are utilized.
SUMMATION STATEMENT:	"I work on an individualized approach, emphasizing mental awareness and movement through motivation . . . that every step has a feeling and emotion behind it."

BEVERLY BROWN DANCENTER

388 Broadway, Studio 5
New York, NY 10013
(212) 966–0709

PROGRAM:	Body and Voice Theatre Workshop
INSTRUCTORS:	Beverly Brown, Roger Tolle
ESTABLISHED:	1976
REGISTRATION FEE:	None
CLASS FEE:	Approximately $65, depending upon length of workshop
SCHEDULE:	2 1½-to-3-hour sessions per week, 2–3 weeks
AUDITING:	Yes, special permission required
AUDITING FEE:	No fee
SCHOLARSHIPS:	Not available
NUMBER OF STUDENTS PER CLASS:	20
STUDIOS:	1
DRESSING ROOMS:	1
SHOWERS:	None
FLOOR:	Marley
ACCOMPANYING INSTRUMENT:	Percussion, voice
BIOGRAPHY:	MS. BROWN created her first body/voice theatre work in 1974 and has since been evolving the aesthetic concepts and training techniques of this unique form of contemporary dance theatre. Six years a soloist with the Erick Hawkins Dance Company and a founding member of the Greenhouse Dance Ensemble, she has been choreographer-in-residence at universities across the United States. MR. TOLLE, a soloist with Dancensemble, was for 4 years a principal dancer with the Concert Dance Company of Boston. He has performed in the works of Anna Sokolow, Art Bauman, Pilibolus, and Sophie Maslow.
CLASS:	The emphasis of each workshop is either technique with improvisation, or technique with repertory. The training is for a theatrical art form encompassing both body movement and vocal sound. The goal is to establish a working situation in which each dancer/singer can progress from his individual starting point. We also work to create a reciprocal environment in which students learn from the responses of other students as well as from the teacher.

SUMMATION STATEMENT: "We are concerned with a form of contemporary theatre which combines a modern dance movement vocabulary with vocal sound textures and chanting, simple percussion and sound tapes."

RITA COLBY BALLET SCHOOL

Mailing Address: 308 West 55th Street
New York, NY 10019
Studio: Carnegie Hall Area

(212) 245–3605

PROGRAM:	Ballet Basics—"Designed for the Adult Beginner"
ESTABLISHED:	1972
REGISTRATION FEE:	None
SCHEDULE:	4 sessions per week
AUDITING:	Not permitted
ENTRANCE REQUIREMENTS:	Telephone interview
CANCELLATION POLICIES:	Notification and make-up arranged within card period
SCHOLARSHIPS:	Not available
NUMBER OF STUDENTS PER CLASS:	12 (private available)
STUDENT BREAKDOWN:	90% female, 10% male; 2% under 18, 40% 18–25, 40% 26–35, 16% 36–45, 2% over 45
STUDIOS:	1
DRESSING ROOMS:	2
SHOWERS:	None
FLOOR:	Wood
ACCOMPANYING INSTRUMENT:	Records
CLASS CARD:	5- and 10-week cards available
WAITING AREA:	Yes
BIOGRAPHY:	MS. COLBY holds a B.S. teaching degree as a dance major. Studies in anatomy, physiology, and kinesiology guided the structuring of this program, originated in 1972, as "Ballet Designed for the Adult Beginner." She is New York trained, with credits in stock, company, Off-Broadway, and children's theatre.
CLASS:	The class provides a program that slowly adapts unaccustomed muscles and joints to classical technique. Class begins with tension-relaxing warm-ups, followed by thorough methodical ballet

barre, stretch, and floor work. Classes are patiently taught, explained, demonstrated, and correlated with terminology enabling the student to enjoy executing the light, lyrical, varied center patterns. Helpful suggestions for improving alignment is tailored to the individual. Optional floor stretch exercises after ballet.

SUMMATION STATEMENT: "The goal of the class is to provide the adult with a comfortable setting where groups can learn in a secure, noncompetitive atmosphere, and where neither professionals nor observers are admitted. Never ignored nor intimidated, the adult has the opportunity to recognize that ballet is a rewarding lfielong pursuit."

CAROL CONWAY SCHOOL OF DANCE

Carol Conway, Director
35 Bond Street
New York, NY 10012
(212) 674–8034

PROGRAM:	Modern
INSTRUCTORS:	Carol Conway, Randall Wilson, Virginia Rutherford
ESTABLISHED:	1974
REGISTRATION FEE:	None
CLASS FEES:	Single classes $6; 10 classes—3 per week $40, 2 per week $45, 1 per week $50
SCHEDULE:	13 1½-hour sessions per week, ongoing
AUDITING:	Permitted
AUDITING FEE:	No fee
ENTRANCE REQUIREMENTS:	Open
CANCELLATION POLICIES:	No refunds, make-up classes available
SCHOLARSHIPS:	Partial work-exchange scholarships available, based on ability and length of study
REQUIRED MATERIALS:	Clothing so teacher can see the body; barefoot
NUMBER OF STUDENTS PER CLASS:	Limited to 10
STUDENT BREAKDOWN:	90% female, 10% male; 1% under 18, 75% 18–25, 24% 26–35, 0% over 35; 1% under 6 months, 20% ½–1 year, 60% 1–2 years, 15% 2–3 years, 4% over 3 years
STUDIOS:	1
DRESSING ROOMS:	2

SHOWERS:	None
FLOOR:	Birds-eye maple
ACCOMPANYING	
INSTRUMENT:	None
CLASS CARD:	$40–$50 cards, valid 10 weeks
BIOGRAPHY:	MS. CONWAY studied with the Pacific Ballet Company, Erick Hawkins, Martha Graham, and Jose Limon; choreography with Lucia Dlugozewski; body placement and ideokinesis with Andre Bernard and Bonnie Cohen. She was a member of the Erick Hawkins Dance Company and a founding member of the Greenhouse Dance Ensemble before establishing her own company in 1974. MS. RUTHERFORD has degrees in art history from Vassar College and drama/dance from the University of Montana. Since coming to New York in 1981, she has studied with Carol Conway, joining the teaching staff in 1983. MR. WILSON was born and raised in Hawaii. He became interested in dance after moving to New York City in 1974. He has studied dance with the Erick Hawkins Dance Company and with Carol Conway. He joined the Carol Conway Dance Company in 1981 and began teaching in the company school in 1983.
CLASS:	The classes are designed to train professional modern dancers and teachers. The classes consist of $1/2$-hour warm-up on the floor, $1/2$-hour center work, and $1/2$-hour across the floor. The program stresses placement, strength, and flexibility; and modern dance as a totality, including dynamics, performance, phrasing, space, and focus.
SUMMATION STATEMENT:	"Our teaching is supportive and students receive individual attention."

MERCE CUNNINGHAM STUDIO

Merce Cunningham, Director
463 West Street, 11th floor
New York, NY 10014
(212) 691–9751

PROGRAM:	Modern—Fundamental through Advanced Levels
INSTRUCTORS:	Merce Cunningham, Susan Alexander, Ruth Barnes, Susana Hayman-Chaffey, Ellen Cornfield,

Barbara Ensley, June Finch, Diane Frank, Meg Harper, Chris Komar, Ann Papoulis, Albert Reid

ESTABLISHED:	1956
REGISTRATION FEE:	$15
CLASS FEES:	Single class $5; 10 classes $35; 13-week semester tuition—$215 and up
AUDITING:	Permitted
ENTRANCE REQUIREMENTS:	Open
CANCELLATION POLICIES:	Refunds only in cases of authenticated illness
SCHOLARSHIPS:	Available by audition; federal financial aid to eligible students
NUMBER OF STUDENTS PER CLASS:	25
STUDENT BREAKDOWN:	80% female, 20% male; 10% under 18, 40% 18–25, 40% 26–35, 10% 36–45, 0% over 45; 15% under 6 months, 10% $1/2$–1 year, 30% 1–2 years, 30% 2–3 years, 15% over 3 years
STUDIOS:	2 studios, media-dance library
DRESSING ROOMS:	2
SHOWERS:	Yes
FLOOR:	Sprung hardwood maple
BIOGRAPHY:	MR. CUNNINGHAM began choreographing independently in 1942. Teaching soon became an important adjunct to his choreography, and he became much in demand for master classes across the United States; for two seasons he taught a weekly class at the School of the American Ballet. In 1953 he established his own company which has toured the United States and abroad.
CLASSES:	The studio offers a program in dance training designed to further the student interested in a professional career, whether as a teacher or as a performer. The program starts with technique, which places emphasis on strength, clarity, and precision, and which is the support for the continuing experience. Cunningham is committed to technique that not only makes demands of students in physical terms but also expects of them an enlarging resilience of the mind.
SUMMATION STATEMENT:	"The major strength of the program lies in its close association with the dance company. Cunningham is concerned that the technique not remain fixed, but a flexible experience. Since we work with the body, the strongest and at the same time the most fragile of instruments, the necessity to organize and understand the way of moving is of great urgency for the dancer."

RUTH CURRIER DANCE STUDIO

Ruth Currier, Director
425 Broome Street, 4th floor
New York, NY 10013
(212) 966-7521

PROGRAM:	Modern Dance
INSTRUCTORS:	Ruth Currier, Jane Brendel, Clay Taliaferro
ESTABLISHED:	1981
REGISTRATION FEE:	$5
CLASS FEE:	Single class $6
SCHEDULE:	5 or 6 1½-to1¾-hour classes per week, 46 weeks per year, ongoing
AUDITING:	Permitted
AUDITING FEE:	No fee
ENTRANCE REQUIREMENTS:	Open
SCHOLARSHIPS:	Partial work-study scholarships available
REQUIRED MATERIALS:	Body-revealing dress
NUMBER OF STUDENTS PER CLASS:	8–25, limited
STUDIOS:	1
DRESSING ROOMS:	2
SHOWERS:	None
FLOOR:	Maple
ACCOMPANYING INSTRUMENT:	Piano, etc.
CLASS CARD:	8, 12, or 20 classes—valid 1 month
BIOGRAPHY:	MS. CURRIER was a soloist in the Jose Limon Company and an assistant to Doris Humphrey. MR. TALIAFERRO studied at the Boston Conservatory, and with Donald McKayle, and was a member of the Jose Limon Company. MS. BRENDEL has studied with Betty Jones and Ruth Currier.
SUMMATION STATEMENT:	"Our studio offers technical and choreographic training in the tradition of Doris Humphrey and Jose Limon."

DANCE CIRCLE

Alfredo Corvino, Director
763 Eighth Avenue
New York, NY 10036
(212) 541-7986

PROGRAM:	Ballet, All Levels
INSTRUCTORS:	Alfredo Corvino, Andra Corvino, Ernesta Corvino
ESTABLISHED:	1969
REGISTRATION FEE:	None
CLASS FEES:	$5 single class, $45 for 10 classes within 2 months
SCHEDULE:	1 or 2 1½-hour sessions per week per level
AUDITING:	Permitted
AUDITING FEE:	No fee
SCHOLARSHIPS:	Not available
REQUIRED MATERIALS:	Women: leotard, tights, slippers. Men: T-shirt, tights, dance belt, slippers
NUMBER OF STUDENTS PER CLASS:	10–25 average, not limited
STUDENT BREAKDOWN:	66% female, 34% male; 66% 26–35, 34% over 45; 10% under 6 months, 30% ½–1 year, 20% 1–2 years, 20% 2–3 years, 20% over three years
VIDEO EQUIPMENT:	Yes
STUDIOS:	2
DRESSING ROOMS:	2
SHOWERS:	No
FLOOR:	Wood
ACCOMPANYING INSTRUMENT:	Piano
BIOGRAPHY:	MR. CORVINO, born in Montevideo, Uruguay, danced with such companies as Ballets Rosse de Monte Carlo, the Jooss Ballet, the Radio City Music Hall Ballet, and the Metropolitan Opera Ballet. He has been director of the Dance Circle Company since its inception and has taught ballet at the Julliard School since 1952. A foremost authority on technique, he has taught and choreographed for many regional ballet companies. ANDRA CORVINO was trained at the Metropolitan Opera Ballet School and subsequently joined the company at age 18. She was also a principal dancer with the Maryland Ballet and made guest appearances with the Royal Ballet of England. Andra also teaches at the Julliard School and performs with the Dance Circle Company. ERNESTA CORVINO was

CLASSES: trained at the Metropolitan Opera Ballet School and danced with such companies as the Maryland Ballet, the Radio City Music Hall Ballet and the American Chamber Ballet. She also teaches at the Inner City Ensemble of Patterson, New Jersey. She currently directs the Dance Circle Company of which she is principal dancer and choreographer. Each class begins with a very thorough barre and center, consisting of a balance of adagio, turning, and jumping combinations. The class consists of a full barre with turns and jumps at the barre.

SUMMATION STATEMENT: "The special brand of ballet taught at the Dance Circle is Alfredo Corvino's own technique, an eclectic blend of the various traditional schools. Emphasis is put on correct placement, musicality, and dynamic movement in a natural and organic way so as to benefit dancers of all styles. Classes are small enough to afford each student individual attention, and the Dance Circle Company provides gifted students with performing opportunities."

DANCE-JUNE LEWIS & COMPANY

June Lewis, Director
48 West 21st Street
New York, NY 10010
(212) 741–3044

PROGRAM:	Modern—Basic Elementary through Level II; Contemporary Technique; General Technique
INSTRUCTORS:	June Lewis, Claude Assante, Howard Hormann, Barbara Mateer, Alyssa Satin, Vivian White
ESTABLISHED:	1972
REGISTRATION FEE:	None
CLASS FEES:	Trial $6; single $5; 10-class card $40 (valid 4 weeks); 15-class card $50 (valid 6 weeks); 20-class card $70 (valid 10 weeks)
SCHEDULE:	$1^1/_4$–$1^1/_2$ hour sessions, ongoing
AUDITING:	Permitted by appointment
AUDITING FEE:	No fee
ENTRANCE REQUIREMENTS:	Placement by evaluation
SCHOLARSHIPS:	Available
NUMBER OF STUDENTS PER CLASS:	Limited to 25

STUDENT BREAKDOWN:	80% female, 20% male; 5% under 18, 53% 18–25, 30% 26–35, 10% 36–45, 2% over 45; 15% under 6 months, 10% 1/2–1 year, 40% 1–2 years, 23% 2–3 years, 12% over 3 years
STUDIOS:	2
DRESSING ROOMS:	2
SHOWERS:	None
FLOOR:	Wood
ACCOMPANYING INSTRUMENT:	Piano, percussion, other
CLASS CARD:	Yes, see fees above
BIOGRAPHY:	Teachers at June Lewis are all either present or former members of Dance-June Lewis & Company or invited guest artists.
CLASSES:	Program is geared to meet the needs of each individual dancer. Classes are geared toward levels of concentration.
SUMMATION STATEMENT:	"Quality, clarity, and excellence."

THE DANCE MOVEMENT

Gail Kachadurian, Director
20 East 17th Street, 8th floor
New York, NY 10003
(212) 724–5645

PROGRAM:	Ballet, Beginner–Intermediate
ESTABLISHED:	1971
REGISTRATION FEE:	None
CLASS FEES:	6-week card $33, 24-week card $60
SCHEDULE:	1 1/4-hour sessions, ongoing
ENTRANCE REQUIREMENTS:	Open
SCHOLARSHIPS:	Not available
NUMBER OF STUDENTS PER CLASS:	20
STUDIOS:	1
DRESSING ROOMS:	2
FLOOR:	Linoleum
ACCOMPANYING INSTRUMENT:	Records
CLASS CARD:	Yes, see fees above
WAITING AREA:	Yes
BIOGRAPHY:	MS. KACHADURIAN studied 10 years with the New York City Ballet Company and has taught

ballet at her own school for 8 years. She has served as choreographer for television and for commercials.

CLASSES:
The objective of the classes is to study ballet as a form of exercise, to personally explore it as an art form, to use it as a form of therapeutic exercise, to break down barriers held within and without the body, to use dance as a vehicle for self-exploration, and to dance to feel better about yourself.

SUMMATION STATEMENT:
"Only through correct alignment and use of the body can one find physical well-being and true health. So many people experience their bodies as alien. We try to find harmony between our mind, spirit, and body."

DANCE NOTATION BUREAU

Jan Hanvik, Bunny Rosens, Directors
505 Eighth Avenue
New York, NY 10018
(212) 736–4350

PROGRAM:	Labnotation, Reconstruction, Kinesiology, Laban Movement Analysis, Music, Benesh Notation
INSTRUCTORS:	Sandra Aberkalns, Karen Barracuda, Jill Beck, Ray Cook, Ed Dilello, Virginia Doris, Ilene Fox, Charles Garth, David Lowenstein, Susanna Reich, Leslie Rotman, Ann Rodiger, Carol Page, Muriel Topaz
ESTABLISHED:	1941
REGISTRATION FEE:	$10
CLASS FEES:	$150–$300 per term
SCHEDULE:	1 to 3 sessions per week, 3–10 weeks, ongoing
AUDITING:	Permitted
AUDITING FEE:	Half-price
ENTRANCE REQUIREMENTS:	Interview; intermediate dance technique
CANCELLATION POLICIES:	Cancellations must be made 10 days prior to commencement of class.
SCHOLARSHIPS:	Available
REQUIRED MATERIALS:	Dance clothes, varied texts
NUMBER OF STUDENTS PER CLASS:	Limited to 12
TOTAL STUDIO ENROLLMENT:	40
STUDENT BREAKDOWN:	65% female, 35% male; 40% 18–25, 30% 26–35,

15% 36–45, 15% over 45; 33% under 6 months,
33% 1/2–1 year, 34% 1–2 years

VIDEO EQUIPMENT:	Yes
STUDIOS:	2
DRESSING ROOMS:	2
SHOWERS:	None
FLOOR:	Sprung wood
ACCOMPANYING INSTRUMENT:	Percussion
WAITING AREA:	Yes

BIOGRAPHY: MS. ABERKALNS is a Benesh Notator with American Ballet Theatre. MS. BARRACUDA, a Julliard graduate, is with Brooklyn College. MR. COOK is a notator and reconstructor at Vassar College. MR. DILELLO is a composer and choreographer. MS. DORIS danced with Agnes DeMille and is a notator and reconstructor. MS. FOX is a notator of Joffrey, Sokolow, Shawn and others. MR. GARTH is a Feuillet notation teacher and a Renaissance dance director. MR. LOWENSTEIN is a certified movement analyst with an M.A. in dance. MS. PAGE is a notation teacher and choreographer. MS. RODIGER is a notator/reconstructor/choreographer. MS. REICH is a certified movement analyst. MS. ROTMAN is a notator, reconstructor, and teacher with an M.F.A. from Sarah Lawrence. MS. TOPAZ is the Bureau's Executive Director and a notator of work by Balanchine, Limon, Tudor, Graham, and Humphrey.

CLASSES: All courses approach the subject matter theoretcially and through movement theory and movement levels, progressing from elementary through advanced levels.

SUMMATION STATEMENT: "We teach dance notation by reading well-known dance works and through creative writing exercises. Our goal is to impart a practical and applicable knowledge of notated dance literature. Full employment as a career notation professional is increasingly an alternative to performing and choreography for those interested in remaining in the dance field."

DANCE THEATRE OF HARLEM

Arthur Mitchell and Karel Shook, Directors
466 West 152nd Street
New York, NY 10031
(212) 690–2800

PROGRAM:	Ballet, Ethnic, Tap, Modern, Exercise, Repertory
INSTRUCTORS:	Vicki Fedine, Mary Hinkson, Arthur Mitchell, Melvin Purnell, Karel Shook, Carol Sumner, Victoria Simon
ESTABLISHED:	1969
REGISTRATION FEE:	$10
CLASS FEE:	$5 per class
SCHOLARSHIPS:	Full, partial and work-scholarships available
NUMBER OF STUDENTS PER CLASS:	25
TOTAL STUDIO ENROLLMENT:	1,100
STUDENT BREAKDOWN:	70% female, 30% male; 40% under 18, 30% 18–25, 20% 26–35, 5% 36–45, 5% over 45; 30% under 6 months, 30% ½–1 year, 25% 1–2 years, 15% 2–3 years, 0% over 3 years
STUDIOS:	3
DRESSING ROOMS:	Yes
SHOWERS:	Yes
ACCOMPANYING INSTRUMENT:	Percussion, piano
CLASS CARD:	Yes

CAL DEL POZO

Caranci Studio
22 West 15th Street
New York, NY 10011
(212) 924–5295

PROGRAM:	Jazz
INSTRUCTOR:	Cal del Pozo
ESTABLISHED:	1977
REGISTRATION FEE:	None
CLASS FEES:	Single class $5, 10-class card $40 (valid 2 months)
SCHEDULE:	1½-hour sessions, ongoing
AUDITING:	Permitted

AUDITING FEE:	None
ENTRANCE REQUIREMENTS:	Open
SCHOLARSHIPS:	Not available
NUMBER OF STUDENTS PER CLASS:	Average 15, not limited
STUDENT BREAKDOWN:	75% female, 25% male; 0% under 18, 50% 18–25, 45% 26–35, 5% 36–45, 0% over 45; 15% under 6 months, 15% ½–1 year, 40% 1–2 years, 30% 2–3 years, 0% over 3 years
STUDIOS:	7
DRESSING ROOMS:	Yes
SHOWERS:	None
FLOOR:	Hardwood
ACCOMPANYING INSTRUMENT:	Records
CLASS CARD:	Yes, see fees above
BIOGRAPHY:	MR. DEL POZO danced with the Miami Ballet Company and Luigi's Jazz Company. His credits include Broadway and Off-Broadway productions, and he has choreographed 4 Broadway shows in the last 3 years.
CLASS:	Classes are geared to theatre dance for actors, models, and dancers.

THE EXERCISE EXCHANGE

Jean Paul Mustone, Director
236 West 78th Street
New York, NY 10024
(212) 595–6475

PROGRAM:	General, Corrective, Stretch, Aerobic
INSTRUCTORS:	14 instructors
ESTABLISHED:	1980
REGISTRATION FEE:	None
CLASS FEES:	Single class $6; 10-class card $45, valid 2 months
SCHEDULE:	Continuous 1-hour classes, 7:30 A.M.–8:30 P.M.
ENTRANCE REQUIREMENTS:	Open
SCHOLARSHIPS:	Not available
NUMBER OF STUDENTS PER CLASS:	15–25
STUDENT BREAKDOWN:	50% 18–25, 40% 26–35, 5% 36–45, 5% over 45
STUDIOS:	1
DRESSING ROOMS:	2

SHOWERS: 1
FLOOR: Carpeted
ACCOMPANYING
  INSTRUMENT: Tapes, records
CLASS CARD: Yes, valid 2 months, 10 classes $45
WAITING AREA: Yes
CLASSES: General emphasizes muscular strength and postural alignment through basic flexibility and range-of-motion exercises; Corrective applies special attention to structural problems and skeletal alignment, especially the spinal column; Stretch improves joint flexibility and muscular elasticity through passive resistance and breathing; Aerobics stress cardiovascular strength and endurance.

JERRI GARNER'S DANCE FOR SINGER-ACTORS ONLY

124 West Houston Street
New York, NY 10012
(212) 254–3951

PROGRAM: Ballet, Jazz, Tap
INSTRUCTOR: Jerri Garner
ESTABLISHED: 1979
REGISTRATION FEE: None
CLASS FEES: Single class $5; 10-class card (valid 1 year) $45; 10-class card (valid 1 month) $40; 10-class card (valid 2 weeks) $35
SCHEDULE: 2 2-hour sessions per week, ongoing
AUDITING: Not permitted
ENTRANCE REQUIREMENTS: Open
SCHOLARSHIPS: Work-scholarships available
NUMBER OF STUDENTS
  PER CLASS: 6–10
STUDENT BREAKDOWN: 50% 18–25, 48% 26–35, 2% 36–45; 75% under 6 months, 15% ½–1 year, 10% 1–2 years
STUDIOS: 1
DRESSING ROOMS: 2
SHOWERS: 1
FLOOR: Battleship linoleum over wood floor
WAITING AREA: Yes
BIOGRAPHY: MS. GARNER has performed as a professional dancer for 10 years on Broadway and touring.

She has choreographed for Off Broadway, London, and for touring companies of such shows as *The Mikado, The Fantasticks,* and *Finian's Rainbow.*

CLASSES: Ballet: Classes are aimed for the beginning adult professional who must learn how to dance in the shortest time possible. Jazz: Daily classes in all styles of jazz, from Busby Berkeley to Bob Fosse, and everything in between. Each class includes a floor warm-up, barre exercises, isolations, floor work, and a dance combination.

SUMMATION STATEMENT: "This dance studio provides a place for singers-actors to learn how to dance in an atmosphere that is congenial and uncrowded."

MARTHA GRAHAM SCHOOL OF CONTEMPORARY DANCE

Martha Graham, Artistic Director
Diane Gray, Director
316 East 63rd Street
New York, NY 10021
(212) 838–5886

PROGRAM: Fundamentals I, II; Elementary, Intermediate, Advanced Martha Graham Technique

INSTRUCTORS: Present and former members of the company

ESTABLISHED: 1925

REGISTRATION FEE: $25 per year

CLASS FEES: Single class $6; 10-class card (valid 30 days) $50; 20-class card (valid 30 days) $85; 20-class card (valid 60 days) $105. Professional rates—$6 per class, $45 for 10 classes.

SCHEDULE: Fundamentals I—13 weeks; other classes are on-going, 1 1/2-hour sessions

AUDITING: Permitted

AUDITING FEE: $3 per class

ENTRANCE REQUIREMENTS: Open

CANCELLATION POLICIES: Make-up sessions available

SCHOLARSHIPS: Financial aid available by audition for 2-year certificate program

NUMBER OF STUDENTS
  PER CLASS: 20–30

STUDENT BREAKDOWN:	85% female, 15% male; 5% under 18, 75% 18–25, 15% 26–35, 5% 36–45
VIDEO EQUIPMENT:	Yes
STUDIOS:	3
DRESSING ROOMS:	2
SHOWERS:	2
FLOOR:	Sprung wood
ACCOMPANYING INSTRUMENT:	Piano
SUMMATION STATEMENT:	"The Martha Graham School is the only school in the world where, for the length of time required to master a craft and perfect a talent, the serious dance student may learn the Martha Graham technique."

ERICK HAWKINS SCHOOL OF DANCE

78 Fifth Avenue
New York, NY 10011
(212) 255–6698

PROGRAM:	Modern
INSTRUCTORS:	Erick Hawkins, Lucia Dlugoszewski, Rand Howard, Cynthia Reynolds, Cori Terry, Cathy Ward
ESTABLISHED:	1952
REGISTRATION FEE:	None
CLASS FEE:	$5 per class
ENTRANCE REQUIREMENTS:	Open to adults
SCHOLARSHIPS:	Not available
NUMBER OF STUDENTS PER CLASS:	15
TOTAL STUDIO ENROLLMENT:	350
STUDENT BREAKDOWN:	60% female, 40% male; 0% under 18, 40% 18–25, 30% 26–35, 25% 36–45, 5% over 45; 30% under 6 months, 40% 1/2–1 year, 25% 1–2 years, 5% 2–3 years, 0% over 3 years
STUDIOS:	1
DRESSING ROOMS:	Yes
SHOWERS:	No
ACCOMPANYING INSTRUMENT:	None
CLASS CARD:	Yes

MELISSA HAYDEN INC.

Melissa Hayden, Director
1845 Broadway
New York, NY 10023
(212) 582–7929

PROGRAM:	Ballet: Adult Beginner thru Advanced/Intermediate
INSTRUCTORS:	Melissa Hayden, Wilhem Burmann, Hilary Cartwright
ESTABLISHED:	1976
REGISTRATION FEE:	None
CLASS FEES:	Single class $5. 10-class card $45. Professional rates—single class $4.50; 10-class card $40; barre only, $3.
SCHEDULE:	1½-hour sessions, ongoing
AUDITING:	Permitted
AUDITING FEE:	None
SCHOLARSHIPS:	Available
NUMBER OF STUDENTS PER CLASS:	35
STUDENT BREAKDOWN:	75% female, 25% male; 10% under 18, 50% 18–25, 40% 26–35, 0% over 35
STUDIOS:	1
DRESSING ROOMS:	2
SHOWERS:	None
FLOOR:	Sprung wood
ACCOMPANYING INSTRUMENT:	Piano
CLASS CARD:	Yes, see fees above
WAITING AREA:	Yes
BIOGRAPHY:	MS. HAYDEN began her career in 1945 when she joined American Ballet Theatre, rising within 9 months to the rank of soloist. She was leading ballerina with the New York City Ballet from 1949 until 1973. Among other honors she has received are the Albert Einstein, the Dance Educators, and the *Dance Magazine* awards and the Handel Medallion. MR. BURMANN toured with the Garden State Ballet and was invited to join the Pennsylvania Ballet as a principal. He danced with the New York City Ballet for 5 years and then as a principal dancer with the Geneva Ballet. He has been ballet master and teacher for the Washington Ballet. MS. CARTWRIGHT performed with England's Royal Ballet and the Sadler Wells Royal

Ballet, with whom she later became ballet mistress. She was associate director of the Royal Winnipeg Ballet and director of the junior company of the Dutch Netherlands Company.

SUMMATION STATEMENT: "The school tries to provide the maximum means and opportunity for students to improve."

HB STUDIO

Muriel Burns, Director
120 Bank Street
New York, NY 10014
(212) 675–2370

PROGRAM:	Ballet for Actors, Jazz, Modern, Yoga
INSTRUCTORS:	Barrie Estes, Randall Faxon Parker, June Eve Story, Gui Andrisano, Harriet All
ESTABLISHED:	1945
REGISTRATION FEE:	$7.50
CLASS FEE:	$66.50 (average)
SCHEDULE:	$1^{1}/_{2}$–$2^{1}/_{2}$ hours per week, 19 weeks, ongoing
AUDITING:	Not permitted
ENTRANCE REQUIREMENTS:	Open (for most classes)
CANCELLATION POLICIES:	No refunds given after term has started and no credit given for classes missed.
SCHOLARSHIPS:	Work-exchange available
NUMBER OF STUDENTS PER CLASS:	15–35
TOTAL STUDIO ENROLLMENT:	Over 3,000
STUDENT BREAKDOWN:	60% female, 40% male; 5% under 18, 45% 18–25, 20% 26–35, 20% 36–45, 10% over 45; 5% under 6 months, 10% $^{1}/_{2}$–1 year, 25% 1–2 years, 40% 2–3 years, 20% over 3 years
STUDIOS:	5
DRESSING ROOMS:	2
SHOWERS:	None
FLOOR:	Dance
ACCOMPANYING INSTRUMENT:	Piano
WAITING AREA:	Yes
SUMMATION STATEMENT:	"The HB Studio began in 1945 and aims for a meaningful dramatic expression of the times and country in which we live. To help establish a theatre of experimentation based on classic tradition,

the Studio is dedicated to the development of individual artists who may actively contribute to a theatre of national character. Conceived as an artistic and working home, it offers an outlet for practice and growth for the professional theatre artist, and an opportunity for the young to establish roots in their intended crafts. The Studio's guiding principle is creative freedom, which has as its logical consequence responsibility to a noble art."

FINIS JHUNG STUDIO

2182 Broadway (at 77th Street)
New York, NY 10024
(212) 874–4740

PROGRAM:	Ballet: Intro to Ballet, Advanced Beginning, Beginning Intermediate, Intermediate, Advanced Intermediate, Advanced; Stretch and Alignment; American Yoga; Video Analysis of Famous Dancers; Music Theory
INSTRUCTORS:	Finis Jhung, Liana Plane, Sally Silliman, Barbara Forbes, Theresa Cornish, Eric Beeler, Bill Brown
ESTABLISHED:	1973
REGISTRATION FEE:	None
CLASS FEES:	Single class $6; 10-class card $55, valid 1 month. Professional rates—$5 per class; 10-class card $45, valid 3 months. Theory—$40 for 4 classes; Video—$10 per lecture, 5 1½-hour sessions per level per week, ongoing; Stretch—2 1-hour classes per week; Yoga—6 1½-hour classes per week; Video—2 1½-hour classes, bimonthly; Theory—4 1½-hour sessions, 4 consecutive Sundays
AUDITING:	Not permitted
ENTRANCE REQUIREMENTS:	Open
CANCELLATION POLICIES:	No refunds
SCHOLARSHIPS:	Work-study available
STUDIOS:	1
DRESSING ROOMS:	2
SHOWERS:	Yes
CLASSES:	Classes emphasize correct placement, strength of movement and performance outlook. Video—A look at what makes the great ones great in slow motion, stop frame. Baryshnikov, Makarova, and

other stars. Theory—The aim of the course is to help the student "hear" the music and learn to use it effectively, to understand the written score through study of basic rhythmic notation; and to develop better communication between dancers and musicians through definition and understanding of musical language. Includes meter, counting, musical markings, the dances, musical phrasing.

SUMMATION STATEMENT: "We try to teach people the way we wish we had been taught—with knowledge and compassion."

LE STUDIO

Edwige Val, Director
152 West 56th Street, 2nd floor
New York, NY 10019
(212) 757-1941

PROGRAM:	Ballet: Beginner–Advanced; Jazz
INSTRUCTORS:	Edwidge Val, Ron Bostic, Anna Youskevitch, Rhett Dennis, Gary Cowan, Jeff Edmund
ESTABLISHED:	1976
REGISTRATION FEE:	None
CLASS FEES:	Single class $5, 10 classes $40
SCHEDULE:	1–1½-hour sessions, ongoing
AUDITING:	Not permitted
ENTRANCE REQUIREMENTS:	Open
NUMBER OF STUDENTS PER CLASS:	Not limited
STUDENT BREAKDOWN:	65% female, 35% male; 0% under 18, 40% 18–25, 40% 26–35, 20% 36–45, 0% over 45
STUDIOS:	3
DRESSING ROOMS:	4
SHOWERS:	Yes
FLOOR:	Wood
ACCOMPANYING INSTRUMENT:	Piano, records
CLASS CARD:	Yes, see fees above
WAITING AREA:	Yes

NANCY MEEHAN DANCE SCHOOL

Nancy Meehan, Director
463 West Street
New York, NY 10014
(212) 929–2143

PROGRAM:	Beginning, Intermediate, and Advanced Modern
ESTABLISHED:	1970
REGISTRATION FEE:	None
CLASS FEES:	10 classes, 3 or more times a week $40; 10 classes 1 or more times a week $45
SCHEDULE:	9 1-hour sessions per week, ongoing
AUDITING:	Not permitted
ENTRANCE REQUIREMENTS:	Open
SCHOLARSHIPS:	Limited number available
NUMBER OF STUDENTS PER CLASS:	11–15
STUDENT BREAKDOWN:	90% female, 10% male; 0% under 18, 50% 18–25, 50% 26–35, 0% over 35; 15% under 6 months, 10% 1/2–1 year, 50% 1–2 years, 25% 2–3 years, 0% over 3 years
STUDIOS:	1
DRESSING ROOMS:	1
SHOWERS:	None
FLOOR:	Maple
ACCOMPANYING INSTRUMENT:	Percussion
WAITING AREA:	Yes
BIOGRAPHY:	All instructors are company members of at least 3 years standing.
CLASSES:	Each class has as its goals the development of clear placement, fluidity, lift, dynamic capabilities, the use of momentum, rhythmic skills—the widest range of each student's unique potential. The class begins with very slow floor movements and breathing patterns designed to release tensions and to clear placement for standing and traveling movements. This is followed by center work with emphasis on all movements being generated in the torso first, particularly the pelvis and then moving out to the limbs. The last part of class is active, quick and uses the whole studio space for traveling patterns which engage the total body.
SUMMATION STATEMENT:	"The school provides for the development of dancers through training involving movements

performed without strain and tension, based on principles of balance and momentum rather than on locking the muscles and joints. An area that is stressed is the true sensation of one's own body weights coupled with an awareness of support for these weights."

MONSALVE STUDIO

Jorge Monsalve, Director
126 Fifth Avenue, 7th floor
New York, NY 10011
(212) 675–8921

PROGRAM:	Ballet: Beginning, Intermediate, Advanced; Dance Exercise
INSTRUCTORS:	Jorge Monsalve, Suzanne Wray, Ani Udovicki
ESTABLISHED:	1973
REGISTRATION FEE:	None
CLASS FEES:	8-class card $36 (valid 2 months); 10-class card $45 (valid 3 months)
SCHEDULE:	1 1/2-hour sessions, ongoing
AUDITING:	Not permitted
CANCELLATION POLICIES:	No refunds; classes may be transferred to another student.
ENTRANCE REQUIREMENTS:	Open
SCHOLARSHIPS:	Partial scholarships available
NUMBER OF STUDENTS PER CLASS:	20
STUDENT BREAKDOWN:	85% female, 15% male; 0% under 18, 35% 18–25, 25% 26–35, 35% 36–45, 5% over 45; 15% under 6 months, 20% 1/2–1 year, 40% 1–2 years, 25% 2–3 years, 15% over 3 years
STUDIOS:	1
DRESSING ROOMS:	2
SHOWERS:	Yes
FLOOR:	Wood
ACCOMPANYING INSTRUMENT:	Piano, sound system
WAITING AREA:	Yes
BIOGRAPHY:	MR. MONSALVE was trained in Chile by Kirov-trained Russian teachers. He performed in classical ballet companies in Chile, Argentina, and Mexico and formed companies that toured Central and

South America. He also choreographed musicals, revues, and for television in Mexico and Buenos Aires. MS. WRAY has studied ballet with former Bolshoi soloist Wadim Aulima and Jorge Monsalve and has taught at the studio for several years. MS. UDOVICKI was trained in the Russian style in Belgrade,Yugoslavia, where she performed in classical ballet companies, as well as with the Boston Ballet Ensemble.

CLASSES:

The purpose of Fundamentals is to introduce basic ballet steps and combinations, terminology, and the purpose of the exercises. Emphasis is on slow, careful work to prevent injuries or the development of bad habits. Beginner and Intermediate classes continue to expand movement vocabulary. Longer and more difficult combinations are presented and students begin to develop style, phrasing, and musicality. Each class offers different combinations for barre and center work. In Advanced classes, extra attention is given to interpretation and style in variations from classical repertoire to awaken the dancer to correct use of physical, emotional, and mental possibilities of the body. Dance Exercise utilizes a combination of various techniques to increase body awareness and develop muscle tone, endurance, and muscular control. Through yoga, modern dance, and calisthenics, students learn to isolate, stretch, and strengthen problem spots in the abdomen, torso, and legs.

SUMMATION STATEMENT:

"Monsalve Studio believes that careful correct training is the basis for all further technical development. Even students who will not become professional dancers deserve individual attention and proper training to avoid injuring themselves and forming bad habits in posture or movement. Students are also trained to concentrate and comprehend combinations quickly, rather than perform movements technically."

NEW YORK SCHOOL OF BALLET

Richard Thomas, Daniel Levans, Directors
Hugh Appet, Associate Director
2291 Broadway (82nd and 83rd Streets)
New York, NY 10024
(212) 799–5445

PROGRAM:	Ballet
INSTRUCTORS:	Richard Thomas, Daniel Levans, Dick Andros, Hugh Appet, Shirley Bassat, Debra Flomine, Ann Inglis
ESTABLISHED:	1969
CLASS FEES:	Single class $5; 10-class card $40 (2 month duration)
SCHEDULE:	1-to-1^{1}/$_{2}$-hour sessions, ongoing
AUDITING:	Yes, from outside studio
CANCELLATION POLICIES:	Card nonrefundable
SCHOLARSHIPS:	At discretion of directors
NUMBER OF STUDENTS PER CLASS:	20–25
STUDIOS:	3
DRESSING ROOMS:	2
SHOWERS:	Yes
FLOOR:	Wood
ACCOMPANYING INSTRUMENT:	Piano
CLASS CARD:	Yes

92ND STREET YM/YWHA DANCE CENTER

Sharon Gersten Luckman, Director
1395 Lexington Avenue
New York, NY 10028
(212) 472–6000, ext. 170

PROGRAM:	Modern, Ballet, Jazz, Aerobics, Exercise
INSTRUCTORS:	Neil Applebaum, Ofra Barak, Art Bridgman, Sandra Cameron, Barbara Canner, Roberta Caplan, Dora Dubsky, Hillary Gal, Christine Greas, Leah Harpaz, Mary Pat Henry, Dan Hogan, Holly Irwin,

Lisa Levart, Peggy Levine, Jane Maloney, Yvonne Mestre, Adrianna O'Reeall, Myrna Packer, Abbie Siegel, Audry Tischler, Jackie Villamil, Barbara Wallace, Nancy Wanich, Claudia Wischner-Reder, Annabelle Gamson, Margie Gillis, Hannah Kahn, Bebe Miller, Mel Wong

ESTABLISHED: 1935

CLASS FEES: Single class $5; 14-week course $85

SCHEDULE: 2-hour sessions, ongoing; special workshops throughout the year

AUDITING: Not permitted

ENTRANCE REQUIREMENTS: Open

CANCELLATION POLICIES: Refunds only in special cases

SCHOLARSHIPS: Work scholarships for adults, scholarships for children

NUMBER OF STUDENTS PER CLASS: 20–25 for adults, limited to 15 for children

STUDENT BREAKDOWN: 25% under 18, 45% 18–30, 25% 31–50, 5% over 50

STUDIOS: 3

DRESSING ROOMS: 2

SHOWERS: Yes

FLOOR: Wood

CLASS CARD: No

WAITING AREA: Yes

CLASSES: For professional level classes, the aim is to provide training by master teachers. For adult classes, the aim is to foster understanding of modern, ballet, and jazz styles as performing art forms. Exercise and Aerobics classes work to stretch, tone, and condition the body through enjoyable rhythmic movement.

SUMMATION STATEMENT: "We teach an enjoyment of dance, an appreciation of the art form and good exercises in a warm, supportive, and spirited atmosphere."

THE OPEN CONSERVATORY
OF THE 5 BY 2 DANCE COMPANY

Jane Kominsky, Director
5 East 16th Street
New York, NY 10003
(212) 242–6837

PROGRAM:	Modern, Beginner–Advanced
INSTRUCTORS:	Jane Kominsky, Bruce Becker, Pamela Anderson, Idelle Packer
ESTABLISHED:	1981
REGISTRATION FEE:	None
CLASS FEES:	Single $4.50; 5-class card $20
SCHEDULE:	1-to-1$^{1}/_{2}$-hour sessions, ongoing
ENTRANCE REQUIREMENTS:	Open
SCHOLARSHIPS:	Not available
NUMBER OF STUDENTS PER CLASS:	10
STUDENT BREAKDOWN:	70% female, 30% male; 0% under 18, 50% 18–25, 50% 26–35, 0% over 35
CLASSES:	Classes are intended to provide a training ground for the professional repertory dancer. Toward that end, style, technique, and Alexander technique are employed.
SUMMATION STATEMENT:	"The Open Conservatory offers excellent training in a challenging and supportive environment with a repertory framework."

SCHOOL FOR CREATIVE MOVEMENT

Hattie and Jack Weiner, Directors
20 West 20th Street
New York, NY 10011
(212) 929–0929

PROGRAM:	Creative Movement, Movement Therapy
INSTRUCTORS:	Lynn Pyle, Theo Benjamin, Susan Pelstein, Joan Lavender, Jack Weiner, Hattie Weiner
ESTABLISHED:	1962
REGISTRATION FEE:	None
CLASS FEE:	$100–$250
SCHEDULE:	1-to-2$^{1}/_{2}$-hour sessions; 3 terms per year

AUDITING:	Not permitted
ENTRANCE REQUIREMENTS:	Open
CANCELLATION POLICIES:	Before third class, prorated refund
SCHOLARSHIPS:	Work scholarships available
NUMBER OF STUDENTS PER CLASS:	Limited to 10
STUDENT BREAKDOWN:	90% female, 10% male; 20% under 18, 20% 18–25, 58% 26–35, 2% 36–45, 0% over 45; 5% under 6 months, 5% 1/2–1 year, 40% 1–2 years, 30% 2–3 years, 20% over 3 years
STUDIOS:	2
DRESSING ROOMS:	2
SHOWERS:	None
FLOOR:	Wood
ACCOMPANYING INSTRUMENT:	Records, drums
WAITING AREA:	Yes
BIOGRAPHY:	All instructors have extensive backgrounds in dance, theatre, anatomy, kinesiology, and psychology.
CLASSES:	All classes work for deep muscular strength and for balancing of muscle usage so that the body doesn't keep working in fixed patterns. In addition, the creative explorations work for the discovery and development of each individual's style of movement. Body problems and blocks to expression are located and corrected.
SUMMATION STATEMENT:	"Each person has the potential for experiencing feelings through their bodies and expressing them through dance. Our techniques allow for release and organization of the impulses to form a personal and artistic dance. This way of working integrates the mind and body, so that fantasies and feelings have a creative way of manifesting themselves."

SCHOOL OF BALLET
DE PUERTO RICO

Paschal Guzman, Director
189 Lexington Avenue
New York, NY 10016
(212) 683–1967

PROGRAM:	Ballet: Fundamentals, Beginner, and Intermediate Adults; Entry and Professional Training for Children. Spanish Dance: Flamenco for Adults, Escuela Bolera to Flamenco Jazz for Children; Dance Exercise and Jazz for Adults.
INSTRUCTORS:	Jacqueline Cottrell, Sima Damestoy, Karlyn De Boer, Mariano Garcia, Paschal Guzman, Dan Holdstein, Barbara Kravitz, Lois Mercedes, Celia Marino
ESTABLISHED:	1970
REGISTRATION FEE:	Children $10.00
CLASS FEES:	Adults: single $6; 10 classes $40; unlimited 30 days $50. Children: 1 class per week $15; 2 per week $26, to a maximum of $50 per month.
SCHEDULE:	Adults, ongoing; children, September to December 31 and January to June 30.
ENTRANCE REQUIREMENTS:	Adult classes are open; children's classes by audition.
CANCELLATION POLICIES:	Credit toward other classes only
SCHOLARSHIPS:	Available to children 10–20 "with real talent"
NUMBER OF STUDENTS PER CLASS:	Limited to 10
TOTAL STUDIO ENROLLMENT:	200
STUDENT BREAKDOWN:	95% female, 5% male; 60% under 18, 30% 18–25, 5% 26–35, 5% 36–45; 10% under 6 months, 20% $1/2$–1 year, 30% 1–2 years, 20% 2–3 years, 20% over three years
STUDIOS:	2
DRESSING ROOMS:	2
SHOWERS:	No
FLOOR:	Wood
ACCOMPANYING INSTRUMENT:	Piano
BIOGRAPHY:	MR. GUZMAN was principal dancer with Pennsylvania Ballet. A master teacher, MS. MERCEDES studied Spanish Dance with Carmencita Lopez and in Spain.
SUMMATION STATEMENT:	"We believe in strict discipline and concentration in

order to achieve professional capability in both Ballet and Spanish dance. Understanding of how the body works and moves goes with proper training of feet, arms, hands, and torso in structured classes that teach a full repertory of styles."

SIMONE'S JAZZ CLASSES

Broadway Dance Studio
28 West 48th Street, 3rd floor
New York, NY 10036
(212) 580–0821

PROGRAM:	Jazz
INSTRUCTOR:	Simone Benthien
ESTABLISHED:	1978
REGISTRATION FEE:	None
CLASS FEES:	$5 per class professional; $6 nonprofessional
SCHEDULE:	5 1½-to-2-hour classes per week
AUDITING:	Permitted
AUDITING FEE:	No fee
ENTRANCE REQUIREMENTS:	Open
SCHOLARSHIPS:	Partial work-study scholarships available
NUMBER OF STUDENTS PER CLASS:	8–15, limited
TOTAL STUDIO ENROLLMENT:	100
STUDENT BREAKDOWN:	90% female, 10% male; 50% under 18, 30% 18–25, 15% 26–36, 5% 36–45; 10% under 6 months, 20% ½–1 year, 20% 1–2 years, 30% 2–3 years, 20% over 3 years
STUDIOS:	2
DRESSING ROOMS:	2
SHOWERS:	No
FLOOR:	Linoleum
ACCOMPANYING INSTRUMENT:	Records
CLASS CARD:	Yes; 10 classes, valid 5 weeks
BIOGRAPHY:	Since the age of 3, MS. BENTHIEN studied with some of New York's most notable teachers. She began her performing career in 1957, dancing in musicals and revues, and in 1960 she formed, choreographed, and performed in a two-member dance act that toured nationally for 10 years. While currently choreographing for revues, she

CLASS:

is now in the process of forming a dance company.

Through encouragement, information, and a complete comprehension of the subject, students can release all abilities and advance with quality. Modern, ballet, and ethnic, as well as a wide variety of jazz styles are utilized throughout class. The warm-ups are powerful workouts and set routines are designed to build strength and endurance, and to correct placement and heighten movement awareness. They consist of center isolations, barre, floor and across-the-floor exercises. The dance combination is worked on for several classes, allowing time to develop a fuller understanding of the techniques, ideas, motivations, and dynamics of the movements.

SUMMATION STATEMENT:

"In an effort to build artists, not just technicians, I am very concerned with style, performance quality, and communication through dance. Special attention is given to each individual's unique search and discovery as they move forward toward their ultimate goals. To be a free artist, one must be the experience and the master of craft. The artist must build a strong and solid technical foundation, while never losing the original joy and love that initiated this study."

STUDIO EGG

Elizabeth Geyer Gottlieb, Director
287 Broadway, 3rd floor
New York, NY 10007
(212) 227–1458

PROGRAM:	Intermediate Ballet for Adults, Children's Ballet, Beginning Jazz, Slimnastics, Aerobics, Physical Theatre, Beginning Tap
INSTRUCTOR:	Elizabeth Geyer Gottlieb
REGISTRATION FEE:	None. Single introductory lesson $10
CLASS FEES:	1 class per week $60; 2 classes per week $115; 3 classes per week $170; 4 classes per week $220; 5 classes per week $270
SCHEDULE:	1 to 5 1-to-1½-hour sessions per week, 15 weeks
ENTRANCE REQUIREMENTS:	Open

SCHOLARSHIPS:	Not available
NUMBER OF STUDENTS PER CLASS:	Limited to 18
VIDEO EQUIPMENT:	Yes
STUDIOS:	1
DRESSING ROOMS:	Yes
ACCOMPANYING INSTRUMENT:	Piano
CLASS CARD:	Yes; valid 15 weeks
BIOGRAPHY:	MS. GEYER was a member of the New York City Ballet Company, and has appeared with her own company at colleges and universities in many states, where she has given master classes and performances. EGG & Dancers has produced several New York seasons, and two television productions, winning Ms. Geyer Gottlieb a Bronze Award for Television Film from the International Film & TV Festival of the Americas, in addition to many grants and commissions for choreography. Her work is now being seen regularly as part of the Young Audiences tour of New York City schools.
CLASSES:	Adult Ballet, all levels—Ongoing Lunch Hour Ballet approaches the art of ballet as a fun meditation for the office worker. Jazz Exercise—An introduction to jazz warm-up, spiced with calisthenics, and topped off with a jazz dance routine. Slimnastics—Invigorating exercises to upbeat music, designed to tone and slim problem areas. Aerobics—Breathing, stretching, jogging, and rythmic repetition of simple dance steps.

TOKUNAGA DANCE STUDIO

874 Broadway, 3rd floor
New York, NY 10003
(212) 255–4641/929–8937

PROGRAM:	Intermediate, Advanced-Professional Ballet for Modern Dancers; Pointe Barre
INSTRUCTOR:	Emiko and Yasuko Tokunaga
ESTABLISHED:	1975
REGISTRATION FEE:	None
CLASS FEES:	Ballet or Pointe Barre $3; Full Ballet Class $5

SCHEDULE:	Ballet—5 2-hour sessions per week; Pointe Barre—2 1-hour sessions per week
ENTRANCE REQUIREMENTS:	Open
SCHOLARSHIPS:	Full- and part-time available
NUMBER OF STUDENTS PER CLASS:	15
STUDENT BREAKDOWN:	85% female, 15% male; 75% 18–25, 25% 26–35; 5% under 6 months, 5% ½–1 year, 20% 1–2 years, 50% 2–3 years, 20% over 3 years
STUDIOS:	1
DRESSING ROOMS:	2
SHOWERS:	None
FLOOR:	Wood
ACCOMPANYING INSTRUMENT:	Tape
CLASS CARD:	No
BIOGRAPHY:	EMIKO and YASUKO TOKUNAGA are sisters. They both have extensive training in classical Japanese dance, classical ballet, and modern. They both have studied Aikido. The Tokunagas have performed extensively throughout the United States with their own company (over 2,000 performances) and have taught extensively as full-time members and artists-in-residence at many colleges throughout the United States and Norway.
CLASSES:	Classes are team-taught. Although classes have mixed levels, dancers are challenged individually since advanced ballet vocabulary is presented always in reference to the basics. Every exercise in class is connected to the final grand allegro-short dance, which employs creative use of space, musicality, technical choices, and performance. In-studio performances of Summer and Winter Works are held twice yearly as cameo performances of new and upcoming choreographers.
SUMMATION STATEMENT:	"We hope to help dancers understand their limitations, realize their potential, and move from center with musical muscular efficiency. Because dancers then understand their individuality, they can work with any company."

SPEECH
SPEECH
SPEECH
SPEECH
SPEECH
SPEECH
SPEECH
SPEECH
SPEECH
SPEECH
SPEECH
SPEECH
SPEECH
SPEECH
SPEECH
SPEECH
SPEECH
SPEECH
SPEECH
SPEECH
SPEECH
SPEECH
SPEECH

ACTORS AND DIRECTORS LAB

412 West 42nd Street
New York, NY 10036
(212) 695–5429

PROGRAM:	Speech, Speaking Voice
INSTRUCTORS:	Sharon Dennis, Patricia Heller, Lynn Singer, Syms Wyeth
ESTABLISHED:	1978
CLASS FEE:	$160
SCHEDULE:	1 session per week, 12 weeks
AUDITING:	Permitted after interview
ENTRANCE REQUIREMENTS:	By interview and audition for advanced classes
CANCELLATION POLICIES:	Advanced notice required; make-up available
STUDIOS:	8, and theatre
DRESSING ROOMS:	Yes
WAITING AREA:	Yes
BIOGRAPHY:	MS. DENNIS studied voice and speech with Marian Rich and Alice Hermes. She is on faculty at the New School and has taught at AADA and at the Performing Arts Repertory. MS. HELLER has taught at HB Studio and at the New School and has worked as a speech coach for a number of Broadway plays. MS. SINGER has a B.A. in literature and a masters in theatre and film from San Francisco State College. She has done innumerable voice-overs for both television and radio. MR. WYETH was educated at Princeton and has taught at the Classic School and at AADA; he is currently on the faculty of the New School.
CLASSES:	Speech enables the student to fulfill the speech demands of any play by eliminating his local dialect and replacing it with either General American or Standard speech. Speaking Voice is designed to lead the performing artist to the discovery of his own vocal presence and the freedom to use it expressively and powerfully. The emphasis is on breath control and opening the throat. Advanced work introduces interpretative skills such as vocal imagery, stress, and resonance.
SUMMATION STATEMENT:	"All art is personal and its value is measured by its inner content. However, without training, a truly responsive performance becomes less likely and more difficult to attain. The lab teaches the artist to

observe life and encourages him to illuminate the
nature of man through behavior."

AESTHETIC REALISM FOUNDATION, INC.

Dorothy Koppelman, Director
141 Greene Street (near Houston Street)
New York, NY 10012
(212) 777–4490

PROGRAM:	Speech, Sincerity, and Yourself
INSTRUCTOR:	Anne Fielding
ESTABLISHED:	1977
CLASS FEE:	$35
SCHEDULE:	1 1½-hour session every two weeks, 16 weeks
AUDITING:	Permitted
ENTRANCE REQUIREMENTS:	Open
SCHOLARSHIPS:	Not available
STUDENT BREAKDOWN:	40% 18–25, 40% 26–35, 20% 36–45
CLASS:	The purpose of this course is to have our voice and speech show who we really are. The class looks technically at the 15 questions in "Is Beauty the Making One of Opposites?" by Eli Siegel, in relation to individual speeches prepared by students; and we study Mr. Siegel's essay "The Alphabet" as a means of knowing the sound of the English language and being able to speak it with ease, depth, and sincerity. Some of our subjects are—power and grace in speech; articulation, or How clear do you want to be?; and projection, or Are people worth talking to?

LESLIE HOBAN BLAKE

Chelsea Area
(212) 255–2234

PROGRAM:	Dialects, Private Classes
REGISTRATION FEE:	None
CLASS FEE:	$25

SCHEDULE:	1-hour sessions by appointment, ongoing
AUDITING:	Not permitted
ENTRANCE REQUIREMENTS:	Audition
CANCELLATION POLICIES:	With prior notice, make-up available
SCHOLARSHIPS:	Full and partial, work-exchange as member of technical crew for showcase
STUDENT BREAKDOWN:	50% female, 50% male; 5% under 18, 15% 18–25, 60% 26–35, 10% 36–45, 10% over 45; 15% under 6 months, 60% 1/2–1 year, 20% 1–2 years, 5% 2–3 years
CLASS CARD:	10-class card available, valid 1 year
BIOGRAPHY:	MS. BLAKE has been a coach for 10 years, an actress for 12 years, and a director for 3 years. She has studied at the Royal Shakespeare Company in England and appeared/directed with/for the Riverside Shakespeare Company, Bandwagon Productions, Quaigh Dramathon, Off-Off Broadway Festival, and the Alabama Shakespeare Festival. She currently directs 5 or 6 showcases and 8 or 9 readings per year through the Dramatists Guild, Women in Theatre, and New Playwrights.

BOB BLUMENFELD

321 West 105th Street
New York, NY 10025
(212) 662–5269

PROGRAM:	Dialects, Private Coaching
ESTABLISHED:	1978
REGISTRATION FEE:	None
CLASS FEES:	Vary between $10–$25
SCHEDULE:	1-hour sessions, ongoing
ENTRANCE REQUIREMENTS:	Open
CANCELLATION POLICIES:	Must notify by night before scheduled session
SCHOLARSHIPS:	Not available
VOCAL CASSETTES:	Students may record sessions.
WAITING AREA:	Yes
BIOGRAPHY:	MR. BLUMENFELD received his master's degree in French from Columbia University and his bachelor's from Rutgers. He is a professional actor and speaks fluent French, German, Russian, and Italian.
CLASS:	Phonetic information and examples are provided.

Students read from text for practice and are corrected as they go, differentiating between their speech and the dialect. Emphasis is on intonation, music, and the language.

SUMMATION STATEMENT: "I teach the student to hear for himself or herself."

CENTER FOR SPEECH AND THEATRE ARTS

200 West 57th Street, Suite 408
New York, NY 10019
(212) 664–0188

PROGRAM:	Dialects, Group and Private Classes: Standard American Speech I, II; Basic Voice Technique; Speech for Commercials; Voice-Over Technique; Foreign Accent Correction
INSTRUCTORS:	Arthur Reel, Laura Darius, Douglas Broyles, Joan Strober, Laurel Lockhart
ESTABLISHED:	1977
REGISTRATION FEE:	None
CLASS FEES:	Varies between $50–$150 for group classes; private $20–$30 per hour
SCHEDULE:	4-to-8-week terms
AUDITING:	Permitted
AUDITING FEE:	No fee
ENTRANCE REQUIREMENTS:	Open
CANCELLATION POLICIES:	Make-ups available; no refunds
SCHOLARSHIPS:	Not available
NUMBER OF STUDENTS PER CLASS:	Limited to 10
STUDENT BREAKDOWN:	55% female, 45% male; 5% under 18, 55% 18–25, 35% 26–35, 5% 36–45, 0% over 45; 40% under 6 months, 30% 1/2–1 year, 30% 1–2 years, 0% over 2 years
BIOGRAPHY:	MS. DARIUS holds a B.A. and M.A. in speech, theatre, and speech education and is a member of AEA, SAG, and AFTRA. MR. REEL is an award-winning playwright; he has taught acting and directed for over 25 years. MR. BROYLES is a former coach of voice and dialects at the Actors Conservatory Theatre and at AADA. MS. STROBER is a working actress, a member of AEA, SAG, and AFTRA; she received her speech training from Alice

Hermes. MS. LOCKHART is a working actress who conducts workshops at SAG and AFTRA.

CLASSES: Standard American—The objectives of the class are to sharpen pronunciation, eliminate regional accents, and develop flowing, correct speech. Basic Technique teaches correct breathing and develops pitch, vocal range, melodic speech, and projection for stage or microphone. Accent Correction teaches technical breakdown of tongue and lip position and use of voice, intonation, and rhythm. Commercials and Voice Over teach the adjustments in voice and speech to suit mood, image, and character of commercial narration. Dialects teaches the variations in articulation appropriate to each dialect, based on changes in tongue position, shapes of vowels, duration, and changes in consonant articulation. Differences in resonation, rhythm, stress patterns, musicality, and personality of the dialects will be covered.

SUMMATION STATEMENT: "We pride ourselves in providing a comfortable supportive learning atmosphere and are truly concerned with the progress of our students. We are dedicated to developing the actor's speech and voice to meet the vocal demands of stage, film, radio, and television and to training the actor in basic acting techniques as well as special techniques required within each specific performing discipline."

JESSICA DRAKE

Upper West Side
(212) 724–3719

PROGRAM:	Standard American Speech, Private Coaching; Dialects for the Stage, Private Coaching
INSTRUCTOR:	Jessica Drake
ESTABLISHED:	1980
REGISTRATION FEE:	5 classes paid in advance
CLASS FEE:	$20 per class
SCHEDULE:	1 1-hour session per week, ongoing
AUDITING:	Not permitted
ENTRANCE REQUIREMENTS:	Working understanding of the English language
CANCELLATION POLICIES:	24-hour notice required to reschedule; no refunds

SCHOLARSHIPS:	Not available
TOTAL STUDIO ENROLLMENT:	10
STUDENT BREAKDOWN:	50% female, 50% male; 60% 18–25, 40% 26–35; 60% under 6 months, 30% 1/2–1 year, 10% 1–2 years
EXERCISE CASSETTES:	Not available; but students are permitted to record exercises during session
WAITING AREA:	Yes
BIOGRAPHY:	MS. DRAKE has been around show business all her life. In addition to her professional credits she has had 7 years of formal training, including a degree from Julliard School of Drama. She has worked with Livui Ciulei and Des McAnuff and at Joseph Papp's Public Theatre; she has also appeared with the Lincoln Center Touring Company in New York City. Her many regional credits include *Sister Mary Ignatius Explains It All for You* in Los Angeles. Television audiences have seen her in "St. Elsewhere," "The Edge of Night," and in commercials. She has been teaching auditioning, speech, dialects, and Shakespeare privately for 4 years both in New York and Los Angeles.
CLASSES:	"I teach Standard American Speech as developed by my mentor, Edith Skinner. Ms. Skinner devoted her life to teaching American actors how to speak onstage with proper American pronunciation—not an affectation of British speech. I work with or without phonetics and I use elements of voice production in the training. Once this technique is mastered, dialects and regionalisms may be acquired with ease. I also coach for accent reduction. Private instruction has proven cost-effective but I also offer an occasional group class. I offer two kinds of Dialect Instruction. The first is a course that teaches several of the most frequently used stage dialects. The second is immediate instruction in a particular dialect you may need for a specific audition or job. I work with tapes and phonetics if the student can apply them. In addition to "emergency" coaching and dialect classes, I have also worked as production dialect coach on *Cloud 9* and *Charlotte Sweet* in Los Angeles and New York."
SUMMARY STATEMENT:	"I believe in the American actor's ability to master any form of dramatic literature. For too long we have lived under the shadow of the English in regard to 'elevated texts.' We have our own form of speech that is every bit as applicable as theirs if

used correctly. There is a body of actors in this country who have mastered this and I want to see that body grow until every actor is unrestricted by his speech capabilities. We can be as skilled with Shakespeare, Chekhov, and Shaw as we are with Williams and Miller."

DRAMA TREE INC.

Anthony Mannino, Director
215 Park Avenue South
New York, NY 10003
(212) 228–3932

PROGRAM:	Speech I–III
INSTRUCTOR:	Geddeth Smith
ESTABLISHED:	1959
AUDITING:	Permitted
AUDITING FEE:	No fee
ENTRANCE REQUIREMENTS:	Open
NUMBER OF STUDENTS PER CLASS:	10
STUDENT BREAKDOWN:	60% female; 40% male; 0% under 18, 60% 18–25, 35% 26–35, 2% 36–45, 3% over 45
STUDIOS:	2
CLASS:	Speech I consists of a study of the vowels, dipthongs, and consonants of English and their representation by means of the phonetic alphabet. Emphasis is on ear training. Speech II provides continued practice in transcription and beginning work on using the phonetic alphabet in dialects, study of English intonation, and some verse reading. Speech III studies spoken language by means of Shakespeare's verse and prose. It includes practical use of intonation, phrasing, breath control, and pitch.

WILLIAM ESPER STUDIO INC.

William Esper, Director
723 Seventh Avenue
New York, NY 10019
(212) 345-0421

PROGRAM:	Voice
INSTRUCTOR:	Martin Waldron
ESTABLISHED:	1956
AUDITING:	Not permitted
SCHOLARSHIPS:	Not available
BIOGRAPHY:	MR. WALDRON is a graduate and former member of the Neighborhood Playhouse. He was formerly associated with John Burrell of the Old Vic and Desmond O'Donovan of the National Theatre of Great Britain. He has been a teacher at the Harlem School of the Arts and a guest artist at Princeton, Cornell, and Duke universities.

KRISTINA FISCHER

155 West 46th Street
New York, NY 10036
(212) 764-1711/873-1091

PROGRAM:	Diction and Public Speaking, Private
ESTABLISHED:	1979
REGISTRATION FEE:	None
CLASS FEE:	$150
SCHEDULE:	One 1/2-1 hour session per week, 10 weeks
ENTRANCE REQUIREMENTS:	Open
CANCELLATION POLICIES:	24-hour notice
SCHOLARSHIPS:	Not available
STUDENT BREAKDOWN:	50% female, 50% male; 25% under 18, 20% 18-25, 20% 26-35, 20% 36-45, 15% over 45

SAM FORBES

325 Central Park West
New York, NY 10025
(212) 865–5591

PROGRAM:	Speaking Voice, Private
ESTABLISHED:	1977
REGISTRATION FEE:	None
CLASS FEE:	$10 per session
SCHEDULE:	1-hour sessions, ongoing
AUDITING:	Not permitted, but a consultation and/or presentation is available
ENTRANCE REQUIREMENTS:	By interview
CANCELLATION POLICIES:	24-hour notice
SCHOLARSHIPS:	Not available
STUDENT BREAKDOWN:	50% female, 50% male; 0% under 18, 55% 18–25, 45% 26–35, 0% over 35; 50% under 6 months, 50% 1/2–1 year, 0% over 1 year
BIOGRAPHY:	MR. FORBES received his theatrical training at Davis Center of the Performing Arts and Circle in the Square. He has studied speech with Edith Skinner and is an expert in the Linklater technique.
CLASS:	The goals of the sessions are to improve basic voice, tone, sounds, color, and breath control skills. The means utilized are review exercises, speech warm-ups, and perfecting the sound at the progression of the student's abilities.
SUMMATION STATEMENT:	"Good speech never draws attention to itself."

SUSAN GRABINA

Chelsea Area
(212) 675–8308

PROGRAM:	Speech, Private Classes
REGISTRATION FEE:	None
CLASS FEE:	$25 per class
SCHEDULE:	45-minute sessions, ongoing
AUDITING:	Permitted
AUDITING FEE:	No fee
ENTRANCE REQUIREMENTS:	Interviews

CANCELLATION POLICIES:	24-hour notice
SCHOLARSHIPS:	Not available
STUDENT BREAKDOWN:	50% female, 50% male; 25% under 18, 25% 18–25, 25% 26–35, 25% 36–45
CLASS CARD:	5 classes, valid 5 weeks
VOCAL CASSETTES:	Provided
BIOGRAPHY:	MS. GRABINA is a Professor of Speech with the City University of New York. She is certified with the American Speech-Language-Hearing Association, has a master of arts degree in speech, and is a doctoral candidate.
CLASS:	The class involves correcting accents, dialects, and voice problems in relation to speech.
SUMMATION STATEMENT:	"Accent- and dialect-free speech is a valuable part of a performer's repertoire. It is a skill that can be learned and used whenever the need for general American speech is required. I instruct students to speak with what is known as general American speech, which is speech that is free of any accent or dialect. Once a student learns this, the student will be able to use that speech pattern whenever he or she so desires."

HB STUDIO

Muriel Burns, Director
120 Bank Street
New York, NY 10014
(212) 675–2370

PROGRAM:	Speech—Beginning, Advanced, Dialects, Foreign Accent Correction, Pattern Shift, Shakespeare
INSTRUCTOR:	Alice Hermes, Milenko Rado, William Maloney
ESTABLISHED:	1945
REGISTRATION FEE:	$7.50
CLASS FEE:	$95 (average)
SCHEDULE:	$1\frac{1}{2}$–$2\frac{1}{2}$ hours per week, 19 weeks, ongoing
AUDITING:	Permitted
AUDITING FEE:	$1.50 for first audit; $4 for subsequent audit of same class
ENTRANCE REQUIREMENTS:	Open (for most classes)
CANCELLATION POLICIES:	No refunds given after term has started and no credit given for classes missed.
SCHOLARSHIPS:	Work-exchange available

NUMBER OF STUDENTS PER CLASS:	15–35
TOTAL STUDIO ENROLLMENT:	Over 3,000
STUDENT BREAKDOWN:	60% female, 40% male; 5% under 18, 45% 18–25, 20% 26–35, 20% 36–45, 10% over 45; 5% under 6 months, 10% 1/2–1 year, 25% 1–2 years, 40% 2–3 years, 20% over 3 years
STUDIOS:	5
VOCAL CASSETTES:	No
SUMMATION STATEMENT:	"The HB Studio began in 1945 and aims for a meaningful dramatic expression of the times and country in which we live. To help establish a theatre of experimentation based on classic tradition, the Studio is dedicated to the development of individual artists who may actively contribute to a theatre of national character. Conceived as an artistic and working home, it offers an outlet for practice and growth for the professional theatre artist, and an opportunity for the young to establish roots in their intended crafts. The Studio's guiding principle is creative freedom, which has as its logical consequence responsibility to a noble art."

PRUDENCE HOLMES

Upper West Side
(212) 595-7273

PROGRAM:	Speech and Dialects, Private
INSTRUCTOR:	Prudence Holmes
REGISTRATION FEE:	None
CLASS FEE:	$30 per class
SCHEDULE:	1-hour sessions
ENTRANCE REQUIREMENTS:	Open
SCHOLARSHIPS:	None
REQUIRED MATERIALS:	Speech book by Edith Skinner
STUDENT BREAKDOWN:	50% female, 50% male; 50% 26–35, 50% 36–45; 50% under 6 months, 40% 1–2 years, 10% 2–3 years
VOCAL CASSETTES:	Student is permitted to record exercises during session.
BIOGRAPHY:	MS. HOLMES is a professor of speech at the New York University School of the Arts and has also taught at Carnegie Mellon University, the Ameri-

CLASS:
can Academy of Dramatic Arts, Process School, Actors TV Studio, and Westwinds. She studied with and served as assistant to Edith Skinner at Julliard. The sessions focus on correcting the individual's speech impediments, regional or foreign dialects, lisps, etc., through the use of the phonetic alphabet, audio taping and ear training. The goal is standard American speech.

SUMMATION STATEMENT:
"I provide a systematic and thorough approach, based on lots of support and positive reinforcement for the student."

GORDON A. JACOBY

c/o William Esper Studio
723 Seventh Avenue
New York, NY 10019
Service: (212) 724–1110
Home: (201) 783–4528

PROGRAM: Stage Dialects, Stage Speech
INSTRUCTOR: Gordon A. Jacoby
ESTABLISHED: 1964
REGISTRATION FEE: None
CLASS FEE: $225 per term
SCHEDULE: 2 1³/₄-hour sessions per week, 12 weeks
AUDITING: Not usually permitted
AUDITING FEE: $10
ENTRANCE REQUIREMENTS: Interview
CANCELLATION POLICIES: Refunds and make-ups available
SCHOLARSHIPS: Not available
REQUIRED MATERIALS: None
NUMBER OF STUDENTS
  PER CLASS: 10
STUDENT BREAKDOWN: 50% female, 50% male; 50% 18–25, 40% 26–35, 10% 36–45; 10% under 6 months, 40% ¹/₂–1 year, 40% 1–2 years, 10% 2–3 years
VOCAL CASSETTES: Students are permitted to record exercises at class.
BIOGRAPHY: MR. JACOBY was a dialect coach and speech teacher for 20 years and has worked at the Manhattan Theatre Club, Public Theatre, Trinity Square, William Esper & Warren Robertson Studios, on films, and in private teaching.

CLASSES:	The course concentrates on the ten dialects most in demand in theatre, film, and commercials, using an approach that proceeds from the sound system through scenes. Classes are small, allowing time for individual work.
SUMMATION STATEMENT:	"There is an explanation of sounds and melody in general, and specifically, in relation to the culture that speaks a different way."

DAVID KRASNER

(212) 982–2718/840–1234

PROGRAM:	Voice, Speech, Alexander Technique; Private and Group
REGISTRATION FEE:	None
CLASS FEE:	$15 per hour
SCHEDULE:	1-to-2-hour sessions, ongoing
ENTRANCE REQUIREMENTS:	Interview
SCHOLARSHIPS:	Not available
BIOGRAPHY:	MR. KRASNER graduated from Carnegie Mellon University and is a student of Edith Skinner. He has trained for 2 years in the Alexander technique and is both a yoga and a health club instructor and a director at AADA.
CLASSES:	The classes are aimed at elimination of any regionalisms or speech impediments. Included are middle work on expanding the tone and range of the speaking voice.
SUMMATION STATEMENT:	"I provide a well-rounded approach to voice and speech as used by actors. An actor's voice is his instrument. It must have flexibility and range to support a character's emotional expression."

DENNIS PATELLA

176 West 87th Street
New York, NY 10024
(212) 874–4153

PROGRAM:	Voice and Body Work; Group and Private
ESTABLISHED:	1977

REGISTRATION FEE: None
CLASS FEE: $15
SCHEDULE: 1 or more 1-hour sessions per week, ongoing
ENTRANCE REQUIREMENTS: By interview; no major voice or body impairments
SCHOLARSHIPS: Not available
NUMBER OF STUDENTS
  PER CLASS: Groups are limited to 6
STUDENT BREAKDOWN: 70% female, 30% male; 0% under 18, 65% 18–25,
                       20% 26–35, 15% 36–45, 0% over 45; 50% under 6
                       months, 25% 1/2–1 year, 25% 1–2 years, 0% over
                       2 years
WAITING AREA: Yes
BIOGRAPHY: MR. PATELLA has worked with Kristin Linklater
                       and Clyde Vinson and has undergone teacher
                       training for this technique.
CLASSES: The goal of the work is a relaxed, responsive,
                       "body-voice" that reveals rather than hides its own
                       truth. The Linklater process starts with breathing
                       work and includes the entire musculature as it ap-
                       plies to vocal production in performance.

MARCELLE RABINOVICH

300 East 56th Street
New York, NY 10022
(212) 758–7464

PROGRAM: Speaking Voice; Private
REGISTRATION FEE: None
CLASS FEE: Dependent on diagnosis
SCHEDULE: 1-hour sessions, ongoing
ENTRANCE REQUIREMENTS: Open
SCHOLARSHIPS: Not available
BIOGRAPHY: MS. RABINOVICH received her bachelor's degree
                       in both pre-med and acting, her master's in speech
                       pathology and audiology, and her Ph.D. in educa-
                       tion.
CLASS: A complete diagnosis of speech and voice prob-
                       lems is conducted. Exercises and practice during
                       each session build on and coordinate with the pre-
                       vious session.
SUMMATION STATEMENT: "My objective is to unlock the speech potential of
                       every student."

WARREN ROBERTSON THEATRE WORKSHOP

Janet M. Doeden, Director
303 East 44th Street
New York, NY 10017
(212) 687–6430

PROGRAM:	Voice Production, Speech and Diction
INSTRUCTOR:	Shauna Kanter, Gordon Jacoby
ESTABLISHED:	1976
REGISTRATION FEE:	$20
CLASS FEES:	$65 for 4 weeks; $90 for 6 weeks
SCHEDULE:	1 2-hour class per week
AUDITING:	Permitted
AUDITING FEE:	$20
ENTRANCE REQUIREMENTS:	Interview
CANCELLATION POLICIES:	No refunds
SCHOLARSHIPS:	Work-study available, terms negotiable
REQUIRED MATERIALS:	None
NUMBER OF STUDENTS PER CLASS:	5+
TOTAL STUDIO ENROLLMENT:	300
STUDENT BREAKDOWN:	50% female, 50% male; 6% under 18, 35% 18–25, 50% 26–35, 6% 36–45, 3% over 45; 10% under 6 months, 90% 1/2–1 year
STUDIOS:	3
DRESSING ROOMS:	2
BIOGRAPHY:	MS. KANTER has taught voice at the New York University School of the Arts, among other colleges. She has also taught regionally and in theatres in New York City. MR. JACOBY has been teaching speech and dialects for 20 years in New York City. He has worked with such theatres as the Roundabout, the Public Theatre, the Manhattan Theatre Club, as well as with many film productions.
CLASSES:	Voice Production—Vocal exercises to release tension in each part of the vocal musculature. Emphasis on breath work, spinal alignment, vocalizing, range expansion, and ear training. Many of the exercises used in the class are drawn from the Linklater technique. Speech and Diction—A class stressing intensive work on American pronunciation; flexibility and mobility in speech patterns to help the actor handle dialogue.

SUMMATION STATEMENT: "WRTW was founded in 1976 to create an environment for the art of acting: to integrate voice, body, emotion, and intellect into a heightened whole in which the actor may develop technique without sacrificing individuality."

CLIFF SEIDMAN STUDIO

704 Broadway (at 4th Street)
New York, NY 10003
(212) 677–8575

PROGRAM: Speaking Voice, Private
ESTABLISHED: 1975
REGISTRATION FEE: None
CLASS FEES: First class $50; each additional class $30; 5 classes (payable at first class) $150
SCHEDULE: 1-to-2-hour sessions, ongoing
ENTRANCE REQUIREMENTS: Open
SCHOLARSHIPS: Not available
BIOGRAPHY: MR. SEIDMAN received his M.F.A. from New York University. He is a former member of the Working Theatre, where he was trained as a teacher by Kristin Linklater, Peter Kass, and Joseph Chaikin for 2 years. He has taught at the American College, the University of Oklahoma, the State University of New York at Fredonia, and at the National Theatre of Spain in Madrid.
CLASS: The detailed and interdependent voice and body exercises are designed to undo habitual tensions that limit the actor's expressive potential. Only when the innate intelligence and intrinsic energies of the body and voice are freed and developed can the actor explore the sensory experience of thoughts, vowels, consonants, and words.
SUMMATION STATEMENT: "My personal interests and research is as much in science as in art. In our evolutionary history, the two were separated. Through my work I am trying to reunify them, reconnecting the body and voice with the creative mind."

CLYDE VINSON STUDIOS

Clyde Vinson, Director
612–619 Eighth Avenue, 4th floor (between 39th and 40th Streets)
New York, NY 10036
(212) 874–4153

PROGRAM:	Voice and Movement, Stage Dialects
INSTRUCTOR:	Clyde Vinson, Gordon Jacoby, Dennis Patella
ESTABLISHED:	1981
REGISTRATION FEE:	First payment due 1 week before term begins
CLASS FEE:	Voice and Movement $390
SCHEDULE:	Voice and Movement, 24 2½-hour sessions
ENTRANCE REQUIREMENTS:	Interview
NUMBER OF STUDENTS PER CLASS:	Limited to 12
TOTAL STUDIO ENROLLMENT:	100+
STUDENT BREAKDOWN:	65% female, 35% male; 60% 18–25, 30% 26–35, 10% 36–45
STUDIOS:	3
DRESSING ROOMS:	Yes
SHOWERS:	No
ACCOMPANYING INSTRUMENT:	Piano
VOCAL CASSETTES:	Not provided; no recording permitted
ACCOMPANIST:	Instructor accompanies
WAITING AREA:	Yes
BIOGRAPHY:	MR. VINSON has taught for more than 25 years in universities and privately in New York. He received his Ph.D. from Northwestern University and spent 2 years with the Working Theatre in New York, a foundation-sponsored training program in voice, movement, and acting founded by Kristin Linklater, Joseph Chaikin, and Peter Kass. He did two years of Alexander technique, is conversant with Rolfing, and has done workshops with Charlotte Selver, Eric Morris, Bob Chapra, and Moshe Feldenkrais. For the past year he has been studying at the Psychosynthesis Institute of New York and believes that work has profound implications for the actor. He has directed both in universities and professionally. Apart from the studios in midtown and work with leading actors in McCann-Nugent productions, his greatest alliance is with the Circle Repertory Company. MR. JACOBY has taught stage dialects and speech for actors for 20

years at the Manhattan Theatre Club, Public Theatre, Roundabout, Chelsea Theatre Company, WPA Theatre, Whole Theatre Company, Trinity Square Repertory, and at the William Esper and Clyde Vinson Studios. MR. PATELLA has taught for 8 years. He has worked directly with Kristin Linklater, Clyde Vinson, Moshe Feldenkrais, and Alvina Kraus. His teaching credits include Circle Rep, Circle-in-the-Square, Bloomsburg Theatre Ensemble, and 4 years of private practice. He is currently on the faculty at City College of New York.

CLASS: The voice and movement work is about consciousness and freedom—about "knowing what you are doing so that you can do what you want." The work on the body consists primarily of easy-to-execute movements designed to make one aware of how he or she functions physically: (1) aware of how one holds feelings and thoughts in the body, (2) aware of what happens in the body on the subtlest level when a task is performed or even when there is an intention to perform it, (3) aware of one's habitual and compulsive way of moving and being in the world and on the stage, and (4) aware of other possibilities which are often easier and more pleasurable—all this, to develop the freedom to make choices as a person and as a character. The desired result is an aligned body free of unnecessary tension that has the capacity to move easily and joyously through the world. Mr. Patella's class is a combination of Feldenkrais movement work and Linklater voice work. The goal is a "body-voice" that reveals rather than hides its own truth.

SUMMATION STATEMENT: "The goal of all the work is to unify and integrate body, voice, thought, and emotion so that the actor is centered and in touch with all parts of the self, with no split between thought and feeling and the expression of it—so that the body and the voice do not mask thought and feeling but reveal it."

VOICE
VOICE
VOICE
VOICE
VOICE
VOICE
VOICE
VOICE
VOICE
VOICE
VOICE
VOICE
VOICE
VOICE
VOICE
VOICE
VOICE
VOICE
VOICE
VOICE
VOICE
VOICE
VOICE
VOICE
VOICE
VOICE

ACTORS AND DIRECTORS LAB

412 West 42nd Street
New York, NY 10036
(212) 695-5429

PROGRAM:	Singing
INSTRUCTOR:	Joseph K. Scott
ESTABLISHED:	1978
CLASS FEE:	$300
SCHEDULE:	12 weeks, ongoing
AUDITING:	Permitted after interview
ENTRANCE REQUIREMENTS:	By interview and audition for advanced classes
CANCELLATION POLICIES:	Advanced notice required; make-up available
STUDIOS:	8; and theatre
DRESSING ROOMS:	Yes
WAITING AREA:	Yes
BIOGRAPHY:	MR. SCOTT holds B.M., M.M., and M.F.A. degrees. He studied at Tanglewood with Boris Goldovsky and Sarah Caldwell, where he sang the premiere of Leonard Bernstein's *Trouble in Tahiti*. His background includes opera, oratorio, concert, musical comedy, straight theatre and solos in many New York churches and temples. He has served for 9 seasons as guest lecturer-demonstrator at Care of Professional Voices, an annual symposium held at Julliard.
CLASS:	Through presenting the acoustical and psychological factors of voice, the emphasis of the course is on the experiential rather than the intellectual. Working from the premise that singing is sustained speech, the knowledge that one cannot hear oneself and using simple word exercises and scales, the teacher guides the student to the most efficient and healthy use of his or her voice on the stage and off.
SUMMATION STATEMENT:	"All art is personal and its value is measured by its inner content. However, without training, a truly responsive performance becomes less likely and more difficult to attain. The lab teaches the artist to observe life, and encourages him to illuminate the nature of man through behavior."

AESTHETIC REALISM FOUNDATION, INC.

Dorothy Koppelman, Director
141 Greene Street (near Houston Street)
New York, NY 10012
(212) 777–4490

PROGRAM:	The Art of Singing—Technique and Feeling
INSTRUCTOR:	Carrie Wilson
ESTABLISHED:	1977
CLASS FEE:	$40
SCHEDULE:	1 1½-hour session every two weeks, 16 weeks
SCHOLARSHIPS:	Not available
NUMBER OF STUDENTS PER CLASS:	Limited to 16
STUDENT BREAKDOWN:	60% female, 40% male; 35% 18–25, 45% 26–35, 20% 36–45; 10% under 6 months, 25% ½–1 year, 30% 1–2 years, 20% 2–3 years, 15% over 3 years
BIOGRAPHY:	MS. WILSON is a graduate of Barnard College and the Neighborhood Playhouse and has studied voice privately for 10 years. She has worked professionally in musical theatre and concerts. She studied Aesthetic Realism with Eli Siegel and has been an Aesthetic Realism consultant for 9 years.
CLASS:	The class studies singing from the point of view of the Aesthetic Realism of Eli Siegel—as oneness of opposites—high and low, power and sweetness, steadiness and flexibility, technique and feeling. Each class consists of discussion, vocal exercises, and the individual presentation of songs (both classical and popular), with criticism by instructor and comments by class members. The aim of the class is to encourage the greatest sincerity simultaneously with the greatest technical faculty.
SUMMATION STATEMENT:	" 'The world, art, and self explain each other—each is the aesthetic oneness of opposites—Eli Siegel.' Courses are not only in the performing arts, but the visual arts, the humanities, poetry and literature, criticism; seminar workshops in the family, business, and drug abuse."

ALBERINI VOCAL STUDIO

160 West 73rd Street
New York, NY 10023
(212) 874–0015/877–6700

PROGRAM:	Vocal Technique, Private
INSTRUCTOR:	Ellen Alberini
ESTABLISHED:	1946
REGISTRATION FEE:	None
CLASS FEE:	$20 per hour
SCHEDULE:	1-hour sessions, ongoing
AUDITING:	Permitted
AUDITING FEE:	No fee
ENTRANCE REQUIREMENTS:	Open
CANCELLATION POLICIES:	24-hour notice, make-ups available
SCHOLARSHIPS:	Not available
STUDENT BREAKDOWN:	65% female, 35% male; 25% under 18, 40% 18–25, 25% 26–35, 10% 36–45, 0% over 45; 10% under 6 months, 10% 1/2–1 year, 40% 1–2 years, 40% 2–3 years, 0% over 3 years
VOCAL CASSETTES:	Provided
ACCOMPANIST:	Instructor accompanies.
BIOGRAPHY:	MS. ALBERINI received her musical training at the New England Conservatory of Music. She studied for several years under Alessandro Alberini and became his vocal assistant. Ms. Alberini has sung in Carnegie Hall, Town Hall, and the Brooklyn Academy of Music and has given numerous recitals throughout New York and New England.
CLASS:	The sessions focus on learning to sing without strain. Vocal exercises including breathing and relaxation techniques are given according to the specific needs of each student. Versatility in style and repertoire, from belt to classical, and a positive singing attitude are emphasized.

LOWELL ALLECKSON

411 West 44th Street
New York, NY 10036
(212) 246–4889

PROGRAM: Vocal Technique, Private
ESTABLISHED: 1979, New York; 1973, regionally
CLASS FEES: $15 per half-hour; $30 per hour
SCHEDULE: 1/2-to-1-hour sessions, ongoing; minimum number of classes—1 lesson per week, 4 weeks
AUDITING: Not permitted
ENTRANCE REQUIREMENTS: Open
CANCELLATION POLICIES: 24-hour notice required
SCHOLARSHIPS: Not available
STUDENT BREAKDOWN: 60% female, 40% male; 0% under 18, 65% 18–25, 35% 26–35, 0% over 35; 25% under 6 months, 15% 1/2–1 year, 60% 1–2 years, 0% over 2 years
VOCAL CASSETTES: Student may record lesson.
ACCOMPANIST: Instructor accompanies.
WAITING AREA: Yes
BIOGRAPHY: MR. ALLECKSON received his B.M.A. from Concordia College and his master's from the University of Colorado. A member of AEA and SAG, he has trained as a singer and has appeared in operas, musical theatre, and plays.
CLASS: "I assess the basic needs of the student by hearing his or her voice. Usually the student wishes to gain more control and flexibility of the voice. I teach a basic classical technique that can be applied to any musical style."
SUMMATION STATEMENT: "The foremost goal is to gain the freedom to release the true potential of the voice."

AMERICAN RENAISSANCE THEATRE

Robert Elston, Artistic Director
112 Charlton Street
New York, NY 10014
(212) 929–4718

PROGRAM:	Musical Comedy and Opera
INSTRUCTOR:	Robert Elston
ESTABLISHED:	1974
REGISTRATION FEE:	None
CLASS FEE:	$28 for 4 weeks
SCHEDULE:	1 2-hour session per week
AUDITING:	Permitted
AUDITING FEE:	$3
ENTRANCE REQUIREMENTS:	Singing audition
SCHOLARSHIPS:	Not available
NUMBER OF STUDENTS PER CLASS:	Average 10, limited to 20
STUDENT BREAKDOWN:	50% female, 50% male; 10% under 18, 40% 18–25, 40% 26–35, 10% 36–45; 25% under 6 months, 25% 1–2 years, 25% 2–3 years, 25% over 3 years
CLASS:	Material covered includes how to beak down an aria, a song, and a scene for emotional content, physical acting, and musical style. The class is designed for musical comedy and cabaret performers, and opera singers.

ASPEN MUSIC SCHOOL

Gordon Hardy, Dean
1860 Broadway, Suite 401
New York, NY 10023
(212) 581–2196

PROGRAM:	Vocal Technique
ESTABLISHED:	1958
CLASS FEE:	$1,180 tuition and fees
SCHEDULE:	1 1½-to-2-hour session per week, 9 weeks
AUDITING:	Not permitted
ENTRANCE REQUIREMENTS:	By application and audition

SCHOLARSHIPS:	Available based on financial need and instructor recommendation
NUMBER OF STUDENTS PER CLASS:	23
STUDENT BREAKDOWN:	60% female, 40% male; 0% under 18, 95% 18–25, 5% 26–35, 0% over 35
ACCOMPANIST:	Provided
CLASS:	The Opera Program of the Aspen Music School provides aspiring young singers the opportunity to further develop acting and voice skills. Students in the Opera Workshop must study privately in courses ranging from diction to stage movement. As well, the program auditions singers for roles in the summer opera.
SUMMATION STATEMENT:	"Faculty and students meet and share in the intimate atmosphere of Aspen. The exchange of points of view from all perspectives through exposure to all aspects of music-making is one of the most unusual and valuable experiences which the Aspen Music School affords."

ROSS BARENTYNE

160 West 73rd Street
New York, NY 10023
(212) 580–2419

PROGRAM:	Vocal Coaching, Private
ESTABLISHED:	1974
REGISTRATION FEE:	None
CLASS FEE:	$30 per hour
SCHEDULE:	1-hour sessions, ongoing
AUDITING:	Permitted
AUDITING FEE:	No fee
ENTRANCE REQUIREMENTS:	30-minute audition, no charge
CANCELLATION POLICIES:	24-hour notice required or payment due
SCHOLARSHIPS:	Not available
TOTAL STUDIO ENROLLMENT:	35
STUDENT BREAKDOWN:	75% female, 25% male; 5% under 18, 25% 18–25, 50% 26–35, 20% 36–45; 10% under 6 months, 25% 1/2–1 year, 40% 1–2 years, 15% 2–3 years, 10% over 3 years
VIDEO EQUIPMENT:	Yes
VIDEO CASSETTES:	Students may purchase their video cassettes.

ACCOMPANIST:	Instructor accompanies.
WAITING AREA:	Yes
BIOGRAPHY:	Educated in Texas, Florida, and Michigan, MR. BARENTYNE has also worked and studied with many of the leading singers and teachers in New York. His students have appeared with the Metropolitan Opera, the New York City Opera, and with many of the leading United States regional opera companies and numerous Broadway shows.
CLASS:	The technique is a flexible one, tailored to the needs of the student, with emphasis on breath and correct vowel formation. The coaching is principally geared toward the relationships between the musical and dramatic (words) elements of a particular song, aria, or role. Strong emphasis is placed on each singer's individual personality and abilities.
SUMMATION STATEMENT:	"I believe that a performer must ultimately learn to depend almost entirely on himself or herself. I try to help each singer discover that 'self' as it relates to singing and performing. This is done in a relaxed, unhurried, but serious atmosphere. An emphasis is placed on emotional and physical aspects of studying and performing. No rigid 'method' is used, but certain underlying principles of good singing and performing are tailored to the individual needs of each student."

EMILY BURCHILL

24 Bennett Avenue
New York, NY 10033
(212) 568–8161

PROGRAM:	Vocal Technique, Private
ESTABLISHED:	1973
REGISTRATION FEE:	None
CLASS FEE:	$15 per half hour; $30 per hour
SCHEDULE:	$1/2$-to-1-hour sessions, ongoing
ENTRANCE REQUIREMENTS:	By evaluation audition
CANCELLATION POLICIES:	24-hour notice to avoid fee penalty
SCHOLARSHIPS:	Not available
STUDENT BREAKDOWN:	75% female, 25% male; 0% under 18, 70% 18–25, 25% 26–35, 5% 36–45, 0% over 45
VOCAL CASSETTES:	Not provided

WAITING AREA:	Yes
BIOGRAPHY:	MS. BURCHILL's professional affiliations include the National Association of Teachers of Singing, the New York Singing Teachers Association, Sigma Alpha Iota, Pi Kappa Lamba, and Phi Delta Kappa. She received her B.M. in applied voice and her M.A. in music education and is currently working on her Ph.D. She has performed recitals in Michigan, Canada, and New York.
CLASS:	Lessons emphasize the efficient use of the vocal mechanism to achieve effective communication through singing. Materials used from the art song repertoire are chosen with respect to the student's interests and abilities. Basic concepts include breath control, tone production, and relaxation of the throat and jaw. Interpretive musical concepts include exploring ideas such as the poetic meaning of texts, phrasing, characterization, and the most appropriate tone quality for a particular song. Periodically, short programs of songs are presented by the students to each other to give performance practice.
SUMMATION STATEMENT:	"The emphasis in my voice lessons is on the musical aspect of songs. Vocal technique is the means for gaining control of the voice so that it will achieve the finest singing quality possible. However, the technique must not overpower the inherent musical aspect of songs, for the two must work together to create effective communication."

JANICE CAVALIER

161 West 54th Street
New York, NY 10019
(212) 265–5316

PROGRAM:	Vocal Technique, Private
ESTABLISHED:	1973
REGISTRATION FEE:	None
CLASS FEE:	$30 per hour
SCHEDULE:	½-hour sessions, ongoing
AUDITING:	Not permitted
ENTRANCE REQUIREMENTS:	Interview

CANCELLATION POLICIES:	Reschedule on more than 24-hour notice; no lessons excused
SCHOLARSHIPS:	Not available
STUDENT BREAKDOWN:	60% female, 40% male; 5% under 18, 60% 18–25, 30% 26–35, 5% 36–45, 0% over 45; 10% under 6 months, 10% 1/2–1 year, 50% 1–2 years, 30% 2–3 years, 0% over 3 years
ACCOMPANYING INSTRUMENT:	Piano
VOCAL CASSETTES:	Students may record exercises at sessions.
ACCOMPANIST:	Provided
WAITING AREA:	No
BIOGRAPHY:	MS. CAVALIER has an extensive singing background and has appeared on television, radio, and with major orchestras and opera companies. She has appeared at all the major New York concert halls, including Carnegie, Alice Tully, Town Hall, and the Brooklyn Academy of Music.
CLASS:	Classes are primarily for dedicated and serious students who want a career in show business or seek personal fulfillment through singing. Beginning students are accepted. Instruction emphasizes the principles of solid vocal technique with a goal of producing consistent and dependable singers. Demonstration of individual vocal techniques and principles are given when necessary.
SUMMATION STATEMENT:	"Singing is a learning experience that requires the same dedication and discipline required of an instrumental soloist, or of a successful artist in dancing or acting. With proper training a singer can increase the size of the voice and maintain a healthy voice that will be dependable and useful for the life of the performer. To teach this technique requires an understanding of the principles of voice production by the teacher and constant application by the student."

LAWRENCE CHELSI

17 Park Avenue
New York, NY 10016
(212) 689–4596

PROGRAM:	Vocal Technique, Private
ESTABLISHED:	1966
REGISTRATION FEE:	None
CLASS FEE:	$15 per hour
SCHEDULE:	1-hour sessions, ongoing
ENTRANCE REQUIREMENTS:	Some vocal and musical talent or "ear"
CANCELLATION POLICIES:	3-hour notice
SCHOLARSHIPS:	Not available
STUDENT BREAKDOWN:	50% female, 50% male; 18% under 18, 44% 18–25, 30% 26–35, 8% 36–45, 0% over 45; 10% under 6 months, 10% 1/2–1 year, 25% 1–2 years, 25% 2–3 years, 30% over 3 years
VOCAL CASSETTES:	Provided
ACCOMPANIST:	Provided
WAITING AREA:	Yes
BIOGRAPHY:	MR. CHELSI has studied piano for 10 years and voice for 8 years. He has hundreds of credits in all areas of vocal performance, including television shows, Broadway musicals and dramas, clubs, commercials, voice-overs, narration, industrial shows, oratorios, operas, concerts, motion pictures, arrangements and compositions, etc. He received an Off-Broadway award for best performer.
CLASS:	A natural approach to vocal production with an emphasis on even, relaxed, resonant production of singing voice, applied to meaningful interpretations of lyrics. Warm-up exercises and discussion of technique as applied to each individual as well as work on purification of vowels to produce a seamless combination of all registers. Emphasis is on breath support, clear diction, and coloring of vowels. Application of these vocalises to repertoire, current music, popular standards, musical comedy, and classics.
SUMMATION STATEMENT:	"I utilize a natural approach to vocal production, so each voice may retain its own personal quality. Each student's repertoire is designed to suit the individual and his possible needs, as determined by his capabilities. This is achieved by application of bel canto ideals, technique, exercises, and im-

agery. A sense of the history of singing is always present."

RUSSELL CHRISTOPHER

Upper West Side
(212) 787–3462

PROGRAM:	Vocal Technique, Private
ESTABLISHED:	1977
REGISTRATION FEE:	None
CLASS FEE:	$30 per hour
SCHEDULE:	1/2-to-1-hour sessions, ongoing
ENTRANCE REQUIREMENTS:	Interview and audition
CANCELLATION POLICIES:	24-hour notice
SCHOLARSHIPS:	Not available
STUDENT BREAKDOWN:	60% female, 40% male; 0% under 18, 50% 18–25, 50% 26–35, 0% over 35
VOCAL CASSETTES:	Students may record lessons.
ACCOMPANIST:	Provided
BIOGRAPHY:	A professional for 25 years, Mr. Christopher began his career with NBC television; has done chorus and nightclub work; worked with the City Opera of San Francisco and the Metropolitan Opera for 19 years.
CLASS:	Goals of the lessons are to expand range with lack of tension, modulating the voice to accomplish the greatest and finest degree of vocal color.
SUMMATION STATEMENT:	"My approach to singing and teaching is basically a conservative one in the bel canto mode. I encourage confidence building with expansive vocal exercises, hard work and no gimmicks."

CLASSICAL VOICE TRAINING

730 Riverside Drive
New York, NY 10031
(212) 368–7534

PROGRAM:	Vocal Technique, Private
INSTRUCTOR:	Emmy Hauser
ESTABLISHED:	1961

CLASS FEE:	$30 per session
SCHEDULE:	1-to-1½-hour sessions, ongoing
ENTRANCE REQUIREMENTS:	Adequate personal and musical background; free audition
SCHOLARSHIPS:	Not available
BIOGRAPHY:	MS. HAUSER's study in Vienna was based on Lilly Lehman's work; she has performed lieder and oratorio repertoire extensively in Europe. She has command of 5 languages and is a long-time student of psychology. Her teaching experience of several decades enables her to help her students to a healthy, beautiful, and free voice production to be used for any kind of music making.

ANNE COTTON

Broadway at 86th Street
(212) 874–4151

PROGRAM:	Vocal Technique, Private
ESTABLISHED:	1968
REGISTRATION FEE:	None
CLASS FEE:	$20 per hour
SCHEDULE:	1-hour sessions, ongoing
ENTRANCE REQUIREMENTS:	Interviews
CANCELLATION POLICIES:	24-hour notice; missed lessons must be made up
VOCAL CASSETTES:	Students may record lessons.
ACCOMPANIST:	Instructor accompanies.
BIOGRAPHY:	MS. COTTON received her M.M. from the University of Illinois and her B.M. from Syracuse University. She has taught at the State University of New York at New Paltz, Millikin University, Skidmore and Bennett Colleges, and for 13 years at her own private studio. She is also currently on the faculty of the American Musical and Dramatic Academy. She has performed in concert, opera, oratorio, musical comedy, and has excellent knowledge of English, Italian, French, German, and Spanish diction.
CLASS:	The goal of lessons is to learn correct posture, correct breathing using the diaphragm, and correct support using the abdominal muscles; and to achieve freedom, resonance, focus, legato line, flexibility, and evenness. Vocalises and songs are

used to develop the technique and artistry of singing.

SUMMATION STATEMENT:

"As an active performer-teacher who received training in both performance and teaching of singing, I work for the development of a strong, healthy technical foundation. I also stress fine musicianship, artistic performance, and good diction. There is an ongoing honest evaluation of the student's progress in a friendly atmosphere stemming from a genuine love for teaching."

THOMAS CULTICE

160 West 73rd Street, #9G
New York, NY 10023
(212) 799–5503

PROGRAM:	Vocal Technique, Private
ESTABLISHED:	1972
REGISTRATION FEE:	None
SCHEDULE:	1 to 4 $1/2$-to-1-hour sessions per week, ongoing
AUDITING:	Not permitted
ENTRANCE REQUIREMENTS:	Audition
CANCELLATION POLICIES:	Make-ups arranged with 24-hour notice
SCHOLARSHIPS:	Not available
STUDENT BREAKDOWN:	60% female, 40% male; 5% under 18, 45 % 18–25, 35% 26–35, 10% 36–45, 5% over 45; 10% under 6 months, 10% $1/2$–1 year, 20% 1–2 years, 30% 2–3 years, 30% over 3 years
ACCOMPANYING INSTRUMENT:	Grand piano
VOCAL CASSETTES:	Students may record lessons.
ACCOMPANIST:	Instructor accompanies.
WAITING AREA:	Yes
BIOGRAPHY:	MR. CULTICE received his B.M. from the University of Michigan, his master's from Indiana University; he is on the faculty of Mannes College, SUNY at Purchase, and he studies with Oren Brown. He has performed in opera, oratorio, recitals, and on television, and has 25 years of teaching experience.
CLASS:	Private lessons include vocalizing and application of technique to repertoire. Method based on principles of voice therapy and bel canto.

SUMMATION STATEMENT: "The class attempts to explore the potentials of the voice and to develop to the fullest extent special attention to proper classification. It includes hard work on breathing, phonation, resonance, and articulation in the main stream of good teaching, wide knowledge of repertoire."

ALEX DAMIEN

449 West 46th Street
New York, NY 10036
(212) 247–8125

PROGRAM: Vocal Technique, Private
REGISTRATION FEE: None
CLASS FEE: $15 per hour
SCHEDULE: 1-hour sessions, ongoing
BIOGRAPHY: MS. DAMIEN started performing professionally as an actress, specializing in classics. After doing the national tour of *Cabaret*, 1969–1970, she returned to New York anxious to sing for her supper and discovered that dramatic singing had never taught her how to count. She contacted Lennie Tristano, a jazz pianist. She studied with him a year and then with Sal Mosca. For 7 years, she has been dealing with the principles of jazz vocals and piano, filling in all those spaces that were previously empty.

CLASS: The lessons try to achieve freedom, independence, and originality. Singing students should have at least 6-months piano training. The singing musician must be as independent as anyone else in a group. Various exercises are used to open up the instrument for a relaxed sound and to help develop intonation by use of scales sung with the metronome. Singers scat sing with instrumentalists and also learn the ways of those such as Billie Holiday and Louis Armstrong. Four standard tunes are broken down to bare-bone structures, the melodies and changes are learned, then the rhythms and jazz begin, and this the student learns to do alone. Accompaniment is provided only when the student is ready to stand on his or her own.

SUMMATION STATEMENT: "As a teacher I use my experience with Lennie and Sal as a basis for developing musicianship. I understand how it is to be at sea as a singer, dependent on coaches and pianists, without a notion about what music is there for."

JAN ERIC DOUGLAS

West End Avenue, at 98th Street
New York, NY 10025
(212) 666–1166

PROGRAM:	Vocal Technique, Private
REGISTRATION FEE:	None
CLASS FEE:	$20 per half-hour
SCHEDULE:	1/2-hour sessions, ongoing
ENTRANCE REQUIREMENTS:	Open
BIOGRAPHY:	MR. DOUGLAS has his doctorate in vocal performance and did further graduate studies at the University of Sorbonne, Paris, and has studied privately with Cornelius Reid. He has ten years' teaching experience and is an active performer. He is currently on the faculties at William Patterson and Wagner colleges.
CLASS:	The goal of the lesson is to gain increased proficiency through an emphasis on singing technique. Instruction deals primarily with vocalises which exercise the vocal registers both independently and conjunctively. Longer lessons to incorporate repertoire may be arranged.

THE DRAMA TREE INC.

215 Park Avenue South, at 18th Street
New York, NY 10003
(212) 228–3932

INSTRUCTOR:	Henry N. Jacobi
CLASS:	The tone must be produced with vigor, shape, essence, and elasticity. We must learn to produce

tone that sounds round, ringing, and even-flowing. The purpose is to use and express oneself to the fullest extent, compatible with the natural ability of the vocalist, taking into account the unique aspects which every voice possesses.

STEPHANIE DUNCAN

340 West 85th Street
New York, NY 10024
(212) 496–6901

PROGRAM:	Vocal Technique, Private
REGISTRATION FEE:	None
CLASS FEE:	$25 per hour
SCHEDULE:	1-hour sessions, ongoing
ENTRANCE REQUIREMENTS:	Open
CANCELLATION POLICIES:	24-hour notice
ACCOMPANIST:	Provided
BIOGRAPHY:	MS. DUNCAN received her B.A. in humanities from Michigan State University and attended Eastman School of Music, mastering vocal performance.
CLASS:	The goal of the class is to develop to the fullest the student's skill and understanding of vocal technique. Based on initial evaluation, we endeavor to incorporate principles of breath, resonance, and freedom from tension through a series of exercises. Repertoire is selected based on the student's range and present abilities.

SHIRLEY EMMONS

12 West 96th Street
New York, NY 10025
(212) 222–5154

PROGRAM:	Vocal Technique, Private
REGISTRATION FEE:	None
CLASS FEE:	$50 per hour
SCHEDULE:	1-hour sessions, ongoing
ENTRANCE REQUIREMENTS:	By audition

CANCELLATION POLICIES:	24-hour notice required
SCHOLARSHIPS:	Available at instructor's discretion
BIOGRAPHY:	MS. EMMONS is a graduate of Lawrence University, Curtis Institute of Music, and Milan's Conservatorio Giuseppe Verdi. Winner of an Obie award and author of *The Art of the Song Recital,* she has taught at Columbia and Princeton universities, and now teaches at the Boston University School for Music as well as in New York. She is one of two women elected since 1922 to the American Academy of Teachers of Singing.

DENNIS ENGLISH

736 West End Avenue
New York, NY 10025
(212) 222–6939

PROGRAM:	Vocal Technique and Coaching
ESTABLISHED:	1973
REGISTRATION FEE:	None
CLASS FEE:	$20 per hour
SCHEDULE:	1-hour sessions, ongoing
AUDITING:	Permitted
AUDITING FEE:	None
ENTRANCE REQUIREMENTS:	Free interview, involving some singing, but not an "audition"
CANCELLATION POLICIES:	24-hour notice required
SCHOLARSHIPS:	Not available
REQUIRED MATERIALS:	Students supply music.
ACCOMPANYING INSTRUMENT:	Piano
VOCAL CASSETTES:	Students are encouraged to record exercises at classes.
ACCOMPANIST:	Instructor accompanies.
WAITING AREA:	Yes
SUMMATION STATEMENT:	"The artistic imagination responds positively to the freeing of vocal technique. Every singer has an obligation first to himself, then to his audience, to demand the freedom which allows the creative imagination to be exercised to the fullest capabilities of the individual; a teacher's 'job' is to develop the technique and encourage that creative process."

WILLIAM ESPER STUDIOS

Classes conducted at
Westrax Recording Studios
484 West 43rd Street
New York, NY 10036
(212) 947–0533

PROGRAM:	Song Interpretation
INSTRUCTOR:	Peter Link
ESTABLISHED:	1956
REGISTRATION FEE:	None
CLASS FEE:	$125 per month
SCHEDULE:	1 4-hour session per week, ongoing
AUDITING:	Permitted
AUDITING FEE:	No fee
ENTRANCE REQUIREMENTS:	Interview
SCHOLARSHIPS:	Available
NUMBER OF STUDENTS PER CLASS:	Limited to 12
TOTAL STUDIO ENROLLMENT:	30
STUDENT BREAKDOWN:	60% female, 40% male; 0% under 18, 50% 18–25, 50% 26–35, 0% over 35; 0% under 6 months, 30% $1/2$–1 year, 40% 1–2 years, 30% 2–3 years, 0% over 3 years
AUDIO EQUIPMENT:	Yes
STUDIOS:	1
ACCOMPANYING INSTRUMENT:	Piano
VOCAL CASSETTES:	Exercise cassettes are provided; student may also record exercises at class.
ACCOMPANIST:	Provided
WAITING AREA:	Yes
BIOGRAPHY:	MR. LINK is a 2-time Tony-Award-nominee composer and director. He has written for film, television, pop music and Broadway, and has directed numerous musicals and cabaret acts. He is the winner of a Drama Desk Award for composition and has had several gold records, including "If You Let Me Make Love To You, Then Why Can't I Touch You?"
CLASS:	The class is a performance class which in the course of a year covers the folowing subjects: Basics, Auditions, Concert Work, Cabaret, Musical Comedy, Television and Recording Studio. At the end of the course the student should be able to

SUMMATION STATEMENT:

walk into any given situation and know how to handle himself or herself as a professional singer. The basic approach to all the various styles is through the lyric. Solid work is done on all kinds of material, from pop to Broadway.

"The class is based primarily on the teachings of Sanford Meisner at the Neighborhood Playhouse. I basically work with whatever individual problems each singer has and within each style clean up the difficulties. The class differs from most New York-based singing classes in that the main objective is not singing on the Broadway stage (although that too is covered). Instead, the student is encouraged and sometimes pushed to have a greater understanding and sense of pop music forms."

MARY FEINSINGER

99 East 4th Street
New York, NY 10003
(212) 674–1194

PROGRAM:	Vocal Technique, Coaching, Sight-Singing
ESTABLISHED:	1977
REGISTRATION FEE:	None
SCHEDULE:	1-hour sessions, ongoing
SCHOLARSHIPS:	Not available
ACCOMPANYING INSTRUMENT:	Piano
VOCAL CASSETTES:	Students may record exercises at classes.
BIOGRAPHY:	MS. FEINSINGER holds degrees from the Julliard School and Barnard College. She is a highly acclaimed singer with extensive nationwide experience in oratorio, opera, recital, and contemporary music. She is also an accomplished pianist and accompanist. She is currently on the voice faculties of the 92nd Street Y and the Hebrew Arts School, as well as on the accompanying staff at Julliard.
CLASS:	The sessions are aimed at imparting a solid technical foundation: developing maximum resonance and ease of production; extending range; smoothing breaks. Also covered is how to apply technique to performance; how to project a song or aria; how

to put across a song dramatically. Appropriate pieces are recommended from all periods including contemporary and avant-garde. A specialization is "singer's languages"—French, German, Italian, and Stage American/English. Sight-Singing classes specialize in difficult cases—students who believe they have a block against learning to read music.

SUMMATION STATEMENT: "I believe a singer does best in an atmosphere of warmth and encouragement, and conduct my lessons accordingly."

JONATHEN FEY

622 Washington Street
New York, NY 10014
(212) 691–3414

PROGRAM:	Voice Acoustices
ESTABLISHED:	1969
REGISTRATION FEE:	None
CLASS FEE:	$25 per session
SCHEDULE:	1-hour sessions, ongoing
BIOGRAPHY:	MR. FEY holds a B.A. in piano and an M.A. in voice pathology. He has studied extensively with Eleanor McClellan.
CLASS:	The acoustical voice is trained to align the muscles, not by changing the voice but by kinesthetic use of a larger pattern of muscles of the rib cage and face. The voice is restored to a natural level and greater efficiency.

FIND YOUR REAL VOICE

160 West 73rd Street
New York, NY 10023
(212) 877–6700, ext. 6-i

PROGRAM:	Vocal Technique, Private
ESTABLISHED:	1973
CLASS FEES:	Sliding scale

SCHEDULE:	45-minute sessions, ongoing
ENTRANCE REQUIREMENTS:	By (free) interview
CANCELLATION POLICIES:	24-hour notice
SCHOLARSHIPS:	Not available
STUDENT BREAKDOWN:	60% female, 40% male; 10% under 18, 55% 18–25, 35% 26–35,0% over 35; 10% under 6 months, 10% ½–1 year, 50% 1–2 years, 20% 2–3 years, 10% over 3 years
ACCOMPANIST:	Instructor accompanies.
WAITING AREA:	Yes
BIOGRAPHY:	20 years of professional experience as a singer-performer in clubs, concerts, movies, recordings, and theatre. Methods based on teacher's own extensive work and study in voice, piano, guitar, acting, gestalt, and bio-energetics. Record producer and songwriter.
CLASS:	Class approach is eclectic, combining traditional and modern techniques with bio-energetics, a documented series of exercises used here to reduce tension and promote a feeling of relaxation with energy. Technical and emotional aspects of singing are combined, resulting in correct vocal production plus easy self-expression. The musical focus is on contemporary singing styles—pop, rock, jazz, Broadway—and those pursuing recording careers.
SUMMATION STATEMENT:	"A voice is the sound of our personality. Because no two people are alike, no two voices are alike. Through a supportive environment, we can learn to make our own unique sound."

RICHARD FOSTER

600 West End Avenue
New York, NY 10025
(212) 874–5979

PROGRAM:	Vocal Coaching
BIOGRAPHY:	MR. FOSTER received his B.M. and M.M. from New England Conservatory of Music and studied with Lucille Monaghan, Felix Wolfe, Nadia Boulanger. He serves as an accompanist and coach for stars of the Metropolitan Opera and the New York City Opera; was an assistant conductor of Central City and St. Paul operas, and was coach

and accompanist for Zero Mostel and Anna Russell. He has made State Department tours throughout Europe with the Schola Cantorum, and he has played continuo with the New York Philharmonic, Royal Philharmonic of London, French National Orchestra, Symphony of the Air, American Symphony, and with the Handel Society.

CLASS: Class consists of coaching singers in opera, oratorio, and song literature. Mr. Foster is a specialist in building a program of songs of all periods, including songs with obligato instruments; vocal chamber music (solo cantatas, vocal duets, etc.); French, German, and Italian diction; and extensive repertoire of American song literature.

GENE FRANKEL
THEATRE WORKSHOP, INC.

36 West 62nd Street
New York, NY 11201
(212) 522–5569/724–7400

PROGRAM: Musical Theatre
INSTRUCTOR: Fred Silver
ESTABLISHED: 1946
SCHEDULE: 1 3-hour session per week, 10 weeks
AUDITING: Permitted following interview
AUDITING FEE: No fee
ENTRANCE REQUIREMENTS: Interview by audition
SCHOLARSHIPS: Limited number available
NUMBER OF STUDENTS
 PER CLASS: Limited to 15
STUDIOS: 2; stage
ACCOMPANIST: Provided
WAITING AREA: Yes
BIOGRAPHY: MR. SILVER has trained, coached, and written for such performers as Barbara Barrie, Sandy Duncan, E.G. Marshall, Roddy McDowell, Jane Olivor, and Gloria Swanson. He was the recipient of the first Rodgers and Hammerstein Award for musical composition for the theatre. He has been musical director for many of the Julius Monk revues and is the composer-lyricist of *Sterling Silver* and *Gay Company*.

CLASS: Total musical-audition preparation for the singer-actor, including how to select material that best shows off the performer's talents and projects his or her abilities and personality; and how to effectively stage the audition.

CLARK GARDNER STUDIO

Clark Gardner, Director-Instructor
595 West End Avenue
New York, NY 10024
(212) 580–8745

PROGRAM: Musical Performance Workshop; Vocal Technique, Private
ESTABLISHED: 1969
REGISTRATION FEE: None
CLASS FEE: $175
SCHEDULE: 1 2-hour session per week, 12 weeks
AUDITING: 1 audit permitted; fee applicable to session
CANCELLATION POLICIES: Advance payments only, nonrefundable
SCHOLARSHIPS: Not available
NUMBER OF STUDENTS
  PER CLASS: Limited to 12
STUDENT BREAKDOWN: 70% female, 30% male; 1% under 18, 30% 18–25, 30% 26–35, 38%36–45, 1% over 45; 5% under 6 months, 5% 1/2–1 year, 60% 1–2 years, 30% 2–3 years, 0% over 3 years
BIOGRAPHY: MR. GARDNER is a professional singer and actor who has performed in opera, theatre, and in concert. He is an original member of Tom O'Horgan's LaMama Experimental Theatre Lab and Tom Eyen's Theatre of the Open Eye. He studied with Sanford Meisner, Robert Modica, and Martha Schlamme.
CLASSES: Musical Performance provides a space wherein the beginning as well as the more advanced actor-singer can discover his or her value as a musical performer, and further develop his or her talent, skills, and creative potential. Performers work at their own level of development. Acting exercises and techniques are explored in order to free or release the entire instrument so that the actor-singer is able to communicate the song he or she

is interpreting. Vocal Technique offers a technical approach to the development of the vocal instrument through vocal exercises designed to expand the power, range, and control of the voice in order to meet the musical and dramatic needs of the singer. The objective is to "build" the voice within an exercise process designed to develop and coordinate the vocal registers. Special emphasis is given to the close relationship between speaking and singing. Exercises based upon this concept are given in order to achieve simple, natural applications.

SUMMATION STATEMENT: "My aim is to prepare the actor-singer to meet the demands of the professional musical theatre and at the same time to help develop further the creative potential of the performing artist."

JULIE GONDEK

811 Ninth Avenue
New York, NY 10019
(212) 246–7060

PROGRAM:	Vocal Technique, Private
ESTABLISHED:	1974 (Los Angeles)
CLASS FEES:	$75 per month for 4 lessons; $25 single lesson or audition preparation
SCHEDULE:	50-minute sessions, ongoing
ENTRANCE REQUIREMENTS:	Interview
CANCELLATION POLICIES:	Lessons missed without notification are forfeited and nonrefundable; lessons can be rescheduled within the same week if sufficient notice is given.
STUDENT BREAKDOWN:	70% female, 30% male; 10% under 18, 50% 18–25, 35% 26–35, 3% 36–45, 2% over 45; 10% under 6 months, 10% 1/2–1 year, 30% 1–2 years, 50% 2–3 years, 0% over 3 years
VOCAL CASSETTES:	Students may record lessons.
ACCOMPANIST:	Instructor accompanies.
WAITING AREA:	Yes
BIOGRAPHY:	MS. GONDEK has been a professional singer for 10 years, primarily in classical music, including opera and commercial opera recordings. She has 4 years experience singing musical comedy, pop, and jazz in clubs and for conventions. She re-

CLASS:

ceived her B.M. and M.M. from the University of Southern California School of Music and Community School of Performing Arts in Los Angeles.

The class aims at eliminating muscle strain in singing by substituting proper breathing skills for improper neck and facial tension, increasing vocal range, resonance, flexibility; improving quality of timbre; resolving vibrato problems; improving singing diction; communicating text; guiding the student in increasing his or her confidence in singing and performance, positive management of nerves, and transfer of technical vocal skills to practice use in songs.

SUMMATION STATEMENT:

"I do not believe all students of one studio should end up sounding alike. While working to enhance the singer's individual sound and quality, however, I believe that a correct, healthy singing technique should be the same among my students, regardless of the preferred musical category."

GRACE NOTES STUDIO

216 West 102nd Street
New York, NY 10025
(212) 222-6632

PROGRAM:	Musicianship and Scat—Group; Vocal Technique—Private
INSTRUCTOR:	Grace Testani
ESTABLISHED:	1979
REGISTRATION FEE:	None
CLASS FEE:	Musicianship $34 per month; Scat $60 per month
SCHEDULE:	Musicianship 1 1-hour session per week, ongoing; Scat 1 2-hour session per week, ongoing
AUDITING:	After placement interview, auditing is encouraged.
AUDITING FEE:	No fee
ENTRANCE REQUIREMENTS:	Interview
SCHOLARSHIPS:	Not available
NUMBER OF STUDENTS PER CLASS:	6
STUDENT BREAKDOWN:	61% female, 39% male; 3% under 18, 69% 18–25, 20% 26–35, 8% 36–45, 0% over 45; 0% under 1 year, 89% 1–2 years, 11% 2–3 years, 0% over 3 years

VOCAL CASSETTES: Provided

ACCOMPANIST: Instructor accompanies.

BIOGRAPHY: MS. TESTANI is currently on the faculties of the SOG Music Studios, the Guitar Study Center, and the Hebrew Arts School. In 1980 she co-led the vocal jazz workshop in UJC's Women in Jazz Festival in New York City. Also a professional singer, Ms. Testani has performed at the Village Gate. Mikell's, and Horn of Plenty; she is also a recording-studio singer. Ms. Testani received her B.A. from New York University.

CLASSES: The aim of the class is to develop skills for vocal improvisation and to expand the student's ear training, as well as to encourage confidence in his or her own creativity. Special exercises are used that employ arpeggios, modes, rhythm and scat vocabulary on standard repertoire. My approach is systematic: from the blues through more complicated progressions to bebop and modal concepts —all on actual songs so that the student develops a jazz repertoire as well.

SUMMATION STATEMENT: "I believe that to be successful in today's competitive music world, a vocalist has to be a musician and has to be able to read, write, arrange, and improvise. Even if the goal is not to be a jazz singer, the ability to scat opens up a whole new world of emotional and musical interpretation. Vocal jazz is moving into its own adolescence and beginning to mature into an art form in its own right. If the jazz tradition is going to continue to evolve, I believe that it is the vocalists that are going to move the music forward."

NANCY GREEN

741 West End Avenue
New York, NY 10025
(212) 724–2800

PROGRAM: Vocal Technique, Private

REGISTRATION FEE: None

CLASS FEE: $25 per hour

SCHEDULE: 1-hour sessions, ongoing

ENTRANCE REQUIREMENTS: Open

ACCOMPANIST:	Instructor accompanies.
WAITING AREA:	Yes
BIOGRAPHY:	MS. GREEN received her M.M. in voice from the New England Conservatory. She has taught voice in association with Harvard University for 4 years and sponsored several student recitals at Harvard. She has performed with the Boston Opera, the Providence Opera, and was an apprentice with the Santa Fe Opera. She is a mezzo-soprano familiar with both classical and popular repertoire. She also teaches Italian, French, and German diction for singing and is a member of NATS.

THOMAS GRUBB

160 West 73rd Street
New York, NY 10023
(212) 787–7965

PROGRAM:	Vocal Technique
ESTABLISHED:	1966
REGISTRATION FEE:	None
SCHEDULE:	By appointment
CANCELLATION POLICIES:	24-hour notice or payment due in full
REQUIRED MATERIALS:	*Singing in French*, Grubb
ACCOMPANIST:	Instructor accompanies
BIOGRAPHY:	MR. GRUBB is Director of the Vocal Literature and the French for Singers programs at the Manhattan School of Music. He collaborates and performs as coach and pianist with leading singers of the Metropolitan and New York City operas and with internationally renowned recitalists. He coached and accompanied the master classes of the late Pierre Bernac in the United States, France, and Canada. He is a Fulbright Scholar and recipient of the Debussy Award of the Alliance Francaise de New York. He received degrees from the University of Rochester, Yale, and the Manhattan School of Music, as well as the École de Piano Magdo Tagliaferro in Paris.
CLASS:	Goals of the work are refinement and supervision of interpretation, style, diction, and general overall presentation. During a session the singer is corrected after uninterrupted hearing; then, after par-

SUMMATION STATEMENT:
ticular corrections are made, a final hearing is usually beneficial.
"I teach adherence to demands of the score, use of interpretive imagination, and dramatic credibility with no gimmicks."

LEWIS HARDEE

The Lambs
3 West 51st Street
New York, NY 10022
(212) 753–4642

PROGRAM: A Workshop for Actors Who Want to Learn to Sing
ESTABLISHED: 1980
REGISTRATION FEE: None
CLASS FEE: $135 per 10-week session
SCHEDULE: 1 2-hour class per week, ongoing 10-week sessions
AUDITING: Not permitted
ENTRANCE REQUIREMENTS: Interview and audition
CANCELLATION POLICIES: Make-up sessions available
SCHOLARSHIPS: Not available
NUMBER OF STUDENTS PER CLASS: Limited to 10
STUDENT BREAKDOWN: 60% female, 40% male; 10% 26–35, 70% 36–45, 20% over 45; 25% 1–2 years, 50% 2–3 years, 25% over 3 years
ACCOMPANYING INSTRUMENT: Piano
CLASS CARD: No
ACCOMPANIST: Provided
WAITING AREA: Yes
BIOGRAPHY: MR. HARDEE holds a B.A. and M.A. in music from the University of North Carolina at Chapel Hill, and did his post-graduate at Columbia University. He is an instructor of music and speech at the American Academy of Dramatic Arts in New York; a member of ASCAP and NATS; director of numerous choruses and musicals; and Musical Director for Penny Bridge Players.
CLASS: The first hour of each session is spent on developing the vocal instrument—beginning with bodily relaxation and control exercises based on Alexander

technique. Second hour is devoted to group singing and solos, followed by critiques.

SUMMATION STATEMENT: "Every effort is made to provide a friendly, positive
atmosphere in which learning can flourish. My stu-
dents regularly appear on television, in nightclubs,
on Broadway, and Off Broadway. A legit method is
emphasized, with mezzo stressed and belt discouraged. Singing repertory is almost entirely
Broadway."

HB STUDIO

Muriel Burns, Director
120 Bank Street
New York, NY 10014
(212) 675–2370

PROGRAM: Singing, Speaking, Vocal Development, Musical
Theatre, Sight Singing, Music of Elizabethan and
Jacobean Theatre

INSTRUCTORS: George Axiltree, Larry Hill, William Maloney, Eliza-
beth Hodes, Gayle Swymer, Jim Tushar, Arabella
Hong Young, Word Baker, Aaron Frankel, Joe
Bousard, Rita Gardner, Carol Hall, Martha
Schlamme, Mary Roof

ESTABLISHED: 1945

REGISTRATION FEE: $7.50

CLASS FEE: $95 (average); advanced classes where accom-
panist supplied $114

SCHEDULE: 1 1/2-to-2 1/2-hours per week, 19 weeks, ongoing

AUDIT: Permitted

AUDITING FEE: $1.50 for first audit; $4 for subsequent audit of
same class

ENTRANCE REQUIREMENTS: Open (for most classes)

CANCELLATION POLICIES: No refunds given after term has started and no
credit given for classes missed.

SCHOLARSHIPS: Work-exchange available

NUMBER OF STUDENTS
   PER CLASS: 15–35

TOTAL STUDIO ENROLLMENT: Over 3,000

STUDENT BREAKDOWN: 60% female, 40% male; 5% under 18, 45% 18–25,
20% 26–35, 20% 36–45, 10% over 45; 5% under 6
months, 10% 1/2–1 year, 25% 1–2 years, 40% 2–3
years, 20% over 3 years

STUDIOS:	5
ACCOMPANYING INSTRUMENT:	Piano
VOCAL CASSETTES:	No
ACCOMPANIST:	Yes
WAITING AREA:	Yes
SUMMATION STATEMENT:	"The HB Studio began in 1945 and aims for a meaningful dramatic expression of the times and country in which we live. To help establish a theatre of experimentation based on classic tradition, the Studio is dedicated to the development of individual artists who may actively contribute to a theatre of national character. Conceived as an artistic and working home, it offers an outlet for practice and growth for the professional theatre artist, and an opportunity for the young to establish roots in their intended crafts. The Studio's guiding principle is creative freedom, which has as its logical consequence responsibility to a noble art."

HENRY N. JACOBI

344 West 72nd Street
New York, NY 10023
(212) 362–6311

PROGRAM:	Vocal Technique, Private
ESTABLISHED:	1939
SCHEDULE:	$1/2$-hour sessions, ongoing
ENTRANCE REQUIREMENTS:	Interview
CANCELLATION POLICIES:	24-hour notice
SCHOLARSHIPS:	Not available
STUDIOS:	3
WAITING AREA:	Yes
BIOGRAPHY:	PROFESSOR JACOBI has had private vocal studios in Berlin and Vienna. In Havana, he held a professorship at the International Music conservatory where he was the voice instructor to the members of the touring Salzburg Opera Guild. He has taught voice for the American Theatre Wing, Robert Whitehead Productions, the American Shakespeare Festival, Lincoln Center Repertory, and at his own Holywood studio. Professor Jacobi

is the author of the forthcoming book, *Building Your Best Voice,* for which Tony Randall supplied the foreword.

GENETTE KAPLAN

3950 Blackstone Avenue
New York, NY 10471
(212) 549–3567/840–8633 (9:00 A.M.–5:00 P.M.)

PROGRAM:	Vocal Technique, Private
ESTABLISHED:	1977
REGISTRATION FEE:	None
CLASS FEE:	$20 per hour
SCHEDULE:	1-hour sessions, ongoing
CANCELLATION POLICIES:	24-hour notice
SCHOLARSHIPS:	Not available
STUDENT BREAKDOWN:	80% female, 20% male; 20% under 18, 30% 18–25, 40% 26–35, 10% 36–45, 0% over 45
VOCAL CASSETTES:	Provided
ACCOMPANIST:	Instructor accompanies.
BIOGRAPHY:	MS. KAPLAN is a graduate of the Peabody Conservatory of Music in Baltimore and the American Theatre Wing in New York.
CLASS:	The goal of the lesson is to teach the student proper breath control, vocal exercises, performance of a song, sight reading, and ear training.
SUMMATION STATEMENT:	"I attempt to show the student the joy of learning how to sing and perform with self-confidence."

DENNIS KISOR

61 Fourth Avenue
New York, NY 10003
(212) 982–1645

PROGRAM:	Vocal Technique, Private
ESTABLISHED:	1978
CLASS FEE:	$25
SCHEDULE:	50-minute sessions, ongoing, Monday–Saturday 11 A.M.–7 P.M.

ENTRANCE REQUIREMENTS: Student takes an introductory class through which we decide whether or not to work together.

CANCELLATION POLICIES: 24-hour notice

SCHOLARSHIPS: Not available

STUDENT BREAKDOWN: 65% female, 35% male; 0% under 18, 60% 18–25, 35% 26–35, 5% 36–45, 0% over 45; 15% under 6 months, 10% 1/2–1 year, 55% 1–2 years, 20% 2–3 years, 0% over 3 years

ACCOMPANIST: Instructor accompanies.

WAITING AREA: Yes

BIOGRAPHY: MR. KISOR has been the Musical Director at Croswell Summer Musical Theatre for 8 years and has appeared in the national tours of *Music Man,* with Tony Randall, and *South Pacific,* with Jane Powell and Howard Keel. He received his M.M. from the University of Michigan in voice and conducting.

CLASS: Each student is evaluated at the first lesson and vocal exercises are assigned to strengthen vocal clarity and production, and to increase range, with great emphasis on breathing. Audition numbers are assigned in order to allow the student to audition within his or her capabilities.

SUMMATION STATEMENT: "Each class is designed for the individual student to help achieve his or her career goals. Honest support and encouragement are present. If a student does not progress, I will recommend another teacher or specialist for the vocal problem."

MITCHELL KRIEGER

66 West 82nd Street
New York, NY 10024
(212) 874–0158

PROGRAM: Vocal Technique, Private

INSTRUCTORS: Mitchell Krieger, Sarah Bachmann

REGISTRATION FEE: None

CLASS FEE: $25 per hour

SCHEDULE: 1-hour sessions, ongoing

ENTRANCE REQUIREMENTS: Open

ACCOMPANIST: Instructor accompanies.

BIOGRAPHY: MR. KRIEGER, a member of the music staff of the New York City Opera, received degrees from the

Manhattan School of Music and from the California Institute of the Arts. He has served as conductor and coach for opera companies in New York, Los Angeles, and Boston. He has been a Conducting Fellow at the Aspen Music Festival, Julliard American Opera Center, and at Boris Goldovsky's workshop at Southeastern Massachusetts University. Mr. Krieger founded the Sinfonia d'Opera, a company dedicated to giving young singers and instrumentalists much-needed experience with the standard operatic repertoire. MS. BACHMANN studied at Julliard and at the Manhattan School of Music. She has sung major roles with the Western Opera, Opera Ensemble of New York, and Encompass Theatre, among others.

CLASS: Work is primarily with operatic material and involves intense instruction in practical application of musical, dramatic, and textual analysis and understanding. The work is toward achievement of true legato, free and facile colorations, and dramatic variety.

SUMMATION STATEMENT: "As professionals, we advocate a total dedication to achieving the highest artistic standards. We believe that no artist ever stops learning, and we always strive to learn from our students as we teach them."

SHELLEN LUBIN

509 West 110th Street
New York, NY 10025
(212) 864–2380

PROGRAM:	Vocal Technique, Private
ESTABLISHED:	1976
REGISTRATION FEE:	None
CLASS FEE:	$20 per hour
SCHEDULE:	1-hour sessions, ongoing
ENTRANCE REQUIREMENTS:	Interview-lesson is offered so we can meet each other and decide if we want to work together.
CANCELLATION POLICIES:	No charge for first cancellation; after that, cancellation must be prior to the day of the lesson.
SCHOLARSHIPS:	None
VOCAL CASSETTES:	Provided

ACCOMPANIST:	Instructor accompanies.
BIOGRAPHY:	MS. LUBIN is currently teaching song performance and song writing as a guest lecturer at Bennington College. Her theatre scores have been produced by the Chelsea Theatre Center, ELT Informal Series, and the WPA Theatre. She has written the book, music, and lyrics for *Molly's Daughters*. She and her songs were featured in Milos Foreman's first American film, *Taking Off*. Her club act has been seen at such spots as Reno Sweeney, Grand Finale, Mikell's , and Tramps.
CLASS:	The performance of a song for an audition, a role, or a club act includes a number of important aspects: breathing, vocal range and technique, choice of material, arrangement of material (including musical style, key, tempo, key changes, etc.), character work, emotional development. With a club act there is also the question of how someone is presenting himself or herself and of how to share with the audience through the songs and patter.
SUMMATION STATEMENT:	"Techniques are tools which must be learned and understood so that when you're actually performing, you don't think about them, but instead live the moment you're playing and share it with whoever your audience is."

MANHATTAN SCHOOL OF MUSIC

120 Claremont Avenue, at 122nd Street
New York, NY 10027
(212) 749–2802, exts. 471 or 472

PROGRAM:	Rudiments of Theory, Sight-Singing, Ear Training, Singer's Performance Workshop
INSTRUCTORS:	Rya Evans Harrell, Ken Gullmartin
CLASS FEE:	$130–$260 per semester
SCHEDULE:	1 2-to3-hour session per week, September–January, January–May
CLASSES:	Rudiments of Theory includes the study of meter, rhythm, treble, and bass clef notation, major and minor scales, melodic and harmonic intervals, fundamental and inverted chord positions and elementary contrapuntal material. Analytic proce-

dures include determination of keys and simple formal designs; cadences; phrase and period forms. Practical application through creative writing. Performance Workshop is a class in which each individual performer explores his psycho-physical makeup as a performing instrument. This develops awareness for the purpose of stimulating and freeing the performer's imagination.

DAN MAREK

210 West 101st Street
New York, NY 10025
(212) 222-1546

PROGRAM:	Vocal Technique, Private
ESTABLISHED:	1968
CLASS FEE:	$18 per lesson; $40 per hour (with accompanist)
SCHEDULE:	1/2-hour sessions, ongoing
AUDITING:	No audit
ENTRANCE REQUIREMENTS:	Excellent voice
SCHOLARSHIPS:	Available at teacher's discretion
STUDENT BREAKDOWN:	60% female, 40% male; 0% under 18, 65% 18–25, 30% 26–35, 5% 36–45, 0% over 45; 10% under 6 months, 5% 1/2–1 year, 35% 1–2 years, 40% 2–3 years, 10% over 3 years
ACCOMPANIST:	Instructor may accompany or accompanist may be provided.
WAITING AREA:	Yes
BIOGRAPHY:	MR. MAREK is on the faculty of the Mannes College of Music, Upsala College, and the City University of New York. He received his master's from Manhattan School of Music and has studied privately with Issac Van Grove, John Bronlee, and Cornelius Reid. He has won many competitions and awards, such as the Liederkranz and the Katherine Turney Long Scholarship at the Metropolitan Opera.
CLASS:	All exercises are designed to develop the student's voice by careful analysis of individual problems.
SUMMATION STATEMENT:	"A voice teacher should be a person who combines technical knowledge with musicality and performing experience. He or she should not be bi-

ased on the side of either science or art. Students of college age are usually not settled technically and therefore the emphasis should be on building a solid and healthy technique. Technical study should always be viewed not as an end but as a means toward freeing the singer for full artistic expression. Repertoire should be chosen well within the ability of the student to provide positive performance experience and not geared toward making a 'reputation' for either the student or the teacher. I believe that the bel canto ideals of balanced registration, smooth scale, power, wide range, and flexibility are still the goals every singer should strive for."

JEAN McCLELLAND

101 74th Street
North Bergen, NJ 07047
(201) 864–9722/(212) 279–9321

PROGRAM:	Vocal Technique, Private
INSTRUCTOR:	Jean McClelland
ESTABLISHED:	1973 (Boston)
REGISTRATION FEE:	None
CLASS FEE:	$25 per hour, Manhattan; $20 per hour, New Jersey
SCHEDULE:	1-hour sessions, ongoing
AUDITING:	Permitted
AUDITING FEE:	None
ENTRANCE REQUIREMENTS:	Interview
SCHOLARSHIPS:	Not available
STUDENT BREAKDOWN:	75% female, 25% male; 60% 18–25, 40% 26–35; 50% 1–2 years, 50% 2–3 years
BIOGRAPHY:	MS. McCLELLAND has performed in opera, theatre, and children's theatre, and has been on the faculty of several performing arts centers and educational institutions in Boston. She holds a B.A. from Vassar and a M.M. from Boston University.
CLASS:	Ms. McClelland teaches the freeing of the natural voice. Her work with students combines natural breath production and vocal relaxation, which aid in the production of a natural sound; clear, unforced diction; and more artistic singing, whether it

be popular or classical. Students with severe tensions or abnormalities (e.g. vocal nodes) find that this technique helps to clear up the problem and lead to vocal health."

SUMMATION STATEMENT: "I do not impose a manufactured sound on students. I used a positive approach and build on strength rather than weaknesses."

WILLIAM METCALF

215 West 92nd Street
New York, NY 10025
(212) 362–3378

PROGRAM:	Vocal Technique, Private
SCHEDULE:	By appointment, Thursday–Saturday
CANCELLATION POLICIES:	24-hour notice
SCHOLARSHIPS:	Not available
VOCAL CASSETTES:	Not provided
ACCOMPANIST:	Provided
BIOGRAPHY:	MR. METCALF received his B.M. from New England Conservatory of Music and from Julliard School of Music. He is a member of the New York City Opera, the Washington Opera Society, and the Miami Opera Guild; he is a soloist with the Boston, Chicago, New York, and San Francisco symphonies. He has appeared in the American premieres of Britten's *Curlew River, Burning Fiery Furnace,* and *Prodigal Son;* and in solo recitals in the United States and Canada. He has recorded for Columbia, Vanguard, and Kapp.

PHIL ORLICK

41 Fifth Avenue
New York, NY 10003
(212) 777–8929

PROGRAM:	Vocal Technique, Private
ESTABLISHED:	1967
CLASS FEE:	$20 per hour

SCHEDULE:	1-hour sessions, ongoing
AUDITING:	No audit
CANCELLATION POLICIES:	24-hour notice
SCHOLARSHIPS:	Not available
STUDENT BREAKDOWN:	50% female, 50% male; 5% under 18, 55% 18–25, 35% 26–35, 5% 36–45, 0% over 45; 40% under 6 months, 40% 1/2–1 year, 20% 1–2 years, 0% over 2 years
VOCAL CASSETTES:	Provided
ACCOMPANIST:	Instructor accompanies.
WAITING AREA:	Yes
BIOGRAPHY:	MR. ORLICK has worked as a nightclub performer, recording artist, and songwriter, and has been trained by foremost private teachers.
CLASS:	The goal of the lessons is to give the student a consistent, fluid, reliable use of his or her singing voice—greater range, better breathing, etc.—in order to grow as a performer; master pop styles (jazz, blues, rock, swing, country, gospel); express lyrics; relate to audiences; and conquer nervousness.
SUMMATION STATEMENT:	"The performance of a song has a structure within which singers can be spontaneous—material must fit the performer, and needn't be the most famous songs. Nervousness is normal until that energy is channeled, which is learnable. The singer must have a handle on several vocal styles; and singing must be a high priority, one of the most exciting activities in the student's life."

DODI PROTERO

257 Central Park West
New York, NY 10024
(212) 874–5396

PROGRAM:	Vocal Technique, Private
SCHEDULE:	1-hour sessions, ongoing
AUDITING:	No auditing
ENTRANCE REQUIREMENTS:	Audition
SCHOLARSHIPS:	Not available
BIOGRAPHY:	MS. PROTERO has been a professional opera singer in Europe, Canada, and the United States. Her credits include Broadway musicals, European

operettas, and recordings for Epic label. She has taught at the Banff School of Fine Arts and at the University of Illinois.

JOSEPH RUBIN

335 Riverside Drive
New York, NY 10025
(212) 662–9201

PROGRAM:	Vocal Technique, Private
ESTABLISHED:	1979
REGISTRATION FEE:	None
CLASS FEE:	$25 per session
SCHEDULE:	1-hour sessions, ongoing
ENTRANCE REQUIREMENTS:	Audition
CANCELLATION POLICIES:	24-hour notice
SCHOLARSHIPS:	Not available
STUDENT BREAKDOWN:	55% female, 45% male; 10% under 18, 50% 18–25, 40% 26–35, 0% over 35; 10% under 6 months, 10% $1/2$–1 year, 80% 1–2 years, 0% over 2 years
ACCOMPANIST:	Provided
WAITING AREA:	Yes
BIOGRAPHY:	MR. RUBIN received his M.M. from the University of Miami, where he was graduate assistant to the chairman of the voice department. He was a cantorial soloist with the Miami Opera.
CLASS:	The purpose of the lessons is to secure the technical skills and functions of the voice. The coordination of the breath and vōice are fundamentally achieved through specific exercises which the student masters through repetition and careful guidance. Literature and interpretation follow, creating the singer who is well rounded both musically and technically.
SUMMATION STATEMENT:	"It is my goal to communicate vocal skills according to the intellect, background, and emotional range of each individual that the studio commits to teach."

CLIFFORD E. SEIDMAN

Astor Place Area
(212) 677–8575

PROGRAM:	Private Voice Training
REGISTRATION FEE:	None
CLASS FEE:	$30 per class; 5 classes $120, payable at first class
SCHEDULE:	1-hour sessions
BIOGRAPHY:	MR. SEIDMAN is an actor with an M.F.A. in acting from the New York University School of the Arts. He is a former member of the Working Theatre, where he was trained as a teacher by Kristin Linklater, Peter Kass, and Joseph Chaikin. He has taught at American University, University of Oklahoma, State University of New York at Fedonia, and at the National Theatre of Spain in Madrid.
CLASS:	The detailed and interdependent voice and body exercises are designed to undo habitual tensions that limit the actor's expressive potential. Only when the innate intelligence and intrinsic energies of the body and voice are freed and developed can the actor explore the connection of feelings, thoughts, movement, and words.
SUMMATION STATEMENT:	"The classes are designed to achieve vocal and physical flexibility, awareness, and spontaneity. Since there is only one student per class I can attend to that student's specific voice and body problems, and provide a set of exercises the student can continue on his or her own."

NEIL SEMER

400 West 43rd Street
New York, NY 10036
(212) 244–6497

PROGRAM:	Vocal Technique, Private
REGISTRATION FEE:	None
CLASS FEE:	$20 per session
SCHEDULE:	1-hour sessions, ongoing
CANCELLATION POLICIES:	Must cancel by 11 P.M. the previous night

SCHOLARSHIPS:	Not available
ACCOMPANIST:	Instructor accompanies.
BIOGRAPHY:	MR. SEMER has worked professionally as a singer, actor, and pianist.
CLASS:	"Half of each class is dedicated to body, breath work, and vocalises designed to open the voice. The other half is spent in practical application of these skills on songs that are of professional use to the performer. Emphasis is on coordinating a healthy, easy vocal production with expressive, theatrical singing that is in line with one's casting potential. Audition material is prepared."

THE SINGING EXPERIENCE

Upper East Side
New York, NY
(212) 472–2207

PROGRAM:	Vocal Technique, Group
INSTRUCTOR:	Linda Amiel Burns
ESTABLISHED:	1977
REGISTRATION FEE:	None
CLASS FEE:	$95
SCHEDULE:	5 sessions totalling 12 hours over a one-month period
AUDITING:	For a fee students can attend the performances at Dangerfield's which are considered workshop sessions.
ENTRANCE REQUIREMENTS:	Open
CANCELLATION POLICIES:	One week prior to workshop, refund or transfer to another workshop
SCHOLARSHIPS:	Not available
NUMBER OF STUDENTS PER CLASS:	20–25
BIOGRAPHY:	MS. BURNS created the workshop because she herself had a song inside screaming to get out. She grew up not far from Broadway's famed Tin Pan Alley where her father owned two famous restaurants. She became a singer and actress and ultimately star of her own radio show. She resides in Manhattan with her two children, both graduates of The Singing Experience.
CLASS:	The purpose of the workshop is for students to

discover themselves through song, to let go of all the self-judgment and criticism that stops them from performing well on stage and in life. This is a workshop about communication—how to connect with your song both vocally and emotionally, how to move an audience, how to be the best you can be. Classes include relaxation exercises, improvisations, group and individual songs, microphone technique, body movement, stage presence—all leading to the final session at a famous cabaret. The atmosphere is supportive and encouraging. This is a workshop where you learn to take risks, explore the many facets of your personality, and gain a tremendous amount of self-confidence.

SUMMATION STATEMENT: "Our philosophy is that of support and encouragement. The belief is that each person has many talents and that they can be brought out through various ways and means, but no one is ever to be torn down or discouraged. Each student is asked not to use the word 'cannot' and to give 100% to the experience. They are taught to trust what comes out of them, whether it be speaking or singing, and to love themselves."

KATHY SOMMER

369 West 51st Street
New York, NY 10019
(212) 245–0232/541–7600

PROGRAM: Vocal Coaching, Private
REGISTRATION FEE: None
CLASS FEES: Vary according to needs
SCHEDULE: 1-hour sessions, ongoing
ENTRANCE REQUIREMENTS: Open
SCHOLARSHIPS: Not available
BIOGRAPHY: MS. SOMMER has played piano for 18 years. She has directed various summer stock companies around the country and has appeared in solo recitals and club acts. She received her B.A. from Yale.
CLASS: The sessions focus on choice of material, musicality, different dramatic approaches to songs, developing a sense of style. I am a pianist, music direc-

tor, arranger—pop, jazz, Broadway, rock 'n' roll, country western—anything that's necessary.

SUE STARCK

160 West 73rd Street
New York, NY 10023
(212) 580–8528/877–6700

PROGRAM:	Vocal Technique, Private
ESTABLISHED:	1966
REGISTRATION FEE:	None
CLASS FEE:	$30 per hour
SCHEDULE:	1-hour sessions, ongoing
AUDITING:	Yes
AUDITING FEE:	No fee
ENTRANCE REQUIREMENTS:	By audition
CANCELLATION POLICIES:	24 hours or full fee billed
SCHOLARSHIPS:	Two scholarships available per year
STUDENT BREAKDOWN:	60% female, 40% male; 5% under 18, 30% 18–25, 30% 26–35, 30% 36–45, 5% over 45; 50% 1–2 years, 50% over 2 years
ACCOMPANIST:	Instructor accompanies.
BIOGRAPHY:	MS. STARCK received her B.A. from the University of California at Fresno/San Francisco and her M.A. in voice at the San Francisco Conservatory of Music.
CLASS:	Sessions approach singing as a total body experience, training the proper muscles and learning to relax the unnecessary ones. The first aim is to free the middle of the voice range, and then widen the range. Material begins with baroque, early Italian songs, and classical music, no matter what the eventual aim is.
SUMMATION STATEMENT:	"Since my performing experience includes opera, oratorio, recitals, and musicals as well as piano literature, I am able to relate to a wide variety of serious students."

SUSAN WINDER

226 East 89th Street
New York, NY 10028
(212) 289–6594

PROGRAM:	Vocal Technique, Private
BIOGRAPHY:	MS. WINDER has been a professional singer and teacher for 12 years. Her training includes several areas of study, including vocal technique, piano, jazz and classical theory, harmony, composition, and Erick Hawkins movement technique.
CLASS:	Lessons involve a study of the placement, breath support, resonance, and other vocal concepts which can be applied successfully to any style of singing so the student will sound like himself or herself, only better.
SUMMATION STATEMENT:	"Singing right is easier than singing wrong; but you need a careful guide through the process of learning to sing correctly."

MISCELLANEOUS
MISCELLANEOUS
MISCELLANEOUS
MISCELLANEOUS
MISCELLANEOUS
MISCELLANEOUS
MISCELLANEOUS
MISCELLANEOUS
MISCELLANEOUS
MISCELLANEOUS
MISCELLANEOUS
MISCELLANEOUS
MISCELLANEOUS
MISCELLANEOUS
MISCELLANEOUS
MISCELLANEOUS
MISCELLANEOUS
MISCELLANEOUS
MISCELLANEOUS
MISCELLANEOUS
MISCELLANEOUS
MISCELLANEOUS
MISCELLANEOUS
MISCELLANEOUS

ACTORS AND DIRECTORS LAB

412 West 42nd Street
New York, NY 10036
(212) 695–5429

PROGRAM:	Directing, Lighting Design, Production Management, Stage Management, Mime
INSTRUCTOR:	Jack Garfein, Todd Elmer, Stefan Niedzialkowski
ESTABLISHED:	1978
CLASS FEES:	Directing $400, others $200
SCHEDULE:	1 session per week, 12 weeks
AUDITING:	Permitted after interview
ENTRANCE REQUIREMENTS:	By interview and audition for advanced classes
CANCELLATION POLICIES:	Advanced notice required; make-up available
STUDIOS:	8; and theatre
DRESSING ROOMS:	Yes
WAITING AREA:	Yes
BIOGRAPHY:	MR. GARFEIN's Broadway credits include *End as a Man*, *Girls of Summer*, *Shadow of a Gunman*. He produced the first major production of *The Price* and *The American Clock*, both of which were invited to the Spoleto Festival and later opened on Broadway. MR. ELMER has designed lights for Off-Broadway productions such as *These Men*, *Flying Blind*, *A Month in the Country*, and *Dark at the Top of the Stairs* at theatres such as the Harold Clurman and the Roundabout. MR. NIEDZIALKOWSKI is a master teacher at Marcel Marceau's school in Paris and Artistic Director of New York's Mimedance Theatre and of the American School of Polish Mime. He has performed as lead actor in the Polish Mime Ballet Theatre for 12 years and cofounded, and directed and performed in, the Warsaw Mime Theatre.
CLASS:	The emphasis of Directing is on making the director aware of the ways that the actor's imagination can be stimulated, the sensitivity of the actor's instrument, and the language. Also covered are conceptualization, staging techniques, casting and working relationships with writers and designers. Lighting is designed to give the student a working knowledge of theatre lighting equipment, the director/designer relationship, the design/production process, basic lighting design principles, and various forms of stage presentations. Production cov-

ers scheduling, budgeting, cash flow, publicity, promotion, box office, company and house management, front of the house and special production needs for opera, dance, and musical theatre. Stage Management acquaints the actor with the assistant stage manager skills; the director with utilization of his stage manager; and preparation of the stage manager in his profession. Mime presents an innovative approach to mime, expanding it out of the traditional vocabulary of mimes such as Marcel Marceau. The technique involves movement forms from dance and acrobatics. The class emphasizes body strengthening, flexibility, coordination and control, and incorporates barre, general, and mime exercises.

SUMMATION STATEMENT: "All art is personal and its value is measured by its inner content. However, without training, a truly responsive performance becomes less likely and more difficult to attain. The lab teaches the artist to observe life, and encourages him to illuminate the nature of man through behavior."

AMERICAN MIME THEATRE

Paul J. Curtis, Director
24 Bond Street
New York, NY 10012
(212) 777–1710

PROGRAM:	Mime
INSTRUCTOR:	Paul J. Curtis and company members
ESTABLISHED:	1952
REGISTRATION FEE:	None
CLASS FEE:	$70 per month
SCHEDULE:	1 2-hour session per week, ongoing
AUDITING:	One audit permitted
ENTRANCE REQUIREMENTS:	Interview and audit
SCHOLARSHIPS:	Not available
NUMBER OF STUDENTS PER CLASS:	12
STUDENT BREAKDOWN:	50% female, 50% male; 90% 18–25, 10% 26–35; 20% 1–2 years, 80% 2–3 years
STUDIOS:	2
DRESSING ROOMS:	Yes

SHOWERS:	Yes
FLOOR:	Wood
BIOGRAPHY:	MR. CURTIS created the medium called American Mime. He founded the American Mime Theatre, the first professional mime theatre of its kind in the United States. Since, he has taught, lectured, performed, and administered all American Mime activities including the development of the art form itself.
CLASS:	The goal of the class is to achieve proficiency in American Mime, the simultaneous blending of acting and moving through a series of exercises unique to this process.
SUMMATION STATEMENT:	"American Mime is a unique performing art created by a particular balance of playwriting, acting, moving pantomime and theatrical equipment. It is entirely different from the pantomime of the French schools and the dance of Eastern mime disciplines. It is a complete theatre medium defined by its own aesthetic laws, terminology, techniques, script material, and teaching methods. Basically it is a medium for nonspeaking actors who, in characterization, perform the symbolic activities of American Mime plays through movement that is both telling and beautiful."

BOND STREET THEATRE COALITION

2 Bond Street
New York, NY 10012
(212) 254–4616

PROGRAM:	Clowning
INSTRUCTOR:	Joanna Sherman
STUDENT BREAKDOWN:	50% female, 50% male; 10% under 18, 50% 18–25, 30% 26–35, 5% 36–45, 5% over 45; 20% under 6 months, 20% 1/2–1 year, 55% 1–2 years, 5% 2–3 years, 0% over 3 years
STUDIOS:	3
BIOGRAPHY:	MS. SHERMAN has taught acrobatics with Theatre Movement, Les Jongleus, and the Joe Price School of Acrobatics; and mask-making and commedia at the Valley Studio in Wisconsin. She has been a faculty member at St. John's and Adelphi

CLASS:

universities and is a member of the Foundation for Community Artists, the International Juggler Association, and the Unicyclist Society of America.

Clown characters are not created, they are uncovered; this work is a liberating potpourri of skills and improvisation aimed at exposing and developing this vulnerable and spontaneous character. This is an important acting class, as it combines the rough and the holy, the true and the fabled, the silent and the boisterous. The apprentice is introduced to many aspects—improvisation, makeup, costume, juggling, slapstick, floor acrobatics, and comedy.

TONY BROWN and KARI MARGOLIS

Classes held at:
135 West 14th Street
New York, NY 10011
Mailing address:
"The Adaptors"
25 St. Johns Place, #3
Brooklyn, NY 11217
(212) 638–7058

PROGRAM:	Corporal Mime: Beginning, Intermediate, and Advanced Levels
INSTRUCTORS:	Tony Brown, Kari Margolis
ESTABLISHED:	1982
REGISTRATION FEE:	None
CLASS FEE:	$175
SCHEDULE:	1 2-hour session twice a week, 12 weeks, ongoing
AUDITING:	Not permitted
ENTRANCE REQUIREMENTS:	New students are required to take a 4-hour orientation class which is offered at the beginning of each 12-week term.
CANCELLATION POLICIES:	No refunds
SCHOLARSHIPS:	Not available
NUMBER OF STUDENTS PER CLASS:	Limited to 12
TOTAL STUDIO ENROLLMENT:	36
STUDENT BREAKDOWN:	50% female, 50% male; 60% 18–25, 40% 26–35;

	10% under 6 months, 10% ¹/₂–1 year, 40% 1–2 years, 40% 2–3 years
STUDIOS:	2
DRESSING ROOMS:	Yes
SHOWERS:	No
FLOOR:	Suspended wood
WAITING AREA:	Yes
BIOGRAPHY:	TONY BROWN and KARI MARGOLIS first joined forces in Paris while at the school of mime master Etienne Decroux. They devoted themselves to his teachings from 1975 to 1978. They then took an active part in creating and performing the repertory of the international mime troupe "Omnibus," based in Montreal, from 1978 to 1982. They are the artistic directors of "Spectra Mime Inc." which houses the performance group "The Adaptors." As founding members of "The Video Art Mime Project" they are actively involved in the creation and production of video mime works.
CLASS:	Based on the technique of Etienne Decroux, this course explores the dramatic power of corporal expression. Classes begin with a thorough warm-up, designed to develop muscular awareness and control. An in-depth study is made of such principles as isolations, counterweights, rhythm and intensity of movements, spatial awareness, and form. The entire body is sensitized to be used as a tool for dramatic expression.
SUMMATION STATEMENT:	"Our teachings are not based on the study of illusions, but rather on the study of the human spirit and how we can find drama in the human form."

COMEDY PERFORMERS STUDIO
NOLA STUDIOS

250 West 54th Street
New York, NY 10019
(212) 362–3054

PROGRAM:	Comedy Technique Class, Master Class, Coaching
INSTRUCTOR:	Lisa Carmel
ESTABLISHED:	1978
CLASS FEE:	$150

SCHEDULE: Technique: Tuesdays 8:00 PM-10:30 PM, Master: Thursdays 8:00 PM-10:30 PM, 7-week session, private coaching by appointment

AUDITING: Free

ENTRANCE REQUIREMENTS: Interview

CANCELLATION POLICY: Class can be made up if student calls within 2 hours of class.

SCHOLARSHIPS: Work-exchange available

NUMBER OF STUDENTS PER CLASS: 10–15

BIOGRAPHY: MS. CARMEL is a professional comedy writer, director and performer. She has appeared in films and has television credits in New York and in London. She has studied with Marilyn Rosen of the Actor's Studio, and with David Shepard, founder of Second City in Chicago.

CLASSES: Comedy Technique Class consists of explorations of different methods of achieving peak comedic performance, with attention to improvisation, comedy timing, delivery, material, stage performance, auditioning and character study. Emphasis is on building stand-up routines, comedy monologues for stage, television or commercial work, using student's own personal and individual style. Masterclass is a continuation of Technique Class and for performers in nightclubs, television or commercials. Attention is given to the finer points in performance, material enhancement and career placement. Well-known comics will be invited to answer questions. The use of video is also incorporated so performers can see themselves perform. Promising students will be given a chance to perform in top comedy clubs and be submitted to casting directors for jobs.

SUMMATION STATEMENT: The Comedy Performers Studio has received extensive coverage on "PM Magazine," "The Today Show," and was the subject of an NBC special on comedy. Workshops were filmed for public television in Europe. Comedy Performers Studio accepts people with strong commitment to the art of comedy and a willingness to achieve goals in all fields of media. Students are provided with individualized directions according to specific needs.

CUMEEZI CENTER

Eric Trules, Director
303 Park Avenue South
New York, NY 10010
(212) 254–4518

PROGRAM:	Clowning
INSTRUCTORS:	The Cumeezis
ESTABLISHED:	1978
REGISTRATION FEE:	None
CLASS FEE:	$45 for 4 sessions
SCHEDULE:	2-hour sessions, ongoing
AUDITING:	No audit
ENTRANCE REQUIREMENTS:	Open
CANCELLATION POLICIES:	No refunds
SCHOLARSHIPS:	Half-price work-scholarships available
NUMBER OF STUDENTS PER CLASS:	10–20
STUDENT BREAKDOWN:	50% female, 50% male; 5% under 18, 60% 18–25, 20% 26–35, 10% 36–45, 5% over 45; 45% under 6 months, 40% 1/2–1 year, 15% 1–2 years, 0% over 2 years
VIDEO EQUIPMENT:	Yes
STUDIOS:	1
DRESSING ROOMS:	Yes
FLOOR:	Hardwood
WAITING AREA:	Yes
BIOGRAPHY:	MR. TRULES, founder and director of the Cumeezis, teaches advanced classes. Beginner and intermediate classes are taught by members of the Company. The Cumeezis have been funded by NEW, NYSCA, and corporate and private sources. They have toured Europe, appeared on television and film, and have performed throughout the area. All teachers are professional clowns.
CLASS:	All classes offer the Cumeezi technique of clowning, which is a physical style for animating movement, perception, and behavior. The technique deals with gesture and individuality of expression rather than circus skills. It is useful for performing artists of all persuasions as well as lay people with no performance background. Makeup is introduced in the final beginner session and costume is begun in the intermediate level. A goal of the inter-

mediate and advanced classes is a public clown appearance.

SUMMATION STATEMENT: "Students are offered an original form of self-expression at the Cumeezi Center. Individuals work according to their talent and effort. There are no tests or graduations except to the advanced level. There is the opportunity for the advanced students to be invited to apprentice with the company. The work may be taken from the Center and used professionally or incorporated into the student's everyday life."

ENSEMBLE STUDIO THEATRE INSTITUTE FOR PROFESSIONAL TRAINING

Annette Holloway, Director
12 West End Avenue
New York, NY 10023
(212) 581–9409

PROGRAM:	Playwriting: Basic, Advanced, One-Act Plays; Directing; Screenwriting
INSTRUCTORS:	Curt Dempster (Basic, Advanced Playwriting, Directing), Stuart Spencer (The One-Act Play), Brother Jonathan Ringkamp (Screenwriting)
ESTABLISHED:	1978
REGISTRATION FEE:	None
CLASS FEE:	$200–$300
SCHEDULE:	1 or 2 3-to-6-hour classes per week, 9 weeks
AUDITING:	Not permitted
ENTRANCE REQUIREMENTS:	Application, interview
CANCELLATION POLICIES:	Refunds given for paid professional work in the field
SCHOLARSHIPS:	Work-exchange available
NUMBER OF STUDENTS PER CLASS:	Limited to 10–15
TOTAL STUDIO ENROLLMENT:	80–100
STUDENT BREAKDOWN:	60% female, 40% male; 0% under 18, 40% 18–25, 50% 26–35, 10% 36–45, 0% over 45; 50% under 6 months, 25% 1/2–1 year, 20% 1–2 years, 5% 2–3 years, 0% over 3 years
BIOGRAPHY:	BROTHER JONATHAN RINGKAMP is a play-

wright member of EST, and EST has produced his plays *Bella Figura* and *The Poisoner of the Wells*. He is a cofounder of the Everyman Company and one of the originators of the street theatre movement in New York City. Films include screenplays for *Rapallo and Sons, The Killing Hour,* and a rewrite for *Bayou.* MR. DEMPSTER founded EST in 1971. As a director, he has staged new plays by Joyce Carol Oates, Tennessee Williams and Frank D. Gilroy. As a playwright, his works include *Déjà Vu* and *Mimosa Pudica,* which was selected for the *1978–79 Best Short Plays.* As an actor, his stage appearances include roles on and off Broadway. MR. SPENCER is the literary manager of EST. His one-act play *The Golden Rose* won the American College Theatre Festival Mid-West Award in 1979, and his most recent play, *Cash,* was produced in EST's Marathon '83.

CLASS:

The One-Act Play is an introduction to playwriting technique, focusing on the unique form of the one-act, culminating in the reading of students' one-acts at the final session. Basic Playwriting surveys the craft of playwriting and deals with the structure of the one-act play, character, dramatic situation, and the individual imagination of the writer. The Playwriting course deals with full-length works and focuses on character exploration and development. Students are expected to finish a new play during the course to be read by professional actors in the final session. Directing comprises two main aspects: investigation of step-by-step elements of directing, and personal guidance and assistance, from script selection to performance on an individual basis. Fee includes use of rehearsal space. In Screenwriting students will write in class and on their own, in addition to lectures, discussions, and analyses of prepared work.

SUMMATION STATEMENT:

"EST's Institute for Professional Training was established as a training ground for the development of new talent and a place where members of the theatre can teach and work at their crafts."

THE FENCING CENTER

Stephen Khindy, Director
40 Charlton Street
New York, NY 10014
(212) 496–8255

PROGRAM:	Fencing, Individual and Group
INSTRUCTORS:	Stan Bardakh, Stephen Khindy, Steven Otero
ESTABLISHED:	1979
REGISTRATION FEE:	None
CLASS FEES:	$40 per month; Individual $15 per hour
SCHEDULE:	1 5-hour session per week, ongoing
ENTRANCE REQUIREMENTS:	Open
CANCELLATION POLICY:	24-hour notice required
SCHOLARSHIPS:	Available
NUMBER OF STUDENTS PER CLASS:	10
STUDENT BREAKDOWN:	40% female, 60% male; 10% under 18, 35% 18–25, 40% 26–35, 10% 36–45, 5% over 45; 30% under 6 months, 40% ½–1 year, 30% 1–2 years
VIDEO EQUIPMENT:	Yes
STUDIOS:	1
FLOOR:	Parquet
WAITING AREA:	Yes
BIOGRAPHY:	MR. KHINDY is the fencing coach for the college of Staten Island and an active member of the AFLA. MR. OTERO studied stage fencing at the HB Studios with Joe Daly for 4 years and was his assistant for 2. He is a member of the Gentlemen Adventurers.
CLASSES:	The goal of the classes is to turn out competent stage fencers who can arrange fights. This is accomplished through stretching and footwork, technical and tactical drills, bouting and individual lessons with staff members. For stage fencing and footwork, choreography with weapons and prepared duels are utilized.
SUMMATION STATEMENT:	"We teach the basic and advanced skills with the 3 fencing weapons—the foil, épée, and sabre—for both individual discipline and competition. We also offer instruction in stage fencing for actors with rapier, dagger, and small sword."

FIGHTS ARE US

J. Allen Suddeth, Director
1261 Broadway, Suite 505
New York, NY 10001
(212) 725–1379/864–1206

PROGRAM:	Stage Combat
INSTRUCTORS:	J. Allen Suddeth, Steve Vaughan
ESTABLISHED:	1979
REGISTRATION FEE:	None
CLASS FEE:	$90 per term
SCHEDULE:	2 1½-hour classes per week, 9 months, ongoing
AUDITING:	Permitted
AUDITING FEE:	No fee
ENTRANCE REQUIREMENTS:	Good physical condition
CANCELLATION POLICIES:	Some refunds
SCHOLARSHIPS:	Partial work-exchange scholarships
REQUIRED MATERIALS:	Workout clothes; equipment provided
NUMBER OF STUDENTS PER CLASS:	Limited to 10
TOTAL STUDIO ENROLLMENT:	30–50
STUDENT BREAKDOWN:	40% female, 60% male; 2% under 18, 40% 18–25, 45% 26–35, 13% 36–45; 20% under 6 months, 40% ½–1 year, 15% 1–2 years, 12% 2–3 years, 12% over 3 years
VIDEO EQUIPMENT:	Yes
VIDEO CASSETTES:	Students may purchase video cassettes.
STUDIOS:	1
DRESSING ROOMS:	Yes
SHOWERS:	2
FLOOR:	Wood
CLASS CARD:	Yes; 10 classes, valid 3 months
WAITING AREA:	Yes
BIOGRAPHY:	MR. SUDDETH has been a professional fight choreographer for 10 years; he is a full member of the Society of American Fight Directors. He has staged fights for Broadway, Off Broadway and at universities across the country. He is stunt coordinator for "One Life to Live," "Guiding Light," "Another World," and "Texas."
CLASS:	The most important thing about stage combat is safety first. We equip a performer with exciting and safe skills which they can use in the real world of theatre and television, where fight directors are not always employed. The sword training is very disci-

plined, and the unarmed and tumbling skills are taught very thoroughly. Our large studio—75' by 35'—is equipped to train with any weapon from any period.

SUMMATION STATEMENT:
"The movement training and self-discipline we stress are important to every performer. Because the teachers are working professionally, all methods are up to date. Video equipment is used to attain the performers' movement sense, line, and timing. The school was founded to fill a gap in training, and because too many people were getting hurt."

THE FIRST AMENDMENT COMEDY THEATRE

Barbara Contardi, Director
2 Bond Street, below West 3rd Street and Broadway
New York, NY 10012
(212) 677–1409

PROGRAM:	Comedy Improvisation
INSTRUCTOR:	Nancy Lombarts and company members
ESTABLISHED:	1979
REGISTRATION FEE:	None
CLASS FEE:	$50 per month
SCHEDULE:	1 2½-hour class per week, 50 weeks per year, ongoing
AUDITING:	Permitted
AUDITING FEE:	$5
ENTRANCE REQUIREMENTS:	Students must be at least 16 years of age.
CANCELLATION POLICIES:	One make-up session permitted
SCHOLARSHIPS:	Full scholarship available for work-exchange
NUMBER OF STUDENTS PER CLASS:	Limited to 10–12
TOTAL STUDIO ENROLLMENT:	22
STUDENT BREAKDOWN:	50% female, 50% male; 50% 18–25, 50% 26–35; 70% under 6 months, 20% ½–1 year, 10% 1–2 years
BIOGRAPHY:	All teachers are professional improvisational actors and have been performing every weekend for the past five years. The First Amendment won the Best Comedy Group in New York Award, judged by critics.

CLASS:	Methods applied are similar to Viola Spolin's, although geared toward improving verbal ability. The emphasis is on developing many characters through improvisation.
SUMMATION STATEMENT:	"We believe anyone can learn improvisation and beginners are mixed with experienced actors. We believe that learning is by 'doing,' and no one is allowed to sit and watch. We have the longest running improvisational theatre in New York."

KAREN C. FLAHERTY

11 East 17th Street
New York, NY 10003
(212) 255–7983

PROGRAM:	Mime, Private
ESTABLISHED:	1977
REGISTRATION FEE:	None
CLASS FEE:	$15
SCHEDULE:	1-to-1½-hour sessions, ongoing
ENTRANCE REQUIREMENTS:	Prior training in dance and/or mime required
SCHOLARSHIPS:	Not available
STUDENT BREAKDOWN:	70% female, 30% male; 0% under 18, 50% 18–25, 40% 26–35, 10% 36–45, 0% over 45
STUDIOS:	2
DRESSING ROOMS:	2
FLOOR:	Wood
BIOGRAPHY:	MS. FLAHERTY has been working in mime for 11 years, specializing in Decroux mime and classical movement. She continues to study ballet and choreograph performance pieces and is a faculty member at Adelphi University.
CLASS:	Each private class is designed to meet the individual's needs—if it is postural realignment, then most of the class time is devoted to physical exercises and verbal explanation relevant to that study. If the student is ready to expand his dramatic comprehension, then mime exercises and improvisations are given.
SUMMATION STATEMENT:	"The movement must be beautiful and in order to enjoy it, the audience has to be comfortable with it and with the performer. It has to be performed with ease, graciousness, generosity, and joy."

GENE FRANKEL
THEATRE WORKSHOP

36 West 62nd Street
New York, NY 10023
(212) 581–2775

PROGRAM:	Writers and Directors Workshop
INSTRUCTOR:	Gene Frankel, Leonard Melfi
SCHEDULE:	1 4-hour session per week, ongoing
BIOGRAPHY:	MR. MELFI's plays include *Birdbath, Lunchtime, Oh! Calcutta,* and *Porno Stars At Home,* which have been produced both on and off Broadway. For MR. FRANKEL's biography, see under Acting.
CLASS:	A uniquely designed 2-part laboratory experience. At each session the first 2 hours are set aside for the reading and analysis of scripts. The second 2 hours are devoted to the problems of the director and the art of production. The more developed scripts and director's projects will be selected for full workshop productions.

HB STUDIO

Muriel Burns, Director
120 Bank Street
New York, NY 10014
(212) 675–2370

PROGRAM:	Costumes, Directing, Makeup, Playwriting, Poetry in the Theatre, Fencing, Mime
INSTRUCTORS:	Herbert Berghof, Dick Longchamps, Kathe Berl, Joseph Daly, Rasa Allan, Walt Witcover, Aaron Frankel, William Packard, Richard Morse
ESTABLISHED:	1945
REGISTRATION FEE:	$7.50
CLASS FEES:	$95–$133 (average)
SCHEDULE:	1 1/2–2 1/2 hours per week, 19 weeks, ongoing
AUDITING:	Permitted
AUDITING FEE:	$1.50 for first audit, $4 for subsequent audit of same class
ENTRANCE REQUIREMENTS:	Open (for most classes)

CANCELLATION POLICIES:	No refunds given after term has started and no credit given for classes missed
SCHOLARSHIPS:	Work-exchange available
NUMBER OF STUDENTS PER CLASS:	15–35
TOTAL STUDIO ENROLLMENT:	Over 3,000
STUDENT BREAKDOWN:	60% female, 40% male; 5% under 18, 45% 18–25, 20% 26–35, 20% 36–45, 10% over 45; 5% under 6 months, 10% 1/2–1 year, 25% 1–2 years, 40% 2–3 years, 20% over 3 years
VIDEO EQUIPMENT:	Yes
VIDEO CASSETTES:	Students may purchase video cassettes.
CUE-CARD SYSTEM:	Yes
STUDIOS:	5
DRESSING ROOMS:	2
SHOWERS:	None
FLOOR:	Dance
ACCOMPANYING INSTRUMENT:	Piano
VOCAL CASSETTES:	No
ACCOMPANIST:	Yes
WAITING AREA:	Yes
SUMMATION STATEMENT:	"The HB Studio began in 1945 and aims for a meaningful dramatic expression of the times and country in which we live. To help establish a theatre of experimentation based on classic tradition, the Studio is dedicated to the development of individual artists who may actively contribute to a theatre of national character. Conceived as an artistic and working home, it offers an outlet for practice and growth for the professional theatre artist, and an opportunity for the young to establish roots in their intended crafts. The Studio's guiding principle is creative freeedom, which has as its logical consequence responsiblity to a noble art."

CLAUDE KIPNIS MIME SCHOOL

Bob Welter, Director
266 Court Street, 3rd floor (mailing address)
Brooklyn, NY 11231
(212) 852–2305/362–5188

PROGRAM:	Mime
INSTRUCTORS:	Lavinia Plonka, Bob Welter
ESTABLISHED:	1978
REGISTRATION FEE:	None
CLASS FEE:	$7.50 per class
SCHEDULE:	1¹/₂-hour sessions, ongoing
AUDITING:	Permitted
ENTRANCE REQUIREMENTS:	Open
CANCELLATION POLICIES:	No refunds
SCHOLARSHIPS:	Available
NUMBER OF STUDENTS PER CLASS:	Average 6; limited to 20
STUDENT BREAKDOWN:	60% female, 40% male; 5% under 18, 60% 18–25, 30% 26–35, 5% 36–45, 0% over 45; 30% under 6 months, 30% ¹/₂–1 year, 30% 1–2 years, 10% 2–3 years, 0% over 3 years
STUDIOS:	1
DRESSING ROOMS:	2
FLOOR:	Wood
WAITING AREA:	Yes
BIOGRAPHY:	MR. WELTER has been a member of the Claude Kipnis Mime Theater for 5 years and is a recipient of the NEA choreographer's grant. MS. PLONKA is a well-known cabaret performer and has studied with Moni Yakim and Claude Kipnis.
CLASS:	The objective of the class is to condition the student through strength and stretch exercises, mime illusions, and methods for developing characters and motivation, including styles and techniques acquired through other mime, dance, and acting systems, which have been passed on from Mr. Kipnis to his company members. This work provides students with the tools to develop improvisational skill and a clean technique.
SUMMATION STATEMENT:	"The Claude Kipnis Mime School approaches the art of mime with a clean, clear technique, using the elements of music, masks, improvisation, ensemble work, costumes, and lighting to develop pantomimes of both comedy and drama."

STEPHEN LUPINO

Sutton Gym
22 East 38th Street
New York, NY 10016
(212) 684–5833/695–6914

PROGRAM:	Stage Combat
REGISTRATION FEE:	None
CLASS FEES:	Private $30 per hour; Semi-Private $20 per hour; Group Classes: 1½-hour class per week $40; 2 1½-hour classes per week $75; 3 1½-hour classes per week $100
SCHEDULE:	1½-hour sessions, ongoing
ENTRANCE REQUIREMENTS:	Open
SCHOLARSHIPS:	Not available
NUMBER OF STUDENTS PER CLASS:	Limited to 5
BIOGRAPHY:	MR. LUPINO is the Sankukai Karate World Champion. The goals of this class are to build confidence and physical fitness, and to relieve tension and stress.

MAGIC TOWNE HOUSE

Dick Brooks, Director
1026 Third Avenue
New York, NY 10021
(212) 752–1165

PROGRAM:	Magic
INSTRUCTOR:	Dick Brooks, Dorothy Dietrich
ESTABLISHED:	1973
CLASS FEE:	$195–$250
SCHEDULE:	2 2½-hour sessions per week, 6–8 weeks, ongoing
AUDITING:	No audit
ENTRANCE REQUIREMENTS:	Open
CANCELLATION POLICIES:	No refund after class commences
SCHOLARSHIPS:	Not available
NUMBER OF STUDENTS PER CLASS:	Limited to 9
VIDEO EQUIPMENT:	Yes

STUDIOS: 3
BIOGRAPHY: MR. BROOKS is the publisher of *Hocus Pocus* magazine. He has appeared on "The David Susskind Show," "You Asked For It," and HBO specials and has performed for celebrities such as David Merrick, John Lennon, Blondie, Barry Manilow, and David Rockefeller. MS. DIETRICH is a nationally known magic star.
CLASS: Classes include basic skills up to the professional level. Many students do work professionally, and some advanced students may be invited to work in our cabaret.

JAY MILLER

71 West 12th Street
New York, NY 10011
(212) 620–0114

PROGRAM: Mime
REGISTRATION FEE: None
ENTRANCE REQUIREMENTS: Open
BIOGRAPHY: MR. MILLER has studied mime with Stefan Niedzialkowski, Claude Kipnis, and Samuel Avital. He has taught at Vassar College, as well as offering workshops for children through the New York public school system.
CLASS: The class covers an overview of mime, technique, improvisation, theatre development, and history of mime and tries to convey a taste of what it would be like to pursue mime as an artist.
SUMMATION STATEMENT: "My class gives the participant a feeling of the art as a whole experience."

NEW YORK PANTOMIME TRAINING CENTER

Moni Yakim, Director
242 West 27th Street
New York, NY 10001
(212) 242–4273

PROGRAM:	Beginner, Intermediate, and Advanced Mime Technique; Mime Acting, Characterization; Gymnastics; Creative Mime (young people)
INSTRUCTORS:	Lindarell Rivera, Laura Fernandez, Ken Emzig, Ron Leifer-Helman, Moni Yakim, Mina Yakim
ESTABLISHED:	1971
REGISTRATION FEE:	None
SCHEDULE:	2 semesters of 15 weeks each, divided into 5-week sections. Summer and short-term intensive workshops also available.
AUDITING:	Not permitted
ENTRANCE REQUIREMENTS:	Open, placement determined by interview
CANCELLATION POLICIES:	No refunds
SCHOLARSHIPS:	Not available
NUMBER OF STUDENTS PER CLASS:	Limited to 20
STUDIOS:	1
DRESSING ROOMS:	2
SHOWERS:	No
FLOOR:	Wood
WAITING AREA:	Yes
BIOGRAPHY:	MS. RIVERA is a guest artist with the Story Concert Players. MR. ZWERLING is a cofounder of the mime duet Mimelight, a guest artist with several theatre companies, including the Singer's Theatre Opera Company. MS. FERNANDEZ studied with Samuel Avital, Moni Yakim, and at the Fools School in Amsterdam. She has performed with the Phasa Beam Mime Company, Mimelight, and at the Public Theatre. MR. EMZIG has studied with Etienne Decroux, Paul Gualin, and Moni Yakim, and is a member of The Joy of Mime. MR. LEIFER-HELMAN's expertise includes composition, gymnastics, dance, and trumpet. MR. YAKIM has been or is on faculty at the Yale Drama School, Stella Adler Theatre Studio, American Opera Center, Julliard, and Circle in the Square. MS. YAKIM studied with

Etienne Decroux and Marcel Marceau, is a former faculty member of the Stella Adler Studio and the Metropolitan Opera Studio.

CLASSES: In Technique, the body is drilled in specific mime skills while developing control, precision, style, range of motion, and flexibility. Study develops the powers of concentration, projection, and acting by working on specific skills in dramatic contexts.

SUMMATION STATEMENT: "The New York Pantomime Training Center is an artistic resource center founded on both classical and innovative contemporary technique to train the body, and on the most profound acting principles to deepen and develop poetic expression."

CONAL O'BRIEN

The Park Royal
23 West 73rd Street
New York, NY 10023
(212) 586–6300

PROGRAM: Stage Combat/Weaponry
ESTABLISHED: 1978
REGISTRATION FEE: None
SCHEDULE: 1 1 and 1½ hour session per week, 10 weeks
AUDITING: Not permitted
ENTRANCE REQUIREMENTS: Student must submit photo and resume
SCHOLARSHIPS: Not available
NUMBER OF STUDENTS
  PER CLASS: 8–10
BIOGRAPHY: MR. O'BRIEN is assistant to B.H. Barry, has taught at Julliard, New York University, Circle in the Square, California School of the Deaf, and is currently fight director for ABC's "All My Children."
CLASS: Through the class, performers acquire basic skills in stage fighting, tumbling, and methods of safety. The course utilizes movement from the actor's viewpoint. Weaponry is covered in the advanced secondary course.
SUMMATION STATEMENT: "The class allows the performer new freedom which can effect all areas of his or her life."

ANTHONY PASSANTINO

Fazil's Dance Centre
743 Eighth Avenue
New York, NY 10019
(212) 448–0799/254–9504/757–6300

PROGRAM:	Fencing; Individual Coaching in All Weapons
ESTABLISHED:	1969
REGISTRATION FEE:	None
CLASS FEE:	$18 per hour; 2-hour intensive session $32
SCHEDULE:	1–2 hour sessions, ongoing; no enrollment necessary
AUDITING:	Permitted by appointment
AUDITING FEE:	No fee
ENTRANCE REQUIREMENTS:	Open
SCHOLARSHIPS:	Not available
STUDENT BREAKDOWN:	20% female, 80% male; 0% under 18, 65% 18–25, 35% 26–35, 0% over 35; 40% under 6 months, 20% $1/2$–1 year, 40% 1–2 years, 0% over 3 years
BIOGRAPHY:	MR. PASSANTINO has been fencing since 1962. He has been a professional actor for 20 years. Prior pupils include Jon Voight, Rip Torn, and four Shakespeare festival companies. Extensive production credits since 1969.
CLASS:	The course aims for increased physical and mental coordination through mastery of the fundamentals of fencing; heightened sense of body awareness and use of the body as a performer's tool; development of a sound fencing technique for recreation and dramatic use, building, nurturing, and integrating the positive aspects of an emerging and maturing performer's personality and technique; building the highest technical standards for rehearsal and performance. This is achieved by extensive drill-work and teaching of the highest standard. The end result is a stronger, more relaxed, more confident human being.
SUMMATION STATEMENT:	"My teaching is intensive, one to one, and seeks to foster the highest standard of technique both for legitimate sport use and theatrical work. Advanced students, after mastering sound fundamentals, are trained in historical weapons of all types. Elements of staging and choreography are stressed and scene work is encouraged."

SALLE BARDAKH

Stan Bardakh, Director
212 West 15th Street
New York, NY 10011
(212) 463–6258/730–1188

PROGRAM:	Fencing, Private
INSTRUCTOR:	Steven Otero
ESTABLISHED:	1981
REGISTRATION FEE:	None
CLASS FEE:	$15 per class
SCHEDULE:	1-hour sessions, ongoing
AUDITING:	Permitted
AUDITING FEE:	No fee
ENTRANCE REQUIREMENTS:	Telephone interview
CANCELLATION POLICIES:	24-hour notice
SCHOLARSHIPS:	Not available
REQUIRED MATERIALS:	Sweat pants, sneakers, dance wear
STUDENT BREAKDOWN:	50% female, 50% male; 0% under 18, 40% 18–25, 50% 26–35, 10% 36–45, 0% over 45; 50% under 6 months, 50% $^1/_2$–1 year, 0% over 1 year
VIDEO EQUIPMENT:	Yes
VIDEO CASSETTES:	Students may purchase their video cassettes.
STUDIOS:	1
DRESSING ROOMS:	2
SHOWERS:	2
FLOOR:	Wood
WAITING AREA:	Yes
BIOGRAPHY:	MR. OTERO studied stage fencing for 4 years at HB Studio with Joe Daly. He became Mr. Daly's assistant for the next 2 years. He is a member of the Gentlemen Adventurers.
CLASS:	The goal of the class is to turn out competent stage fencers who can arrange fights. This is accomplished through footwork and choreography with weapons. The emphasis is on safety.
SUMMATION STATEMENT:	"I am an actor who teaches fencing, therefore I know the special needs of the actor."

SALTUS FENCING CLUB

McBurney YMCA
215 West 23rd Street
New York, NY 10011
(212) 741–9224

PROGRAM:	Fencing, Group and Individual
INSTRUCTOR:	Richard Gradkowski
ESTABLISHED:	1923
REGISTRATION FEE:	None
SCHEDULE:	1 1½-hour session per week, ongoing
AUDITING:	Permitted
AUDITING FEE:	No fee
ENTRANCE REQUIREMENTS:	Student must have a YMCA membership
NUMBER OF STUDENTS PER CLASS:	6–8; or individual
STUDENT BREAKDOWN:	50% female, 50% male; 10% under 18, 70% 18–25, 20% 26–35
DRESSING ROOMS:	Yes
SHOWERS:	Yes
WAITING AREA:	Yes
BIOGRAPHY:	MR. GRADKOWSKI is a fencing master and fencing official licensed by the International Fencing Federation. He received his diploma from the United States Academy of Armes. He is also a black belt in Japanese fencing, and a member of the Society of American Fight Directors.
CLASS:	The goal of each class is to develop a holistic appreciation of the physical, emotional, and social values of the art of swordplay. Within a structuring framework, the individual needs of each student are fulfilled and his development is encouraged.
SUMMATION STATEMENT:	"Our school stresses perfection in technical execution, as well as understanding of the basic concepts of swordsmanship."

SCHOOL OF THE RIVERSIDE SHAKESPEARE COMPANY

165 West 86th Street
New York, NY 10024
(212) 877–6810

PROGRAM:	Stage Combat
INSTRUCTOR:	Joel Leffert
BIOGRAPHY:	MR. LEFFERT, a graduate of Brown University, began his fight training with the HB Studio 7 years ago. He is RSC's resident fight director.
CLASS:	The class emphasizes a basic knowledge of stage weaponry—broadsword, rapier, and dagger—and choreography of duels. The class also exercises one's physical skills of balance, agility, coordination, and endurance.

STOREFRONT BLITZ

Rusty Blitz, Director
506 West 42nd Street
New York, NY 10036
(212) 244–4575

PROGRAM:	Comedy
ESTABLISHED:	1969
REGISTRATION FEE:	None
CLASS FEE:	$50 per month
SCHEDULE:	1 2-hour session per week, ongoing
AUDITING:	Permitted
AUDITING FEE:	$10
ENTRANCE REQUIREMENTS:	Open
CANCELLATION POLICIES:	Make-ups available
SCHOLARSHIPS:	Not available
NUMBER OF STUDENTS PER CLASS:	20
STUDENT BREAKDOWN:	50% female, 50% male; 0% under 18, 50% 18–25, 25% 26–35, 15% 36–45, 10% over 45
BIOGRAPHY:	MR. BLITZ is a nightclub comedian and musical comedy actor who has appeared on and off Broadway in such shows as *A Funny Thing Happened*

on the Way to the Forum and Three Penny Opera.
He has worked with Mel Brooks and Gene Wilder
and has studied with Harold Clurman. Mr. Blitz is
also a junior high school teacher.

CLASS: The purpose of the class is to teach the student to
think on his feet and in funny terms, working with
improvisation and critique. As a "final," a written
scene or stand-up routine is submitted.

SUMMATION STATEMENT: "The comedian must have a high energy level,
must leave no spaces for the audience to have a
chance to think . . . get up on the stage and go . . . "

WOMEN'S INTERART

Margot Lewitin, Artistic Director
549 West 52nd Street
New York, NY 10019
(212) 246–1050

PROGRAM: Film Production, Video, Writing, Actors/Directors
Lab, Theatre Workshop
INSTRUCTORS: Ellen Horde, Muffis Meyer, Corrine Jacker, Margot
Lewitin, Shirley Clarke
ESTABLISHED: 1971
REGISTRATION FEE: None
CLASS FEE: Full year, full-time $4,100; Film Production $1,500;
Acting $250
AUDITING: Not permitted
ENTRANCE REQUIREMENTS: Open
SCHOLARSHIPS: Financial aid is available to eligible students en-
rolled in Empire State College.

NUMBER OF STUDENTS
  PER CLASS: 12–14
STUDENT BREAKDOWN: 70% female, 30% male; 0% under 18, 60% 18–25,
30% 26–35, 10% 36–45, 0% over 45; 0% under 1
year, 60% 1–2 years, 40% 2–3 years, 0% over 3
years
BIOGRAPHY: MS. HORDE and MS. MEYER are the directors of
Grey Gardens with the Mayales Brothers. MS.
JACKER is a playwright-in-residence at Yale and
an Obie Award winner. MS. LEWITIN is an actress
and director and the artistic director of the Wom-
en's Interart Center. MS. CLARKE is an award
winning director of film and video, including The
Connection and The Cool World.

CLASSES:
Through participation in film, theatre, and video projects, students acquire the specific tools and skills that ensure practical command of the media. The hands-on training will range from thorough acquaintance with 16 mm film NS ³/₄" video equipment to immersion in the theatrical process through production apprenticeships. In addition, continuing workshops in writing, acting, and directing will serve as focal points for exploration of the integrated media idea. Classes are open to men and women.

SUMMATION STATEMENT:
"The Integrated Media Arts Program is a year-long exploration of narrative form and dramatic imagery in three allied but distinct art forms—theatre, film, and video. The curriculum is designed in accordance with our belief that a need exists for a program in which these media can be studied in conjunction with, rather than in isolation from, one another."

YOUNG PEOPLE
YOUNG PEOPLE
YOUNG PEOPLE
YOUNG PEOPLE
YOUNG PEOPLE
YOUNG PEOPLE
YOUNG PEOPLE
YOUNG PEOPLE
YOUNG PEOPLE
YOUNG PEOPLE
YOUNG PEOPLE
YOUNG PEOPLE
YOUNG PEOPLE
YOUNG PEOPLE
YOUNG PEOPLE
YOUNG PEOPLE
YOUNG PEOPLE
YOUNG PEOPLE
YOUNG PEOPLE
YOUNG PEOPLE
YOUNG PEOPLE
YOUNG PEOPLE
YOUNG PEOPLE
YOUNG PEOPLE

ACTORS INSTITUTE

5 West 19th Street, 3rd floor
New York, NY 10011
(212) 924–8888

PROGRAM:	Teen Acting Class, One-Day Teen Acting Workshop
INSTRUCTORS:	R. Abernathy, B. Winn

STELLA ADLER
CONSERVATORY OF ACTING

130 West 56th Street
New York, NY 10019
(212) 246–1195

PROGRAM:	Acting, Dancing, Saturday Theatre Workshop
CLASS FEE:	$150
SCHEDULE:	1 1½-hour session per week, 12 weeks
CLASS:	Acting & Dancing are designed not only to train talented youngsters intent on preparing seriously for the stage, but also to stimulate the development of personality through inspired self-confidence, good physical bearing, and a growing awareness of our cultural heritage. In the Workshop, students are prepared to perform before an invited audience. This course includes the technique of rehearsal, advanced movement, outside characterization, and theatrical makeup and is designed for ages 12–17.

AESTHETIC REALISM FOUNDATION, INC.

141 Greene Street (near Houston Street)
New York, NY 10012
(212) 777–4490

PROGRAM:	Acting Begins Early
INSTRUCTOR:	Anne Fielding

ESTABLISHED: 1980
REGISTRATION FEE: None
CLASS FEE: $3 per class
SCHEDULE: 1½-hour sessions bimonthly, ongoing
ENTRANCE REQUIREMENTS: Open
NUMBER OF STUDENTS
  PER CLASS: Limited to 20
STUDENT BREAKDOWN: 60% female, 40% male; 100% under 18
BIOGRAPHY: MS. FIELDING is an Aesthetic Realism Consul-
                                tant, a teacher of speech and acting and has
                                taught musical comedy at the HB Studio.
CLASS: Through exercises, improvisations, and scenes,
                                persons 6 to 16 study the meaning of this sen-
                                tence: "Everybody wants to be himself, and that
                                means being other things besides himself." Sub-
                                jects covered are —How many characters are in
                                you? six dramatic gestures, Do you want to have a
                                great emotion? and freedom and order in rehears-
                                ing and performing a play.

ALVIN AILEY
AMERICAN DANCE CENTER

1515 Broadway
New York, NY 10036
(212) 997–1980

PROGRAM: Children's Ballet I, IA; Modern I, II, III; Ethnic
                                Dance I, II
REGISTRATION FEE: None
CLASS FEE: Single class $5
SCHEDULE: 1½-hour sessions, ongoing
AUDITING: Not permitted
ENTRANCE REQUIREMENTS: Open
CANCELLATION POLICIES: No transfers, refunds, extensions

BALLET ACADEMY EAST

340 East 79th Street
New York, NY 10021
(212) 861–5204

PROGRAM:	Children's Ballet, Pre-Ballet/Creative Movement
REGISTRATION FEE:	None
CLASS FEE:	1 class per week—$215 for a season; 2 classes per week $210; 3 classes per week $205 for a season
CLASSES:	The Pre-Ballet/Creative Movement division is geared toward children 4–6 years of age and combines basic ballet technique with imagery and teaching tools understandable and inspiring to the age group.

BALLET HISPANICO SCHOOL OF DANCE

167 West 89th Street
New York, NY 10024
(212) 362–6710

PROGRAM:	Ballet, Spanish, Modern, Systematic Dance
REGISTRATION FEE:	None
CLASS:	Through movement, a student learns a new means of self-expression. Through classwork, a student learns skills of discipline and concentration. By working together, all students form friendships beyond economic or ethnic ties. The school gives every student a sense of identity and dignity to carry with them into their daily lives.

DANCE CLASSES FOR CHILDREN

219 West 19th Street
New York, NY 10011
(212) 254-0286

PROGRAM:	Dance, Beginning and Advanced
INSTRUCTOR:	Ellen Robbins
ESTABLISHED:	1966
REGISTRATION FEE:	None
CLASS FEE:	$80
SCHEDULE:	1 1-to-1½-hour session per week, 15 weeks
AUDITING:	First class on a trial basis
ENTRANCE REQUIREMENTS:	Open
SCHOLARSHIPS:	Not available
NUMBER OF STUDENTS PER CLASS:	Limited to 10
STUDENT BREAKDOWN:	85% female, 15% male; 100% under 18; 0% under 1 year, 10% 1–2 years, 80% 2–3 years, 10% over 3 years
STUDIOS:	1
DRESSING ROOMS:	2
SHOWERS:	2
FLOOR:	Wood
ACCOMPANYING INSTRUMENT:	Drums, records

DANCE-JUNE LEWIS & COMPANY

48 West 21st Street
New York, NY 10010
(212) 741-3044

PROGRAM:	Modern Dance for Children
CLASS:	Classes for children ages 4–11
FOR FURTHER INFORMATION:	See Dance

DRAMA TREE INC.

215 Park Avenue South
New York, NY 10003
(212) 228–3932

PROGRAM: Acting Technique for 14–16 Year Olds
INSTRUCTOR: Anthony Mannino
CLASS: Acting fundamentals are adapted to varying needs
                    and capabilities of young adults and will lay the
                    foundation for later training in the adult advanced
                    classes.

GENE FRANKEL WORKSHOP

36 West 62nd Street
New York, NY 10023
(212) 581–2775

PROGRAM: Young People's Acting Workshop I, II
INSTRUCTOR: Judith Seto
SCHEDULE: 1 2-hour session per week, ongoing
BIOGRAPHY: MS. SETO is an experienced teacher and author
                    of *The Young Actors Handbook,* an anthology of
                    scenes and monologues for teen-agers and young
                    adults.
CLASSES: Level I—Through theatre games and improvisa-
                    tion, young actors learn to perform truthfully by
                    making full use of their own resources—mind,
                    body, voice, feelings, imagination—in unison.
                    Spontaneous interaction will be stressed. Level
                    II—This class covers developing a character dif-
                    ferent from oneself through improvisation and
                    scene work. Emphasis is on the process of ap-
                    proaching any role.

MARTHA GRAHAM SCHOOL OF CONTEMPORARY DANCE

316 East 63rd Street
New York, NY 10021
(212) 838–5886

PROGRAM:	Children, Children Beginner, Teens Beginner, Teens Advanced
FOR MORE INFORMATION:	See Dance

HB STUDIO

Muriel Burns, Director
120 Bank Street
New York, NY 10014
(212) 675–2370

PROGRAM:	Acting for Children 9–14, Acting for Teen-agers
INSTRUCTORS:	Marlene Mancini, Judy Leak, Edward Morehouse
ESTABLISHED:	1945
REGISTRATION FEE:	$7.50
CLASS FEE:	$95
SCHEDULE:	$1^1/_2$–$2^1/_2$ hours per week, 19 weeks, ongoing
AUDITING:	Permitted
AUDITING FEE:	$1.50 for first audit; $4 for subsequent audit of same class (no adult auditors)
ENTRANCE REQUIREMENTS:	Open (for most classes)
CANCELLATION POLICIES:	No refunds given after term has started and no credit given for classes missed.
NUMBER OF STUDENTS PER CLASS:	15–35
TOTAL STUDIO ENROLLMENT:	Over 3,000
STUDENT BREAKDOWN:	60% female, 40% male; 5% under 18, 45% 18–25, 20% 26–35, 20% 36–45, 10% over 45; 5% under 6 months, 10% $^1/_2$–1 year, 25% 1–2 years, 40% 2–3 years, 20% over 3 years
VIDEO EQUIPMENT:	Yes
VIDEO CASSETTES:	Students may purchase video cassettes.
CUE-CARD SYSTEM:	Yes
STUDIOS:	5
WAITING AREA:	Yes

SUMMATION STATEMENT: "The HB Studio began in 1945 and aims for a meaningful dramatic expression of the times and country in which we live. To help establish a theatre of experimentation based on classic tradition, the Studio is dedicated to the development of individual artists who may actively contribute to a theatre of national character. Conceived as an artistic and working home, it offers an outlet for practice and growth for the professional theatre artist, and an opportunity for the young to establish roots in their intended crafts. The Studio's guiding principle is creative freedom, which has as its logical consequence responsibility to a noble art."

92nd STREET YMHA DANCE CENTER

1395 Lexington Avenue
New York, NY 10028
(212) 427–6000

PROGRAM: Children's Ballet, Modern, Jazz, Tap
CLASSES: The aim of the classes is to increase student's enjoyment of movement and physical coordination and to allow them a chance to express themselves creatively.
FOR FURTHER INFORMATION: See Dance

ON CAMERA ACTING STUDIO

Marsha Michaels, Director
155 West 72nd Street
New York, NY 10023
(212) 877–2170

PROGRAM: Commercial Acting Class for Children
ESTABLISHED: 1977
REGISTRATION FEE: None
CLASS FEE: $80 per term
SCHEDULE: 1 2-hour class per week, 9 months per year; not ongoing

AUDITING:	Not permitted
ENTRANCE REQUIREMENTS:	Students age 5 and up may submit their application via mail.
CANCELLATION POLICIES:	No refunds; no make-up sessions
SCHOLARSHIPS:	Not available
NUMBER OF STUDENTS PER CLASS:	Limited to 10
STUDENT BREAKDOWN:	60% female, 40% male; 100% under 18.
VIDEO EQUIPMENT:	Yes
VIDEO CASSETTES:	Students may buy their video cassettes.
CUE-CARD SYSTEM:	Yes
STUDIOS:	1
BIOGRAPHY:	MARSHA MICHAELS has appeared in commercials, soap operas, and Off Broadway. Other professional actors and/or casting directors are invited to teach on occasion.
CLASS:	The classes are taught in such a way that each student is prepared to audition successfully for commercials at the end of the term. Students are videotaped, tapes are played back, and students receive constructive criticism throughout the course.
SUMMATION STATEMENT:	"The On Camera Acting Studio is the only school specializing in training children to perform in commercials."

WARREN ROBERTSON THEATRE WORKSHOP

303 East 44th Street
New York, NY 10017
(212) 687–6430

PROGRAM:	Young People's Workshop
INSTRUCTOR:	Joyce Urman
CLASS FEES:	6 to 8 years old $40 per month; 9 to 11 years $50 per month; 12 to 17 years $80 per month
SCHEDULE:	1 1-to-2½-hour session per week, ongoing
BIOGRAPHY:	MS. URMAN is the founder and artistic director of the Bag-A-Tale Players, which was selected as the resident children's theatre company at Lincoln Center for 1981-82
CLASS:	Classes cover acting, improvisation, and creative dramatics.

SCHOOL OF BALLET DE PUERTO RICO

189 Lexington Avenue
New York, NY 10016
(212) 683–1967

PROGRAM:	Ballet, Spanish, Modern/Jazz, Tap
SCHOLARSHIPS:	Offered to talented Hispanic and other children 10 to 20
CLASSES:	"We evaluate classes twice a year and promote those students who need more work or are aiming at professional careers. In Spanish dance, children learn the Escuela Bolera technique."

THE LEE STRASBERG THEATRE INSTITUTE

115 East 15th Street
New York, NY 10003
(212) 533–5500

PROGRAM:	Basic Techniques of the Method, Play Production Workshop, ages 13–17; Special Children's Program, ages 6–13
CLASSES:	Technique class teaches the young actor to behave logically and truthfully through the use of relaxation, sensory exercises, scene work, and improvisation. Emphasis on individual problems of expression, stage presence, and personality growth. The Workshop provides the actor with an opportunity to work with a director in the rehearsal and performance of scenes and plays for an invited audience.

THIRD STREET MUSIC
SCHOOL SETTLEMENT

Robert Christensen, Director
235 East 11th Street
New York, NY 10003
(212) 777-3240

PROGRAM:	Music, Dance, Drama, Visual Arts
INSTRUCTORS:	Approximately 70
ESTABLISHED:	1894
REGISTRATION FEE:	Annual, $15
CLASS FEE:	Fees vary from $60 to $210 per semester
SCHEDULE:	16-week terms
SCHOLARSHIPS:	Available
SUMMATION STATEMENT:	"The school believes that the arts are a life-enriching experience crossing all economic barriers. It has served as a prototype for hundreds of similar institutions around the country. In addition to its core program of instruction and training in the arts, the school presents a performance series, Music Downtown, which attracts 10,000 people to its auditorium each year; an outreach program serving handicapped children, preschoolers, senior citizens, and the public school sector; and similar endeavors."

TOTS TO TEENS
STAGEMOM WORKSHOP

404 Riverside Drive
New York, NY 10025
(212) 662-1029

PROGRAM:	Workshop for Parents of Performing Children
INSTRUCTOR:	Coralie Geiwitz
ESTABLISHED:	1980
CLASS FEE:	Private $50; Semiprivate $25; Group $15
SCHEDULE:	1 3-hour workshop
ENTRANCE REQUIREMENTS:	Open
BIOGRAPHY:	MS. GEIWITZ has been an arts administrator for almost 10 years, involved with coordinating and

arranging children's productions and events for such facilities as the Kennedy Center and Wolf Trap Farm; and for 3 years, as a parent of a working child, she has been involved in the field of print-work and modeling opportunities for youngsters.

CLASS:
The goal is to determine how, where, when, and if a parent should begin their child in the fields of acting and modeling. By sharing information on procedures, expectations, resources, financial aid, emotional realities, and ways to reduce expenditures without sacrificing quality, they can attain entrance in this work for minors. They learn what is expected of them and what they can expect from the industry.

SUMMATION STATEMENT:
"This workshop is to make parents aware of the time and support necessary to follow through in this particular field."

WEIST-BARRON
SCHOOL OF TELEVISION

35 West 45th Street
New York, NY 10036
(212) 840–7025/840–0006

PROGRAM:
Children's Commercial, Soap Technique, Teen Acting

FOR FURTHER INFORMATION:
See Acting

CALIFORNIA
CALIFORNIA
CALIFORNIA
CALIFORNIA
CALIFORNIA
CALIFORNIA
CALIFORNIA
CALIFORNIA
CALIFORNIA
CALIFORNIA
CALIFORNIA

ALL DISCIPLINES
ALL DISCIPLINES
ALL DISCIPLINES
ALL DISCIPLINES
ALL DISCIPLINES
ALL DISCIPLINES
ALL DISCIPLINES
ALL DISCIPLINES
ALL DISCIPLINES
ALL DISCIPLINES
ALL DISCIPLINES
ALL DISCIPLINES
ALL DISCIPLINES
ALL DISCIPLINES
ALL DISCIPLINES
ALL DISCIPLINES
ALL DISCIPLINES
ALL DISCIPLINES
ALL DISCIPLINES
ALL DISCIPLINES
ALL DISCIPLINES
ALL DISCIPLINES
ALL DISCIPLINES
ALL DISCIPLINES

AMERICAN CONSERVATORY THEATRE

450 Geary Street
San Francisco, CA 94102
(415) 771–3880

PROGRAM:	Summer Training Congress
INSTRUCTORS:	ACT trainers, company members, guest teachers
REGISTRATION FEE:	Nonrefundable application fee $30
CLASS FEE:	$1,500
SCHEDULE:	8 hours a day, 5 days a week, 10 weeks
ENTRANCE REQUIREMENTS:	California residents are required to audition; all applicants must send a picture and resume, two letters of recommendation, and must also complete an application form. Minimum age 17.
SCHOLARSHIPS:	Guaranteed Student Loans available; ACT tuition scholarships (based on need) $100–$300; ACT tuition fellowships (based on talent) $100–$1,500.
CLASS:	Days begin with technical practice—voice production, dance, or phonetics and ear training; followed by physical classes, i.e., yoga, Alexander technique, stage combat; afternoon schedules involve acting, theatre games, scene study, and seminars with guest lecturers on art and theatre history. Students are divided into two sections to ensure maximum individual attention.

FRAN BENNETT

Los Angeles Area
(213) 663–5991

PROGRAM:	Voice Production and Movement, Private
INSTRUCTOR:	Fran Bennett
ESTABLISHED:	1966
REGISTRATION FEE:	None
CLASS FEE:	$40 per session
SCHEDULE:	1-hour sessions
AUDITING:	Not permitted
ENTRANCE REQUIREMENTS:	Interview
CANCELLATION POLICIES:	8-hour notice required
SCHOLARSHIPS:	Not available
REQUIRED MATERIAL:	Comfortable clothes

STUDENT BREAKDOWN:	75% female, 25% male; 1% under 18, 10% 18–25, 30% 26–35, 40% 36–45, 9% over 45
ACCOMPANYING INSTRUMENT:	Piano
VOCAL CASSETTES:	Students are permitted to record exercises at session.
WAITING AREA:	Yes
BIOGRAPHY:	MS. BENNETT was voice and movement director and a member of the acting company at the Guthrie Theatre in Minneapolis for 12 years. She is a working actress currently teaching voice production at the California Institute of Arts in Valencia. She was trained by Kristin Linklater in her first teacher training program in 1965.
CLASS:	The goal of each class is to free the student's natural voice by eliminating tensions which inhibit its freedom.
SUMMATION STATEMENT:	"The approach is the Iris Warren-Kristin Linklater one. It is the same work that is taught in most of the schools and regional theatres in the United States and at the London Academy of Dramatic Arts.

DELL 'ARTE SCHOOL OF MIME & COMEDY

Alain Schons, Director
Box 816
Blue Lake, CA 95525
(707) 668–5411/668–5782

PROGRAM:	Mime and Comedy Performance
INSTRUCTORS:	Ralph Hall, Alain Schons, Jan Lapiner, Joan Schirle, Michael Fields, Donald Forrest, Gale Mackey, Sandra Archer
ESTABLISHED:	1975
REGISTRATION FEE:	None
CLASS FEE:	$2,650 per year
SCHEDULE:	5 3-hour sessions per week, 9 months per year, ongoing
AUDITING:	Not permitted
ENTRANCE REQUIREMENTS:	Applicants must be 18 years of age and submit 3 letters of recommendation.
SCHOLARSHIPS:	Not available

NUMBER OF STUDENTS PER CLASS:	Limited to 24
TOTAL STUDIO ENROLLMENT:	30
STUDENT BREAKDOWN:	55% female, 45% male; 2% under 18, 70% 18–25, 28% 26–35, 0% over 35; 0% under 1 year, 90% 1–2 years, 10% 2–3 years, 0% over 3 years
STUDIOS:	3
DRESSING ROOMS:	1
SHOWERS:	None
FLOOR:	Wood
ACCOMPANYING INSTRUMENT:	Piano
BIOGRAPHY:	MR. HALL is an actor specializing in mime and physical comedy. He is a graduate of L'Ecole Jacques Lecoq in Paris. His specialty skills are puppetry and ventriloquism. MR. SCHONS is a designer and director dedicated to physical performance. He has taught at the University of Paris and designed for the Dell 'Arte Players Company for the past 8 years. MS. SCHIRLE is a certified teacher of Alexander technique, an actress, and a dancer. She is cofounder of Dell 'Arte Players Company. MR. FIELDS is an instructor of classical line and Linklater vocal techniques, an actor, and a director. He is a cofounder of the Dell 'Arte Players Company. MR. FORREST is an actor, acrobat, and a juggler. He has worked with the Bay City Reds, Pickle Family Circus, San Francisco Mime Troupe, and the Dell 'Arte Players Company. MS. ARCHER, an actress and director, is a commedial specialist. Ms. Archer established herself as a leading actress in the San Francisco Mime Troupe shows of commedia dell'arte. MS. LAPINER is a dancer and choreographer. She has worked with the San Francisco Mime Troupe and the Actor's Workshop. Her specialty is teaching dance to actors. MS. MACKEY is a gymnastic instructor in vaulting and floor acrobatics. He is a competition coach at Six Rivers Gymnastic in Eureka.
CLASS:	The school curriculum is divided into two programs. Those programs are designed for young professionals who have chosen performing as their profession. Studies are full time. The basic program is 9 months; the advanced program is 6 months. Emphasis of both programs is on performance.
SUMMATION STATEMENT:	"Dell 'Arte was founded to promote the art and the physical life of the performer. Dell 'Arte established

itself in a remote area of the California coast in order to give students, performers, and faculty the opportunity to work in a rural setting away from the distractions of urban life. Its commitment to artistic and economic independence is anchored in the tradition of grass-roots theatre. The artistic and educational philosophy of the school is designed to promote the development of the individual as a creator of stage material; as a result, a great deal of attention is given to the needs of the individual."

JESSICA DRAKE

Hollywood-Santa Monica area
(213) 396–7033/654–8040

PROGRAM:	Private Coaching: Audition Techniques, Basic Shakespeare, Standard American Speech, Dialects for the Stage
ESTABLISHED:	1980
REGISTRATION FEE:	None
CLASS FEE:	$20–$25 per class
SCHEDULE:	1-hour sessions
AUDITING:	Not permitted
ENTRANCE REQUIREMENTS:	Acting—open; Speech—working understanding of the English language
CANCELLATION POLICIES:	24-hour notice required to reschedule; no refunds
SCHOLARSHIPS:	Not available
TOTAL STUDIO ENROLLMENT:	11
STUDENT BREAKDOWN:	Acting—75% female, 25% male; 10% 18–25, 40% 26–35, 30% 36–45, 20% over 45; 100% under 6 months; Speech—50% female, 50% male; 60% 18–25, 40% 26–35; 60% under 6 months, 30% $1/2$–1 year, 10% 1–2 years
EXERCISE CASSETTES:	Not available; but students are permitted to record exercises during session.
BIOGRAPHY:	MS. DRAKE has been around show business all her life. In addition to her professional credits she has had 7 years of formal training, including a degree from the Julliard School of Drama. She has worked with Livui Ciulei and Des McAnuff and Joseph Papp's Public Theatre; she has also appeared with the Lincoln Center Touring Company in New York City. Her many regional credits in-

clude *Sister Mary Ignatius Explains It All for You* in Los Angeles. Television audiences have seen her on "St. Elsewhere," "The Edge of Night," and in commercials. She has been teaching auditioning, speech, dialects, and Shakespeare privately for 4 years both in New York and Los Angeles.

CLASSES:

Audition Techniques is designed to help actors with each phase of preparation. "I help them find unique material that works well for them, stage that material, and tackle any other problems they may have with auditioning. I work in 4 sessions. The first 2 are devoted to material selection and the second 2 to staging that material." The goal of the class is to help you—on a one-session-at-a-time basis—present material that will get you the kind of roles you want. Basic Shakespeare is designed to give the novice a working understanding of Shakespearean texts. Beginning with basic structure (iambic pentameter), and concluding with a fully applied ability to act the text, the actor learns to understand and interpret the directions Shakespeare has given through the structure of his verse. Work begins with sonnets and simple passages and goes on to soliloquies. This class is one-on-one and can be adapted to meet individual needs. "I teach Standard American Speech as developed by my mentor, Edith Skinner. Ms. Skinner devoted her life to teaching American actors how to speak onstage with proper American pronunciation—not an affectation of British speech. I work with or without phonetics and I use elements of voice production in the training. Once this technique is mastered, dialects and regionalisms may be acquired with ease. I also coach for accent reduction. Private instruction has proven cost-effective, but I do also offer an occasional group class. I offer two kinds of dialect instruction. The first is a course that teaches several of the most frequently used stage dialects. The second is immediate instruction in a particular dialect you may need for a specific audition or job. I work with tapes and phonetics if the student can apply them. In addition to 'emergency' coaching and dialect classes, I have also worked as production dialect coach on *Cloud 9* and *Charlotte Sweet* in Los Angeles and New York."

SUMMATION STATEMENT:

"I want to pass along what I have learned about

auditioning over the years as a result of having done them under so many different circumstances. Auditioning is a skill—the most important one there is since you have to audition to get the job. Too many actors dread this experience, when with the proper prepartation, it can be an enjoyable part of an actor's job. I work on a one-to-one basis because how each person successfully auditions is a very individual thing. I want to be able to tailor my techniques to your needs. You can be confident, relaxed, and ready in an audition. The technique of performing Shakespeare is a real skill. It is not the exclusive domain of the British actor. A haphazard approach to Shakespearean text leads to disaster, but with a working understanding of his language and his technique, the principles of good acting applied will bring successful work into being. It is vital for American actors to realize the need to acquire these basic skills so we can have our own Shakespearean theatre, and stop looking to the British as the final word on the subject. Anyone can master a dialect. It is an ability that broadens possibilities for the actor. Whether or not you can use phonetics or have a 'good ear,' they can be learned through sheer concentration on the sounds and the way they are made. A dialect should be a key into a character, it tells you a lot about that character. I want to teach actors to use it as a tool, not to let it lock them up for fear of doing it incorrectly."

THE DRAMA STUDIO
LONDON AT BERKELEY

The Julia Morgan Theatre
2640 College Avenue
Berkeley, CA 94704
(415) 549–1118

PROGRAM: Acting, Speech, Voice Production, Singing, Audience Communication, Improvisation, Mime, Mask Work, Period Movement, Dance for Actors, Theatre Combat, Characterization Study, Text Study,

	Acting Styles, Shakespeare, Stage Makeup, Television and Radio Acting, Cabaret, Positive and Lateral Thinking, Audition/Interview Techniques
INSTRUCTORS:	Approximately 30 faculty members
ESTABLISHED:	1966 in London; 1980 in the United States
CLASS FEE:	$4,675 per academic year
SCHEDULE:	Full time only. 2 intakes per year—spring, March to December; fall, August to June. DSL offers a 1-year full-time acting program, a 1-year full-time directing program, and a summer program for actors.
ENTRANCE REQUIREMENTS:	By personal interview, which will consist of a number of acting and voice exercises, some sight-reading and other tests designed to determine the candidate's suitability. Some prepared work is required. Applicants must be over 20 years of age.
SCHOLARSHIPS:	A number of scholarships and prizes are available.
STUDIOS:	1 studio-theatre 4 rehearsal studios, student lounge, library, study room, wardrobe, scene deck, prop room.
DRESSING ROOMS:	Yes
SUMMATION STATEMENT:	"The primary objective of the course is the thorough preparation of the student for a career in the theatre. The Drama Studio relates the student's work to the realities of the profession as it exists today or might exist in the future. The training covers contemporary, period, and classical dramatic presentation, involving frequent student productions to develop the student's breadth and flexibility as an actor before vastly different audiences and in various media."

EUBANKS CONSERVATORY OF MUSIC AND ARTS

Dorothy Webley, Chairman; Rachel Eubanks, President
4928 Crenshaw Boulevard
Los Angeles, CA 90043
(213) 291–7821

PROGRAM:	Music, Dance, Language, Drama
INSTRUCTORS:	35 faculty members
ESTABLISHED:	1951
CLASS FEE:	Drama (2 years) $2,500; Dance (4 years) $4,500; Music (4 years) $6,000

ENTRANCE REQUIREMENTS: By application
SCHOLARSHIPS: Available
NUMBER OF STUDENTS
   PER CLASS: 2–10
VIDEO EQUIPMENT: Yes
STUDIOS: 12 studios, 2 recital studios, 3 lobbies, student store, library
DRESSING ROOMS: 2
FLOOR: Hardwood
SUMMATION STATEMENT: "The Eubanks Conservatory of Music and Arts program is designed to provide a complete music and arts education for all students through its general music and arts program, sponsoring orchestras and chorus and helping to make individuals aware of their special aptitudes and talents through orientation and guidance. The classes afford the student group expression, performance techniques, objectivity in observation, and exposure to different musical cultures."

FILM ACTORS WORKSHOP

Tony and Barbara Barr, Directors
5004 Vineland Avenue
North Hollywood, CA 91601
(213) 766–5108

PROGRAM: Acting, Camera Technique
INSTRUCTORS: Tony Barr, Eric Kline, Seth Pinsker, David Payner
ESTABLISHED: 1960
REGISTRATION FEE: $40 (includes textbook)
CLASS FEE: $120 per month
SCHEDULE: 2 3-hour sessions per week
AUDITING: Not permitted
SCHOLARSHIPS: Not available
NUMBER OF STUDENTS
   PER CLASS: Limited to 14–16
STUDENT BREAKDOWN: 60% female, 40% male; 90% 18–25, 10% 26–35; 30% 1/2–1 year, 60% 1–2 years, 10% 2–3 years
VIDEO EQUIPMENT: Yes
STUDIOS: 2
BIOGRAPHY: MR. BARR is currently the vice-president of drama programming at DBS Television; he has appeared in features and television, and is a producer and

CLASSES:

associate producer. MR. KLINE received his B.A. from the University of California and Berkeley and M.A. from San Francisco State University. He has 10 years experience as an editor and writer.

The goal of the acting class is to develop acting values and techniques as they relate to performing on camera as opposed to in a theatre. Camera Technique familiarizes the actor with the vocabulary of the sound stage and television studio and acquaints the actor with specific technical skills for working in front of the camera. Scenes are videotaped for examination and evaluation.

SUMMATION STATEMENT:

"We teach the actors to work simply, for maximum effectiveness before the camera and to work from themselves, moment to moment, because this is what the intimacy of the camera demands. We teach through the kinds of scenes actors are hired for in television and movies, principally from teleplays, features, and novels. FAW provides a direct, pragmatic approach which encompasses the inner acting needs as well as the technical needs of work before the camera."

CAROL FRIEDENBERG

3643 California Street
San Francisco, CA 94110
(415) 221–4830

PROGRAM:	Speech and Voice Therapy, Private
ESTABLISHED:	1979
REGISTRATION FEE:	None
CLASS FEE:	$50 per hour
SCHEDULE:	1-hour sessions, ongoing
ENTRANCE REQUIREMENTS:	Open
SCHOLARSHIPS:	Not available
STUDENT BREAKDOWN:	50% female, 50% male; 25% under 18, 25% 26–35, 25% 36–45, 25% over 45; 100% under 6 months
VOCAL CASSETTES:	Students permitted to record exercises at session
BIOGRAPHY:	MS. FRIEDENBERG received her B.S. in speech pathology from the University of Minnesota, and her M.S. in speech pathology from the University of Wisconsin. She has 17 years experience work-

ing in hospitals, particularly with voice problems in adults, including vocal strain, vocal nodules, hoarseness, breathiness, poor projection, lack of inflectional variety, etc. Though the majority of her clients come upon referral from their ear, nose, and throat doctor, an increasing number of performers experiencing vocal difficulty are being referred by vocal coaches.

CLASS: All therapy is individual, reviewing medical and physical production aspects of the voice, working with a tape recorder to obtain the best quality voice production with an appropriate minimal amount of effort. Sessions emphasize proper resonance and and placement of the voice with exercises geared to facilitate the use of correct voice production in spontaneous conversation and professional use as soon as possible.

SUMMATION STATEMENT: "My work came as a result of my specialization in more severe voice disorders over the past 14 years. Individuals with concerns regarding the voice—from the severe extreme of laryngeal cancer, to the less severe but very important complaints of hoarseness or excessive nasal resonance, or lack of adequate volume, vocal strain or effort needed to produce voice—have been seen and treated as part of my work in the departments of Otolaryngology at two university medical centers and two hospitals over the past 17 years. I have become increasingly concerned with the special needs and pressures related to performing and having a clear, effortless voice which is reliable for use in many contexts."

ESTELLE HARMAN ACTORS WORKSHOP

Estelle Harman, Director
522 North La Brea
Los Angeles, CA 90036
(213) 931–8137

PROGRAM: Acting, Camera Technique, Scene Rehearsal, Reading and Vocabulary, Psychology for the Actor, Group Dynamics, Theatre History, Theatre Literature, Film and Play Analysis, Field Study, Voice and Speech, Effective Speech, Dialects, Reader's Theatre, Play Production, Singing for the Actor, Musical Theatre, Cold Reading, Improvisational Theatre, Actor Sensitivity, Body and Dance for the Actor, Mime, Camera Acting Skills, Commercials, Technical Stage Production, Drama Digest, Teen Actors Workshop.

INSTRUCTORS: Estelle Harman, Samuel Harman, Ari Barak, Susan Harris, Judy Heinz, Mark Duke, Paul Morse, Dan Currie, Eden Harman, Carla Meyer, Myrna Gawryn, Paul Carleton

ESTABLISHED: 1957

CLASS FEES: Full time $1,005; three-quarter time $810; one-half time $595; one-quarter time $375

AUDITING: Not permitted

SCHOLARSHIPS: Pell Grant, National Direct Student Loan, and California Student Loan

NUMBER OF STUDENTS PER CLASS: 20–30

STUDENT BREAKDOWN: 50% female, 50% male; 5% under 18, 69% 18–25, 25% 26–35, 1% over 45

VIDEO EQUIPMENT: Yes

STUDIOS: 3 studios, 3 theatres, library, lounge, scene dock

DRESSING ROOMS: Yes

BIOGRAPHY: MS. HARMAN was formerly the head of talent and screen test director at Universal Studios, and an instructor in theatre arts at the University of California. She is the founding director of Circle Theatre and Harman Avenue Theatre; A.A., B.A., M.A., from the University of Southern California; member SAG, AFTRA, AEA, AETA, ANTA, IPA, AFI, Zeta Phi Eta, Mortar Board. MR. HARMAN is a professor in the department of psychology at Los Angeles Community College. He is a management consultant and licensed psychologist; A.A., B.A., M.A., Ph.D., from the University of Southern California. MS. HEINZ's professional experience includes acting, directing, and producing for film, stage and television; B.A., M.F.A. from the University of Southern California; member SAG, AFTRA, AEA. MR. DUKE has practical experience as both an actor and director. Worked in improvisational theatre with Cork Howard and the L.A. Connection; B.A., University of Texas; graduate, EHAW. MR. BARAK has film, stage, and television experience as an actor and dancer in Israel, Europe, the Orient, and Hollywood; graduate, EHAW. Member SAG, AFTRA, AEA. MR. MORSE is an author-composer with 6 plays and short operas produced in New York City and Hollywood. Writer-director with local touring companies; B.A. from the University of California at Los Angeles. MR. CURRIE has practical experience in stage and television, including 65 commercials. Chairman of drama at University of Wisconsin, and drama staff at Pasadena City College, Mt. San Antonio College. MR. HARMAN has practical experience as an actor and director in stage, television, and platform speaking. Founding director of CATCO Productions, currently producing Eden's original play. Graduate EHAW; member AFTRA, IPA. MS. MEYER has practical experience in stage, radio, television, and commercials. She has been a dialect coach for Broadway, Off-Broadway, and touring company productions. Executive director, Ensemble Studio Theatre. News and host for WNET in New York City. Instructor, Webster College, Neighborhood Playhouse, American Conservatory Theatre, and the University of California at Irvine. B.F.A., Carnegie Mellon; member SAG, AEA, AFTRA, CAM, and Women in Film. MS. GAWRYN is a dance instructor at Long Beach State University; administrator and instructor at the Room to Move School of Dance; casting director, Roland Dupre School of Dance; and choreographer, Company Theatre, Hollywood. MS. HARRIS is an instructor in drama for gifted students at Le Conte Junior High and in acting at California State Univesity at Northridge. Practical experience in educational and industrial films and stage. Member SAG, AFTRA; graduate, EHAW. MR. CARLETON is resident technical director at the Alexander Fine Arts Theatre and the Oak Grove Theatre. Training at Concord College; Bulmershe College, England; and Cornish Institute for the Arts; graduate, EHAW.

LORAINE HULL

Hollywood, CA
(213) 851–6210

PROGRAM:	Scene Study, Acting Technique, Private Coaching Actors/Directors/Teachers/Writers Class, Teen Acting, Youth Creative Dramatics, Youth Play Production
ESTABLISHED:	1973
CLASS FEE:	Scene Study; Technique; A/D/T/W Class—$200; Private coaching $50 per hour; Teen Acting and Youth Play Production—$200; Youth Creative Dramatics—$100
AUDITING:	Permitted
AUDITING FEE:	Scene Study/Technique—$15 per class; Youth Classes—$10 per class
SCHEDULE:	1 4-hour session per week, 12 weeks, ongoing
ENTRANCE REQUIREMENTS:	Adult classes—interview, audition, application. Applicants must be 18 years and older and have previous training. Youth classes—interview. Teen Acting open to applicants 13–18; Creative Dramatics 6–12; Play Production 11–18. Play Production students must be enrolled in the acting class.
CANCELLATION POLICIES:	Make-up session available
SCHOLARSHIPS:	Partial work-exchange scholarships available
NUMBER OF STUDENTS PER CLASS:	Adult—limited to 12; Youth—limited to 15
TOTAL STUDIO ENROLLMENT:	80
STUDENT BREAKDOWN:	Adult classes—50% female, 50% male; 0% under 18, 50% 18–25, 20% 26–35, 20% 36–45, 10% over 45; 50% under 6 months, 20% 1/2–1 year, 20% 1–2 years, 10% 2–3 years, 0% over 3 years. Youth classes—75% female, 25% male; 100% under 18; 30% under 6 months, 30% 1/2–1 year, 30% 1–2 years, 10% 2–3 years, 0% over 3 years
BIOGRAPHY:	MS. HULL studied professionally with Lee Strasberg, Herbert Berghof and others in New York City. She was a professor at the University of Wisconsin Center, Fond du Lac, and Ripon College in Wisconsin. It was at Ripon where she was selected to represent the American Theatre Association at the International Congresses in Sweden, Monaco, and Oklahoma. While in Monaco, she conducted acting and directing workshops as a guest of Prince Ranier and Princess Grace, and

founded the North American Regional Theatre Alliance. She is currently a member of the Ensemble Studio Theatre and of the Actors Studio's directors and writers units in both Los Angeles and New York; she continues to teach acting, directing, and writing at the Strasberg Institute.

CLASSES: Format of Scene Study includes preparing and learning the role, breakdown of the script, applying method exercises and techniques to the role, and stages of rehearsal. Fundamentals to be covered in Acting Technique include understanding the method, concentration, sensory responses, improvisation, exercise of will, objectives, situations, scene work, interpretation, breakdown of the script, cold readings, audition technique. Actors/Directors/Teachers/Writers Class: Course members will be guided through the stages of rehearsal and the structuring of homework based on method exercises, along with research and examination of the text and writer's intent. Experimentation is encouraged with writer's original scripts and directing projects. Teen Acting covers "Bodily Language"—relaxation, sensory awareness, concentration exercises, beginning sense memory work, movement and sound, self-awareness—improvisation, threatre games, scene study, film techniques, cold readings. Creative Dramatics includes warm-up exercises, theatre games, movement, exploration of relationships with nature, creative story plays, improvisation work, etc. Youth Play Production will provide actor with an opportunity to work with a director in the rehearsal and performance of selected scenes and plays for an invited audience.

SUMMATION STATEMENT: "This session is a unified approach to all aspects and fundamentals of the Method—to inspire creativity, imagination, a deeper theatrical appreciation, and higher theatrical standards at all levels."

WILLIAM GEORGE MACMILLAN

P.O. Box 480306
Los Angeles, CA 90048
(213) 698–8480

PROGRAM:	Scene Study, Psychic Play Analysis, Psychic Improvisation—Young People
INSTRUCTORS:	William George MacMillan; Karen Wescott, assistant
REGISTRATION FEE:	Scene Study and Psychic Improvisation—none; Play Analysis—$10
CLASS FEES:	Scene Study $250; Play Analysis $150; Psychic Improvisation $200
SCHEDULE:	Scene Study—1 3-hour class per week, 10 weeks, ongoing; Play Analysis—weekend seminar, Friday night, all day Saturday; Psychic Improvisation—1 or 2 2-to-3-hour classes per week, 5–10 weeks, ongoing
AUDITING:	Scene Study and Psychic Improvisation—permitted; Play Analysis—not permitted
AUDITING FEE:	$20
ENTRANCE REQUIREMENTS:	Interview and audition
CANCELLATION POLICIES:	No refunds after second session
SCHOLARSHIPS:	Partial work-exchange available
NUMBER OF STUDENTS PER CLASS:	Scene Study—limited to 15; Play Analysis—limited to 17
STUDENT BREAKDOWN:	Scene Study—65% female, 35% male; 3% under 18, 30% 18–25, 40% 26–35, 20% 36–45, 7% over 45; 30% under 6 months, 0% 1/2–1 year, 5% 1–2 years, 15% 2–3 years, 50% over 3 years. Play Analysis—50% female, 50% male; 2% under 18, 35% 18–25, 35% 26–35, 18% 36–45, 10% over 45. Psychic Improvisation—70% female, 30% male; 3% under 18, 17% 18–25, 50% 26–35, 24% 36–45, 6% over 45; 23% under 6 months, 25% 1/2–1 year, 35% 1–2 years, 7% 2–3 years, 10% over 3 years
VIDEO EQUIPMENT:	Yes
BIOGRAPHY:	MR. MACMILLAN received his M.F.A. from Boston University. He has worked in numerous professional capacities—as a puppeteer, playwright, parapsychologist, lecturer, and as the director of two film shorts, and of the Psychic Repertory Theatre; he has worked as an actor in film, theatre,

television, industrials, commericals, and as a contract player on "General Hospital." MS. WESCOTT is a parapsychologist counselor, lecturer, mystery writer, and a songwriter/playwright who has produced 2 musicals. She has 2 one-woman shows which she performs in repertory.

CLASSES:
Students bring in scenes and monologues for critiquing.

SUMMATION STATEMENT:
"My approach is to be responsive to each individual's needs, challenging the individual to grow and fulfill his or her potential."

KRELL MUSIC STUDIO

Glenn Krell, Director
10755 Pico Boulevard
Los Angeles, CA 90064
(213) 474–5151/279–1500/282–8133

PROGRAM:	Vocal Technique—Private Instruction
INSTRUCTORS:	Gralin Jerald, Diane Gordon
ESTABLISHED:	1957
REGISTRATION FEE:	None
CLASS FEE:	$43 per month
SCHEDULE:	1 1/2-hour class per week, ongoing
AUDITING:	Permitted
AUDITING FEE:	No fee
ENTRANCE REQUIREMENTS:	Open
CANCELLATION POLICIES:	Must cancel 24 hours in advance
SCHOLARSHIPS:	Not available
TOTAL STUDIO ENROLLMENT:	125
STUDENT BREAKDOWN:	50% female, 50% male; 80% under 18, 5% 18–25, 10% 26–35, 5% 36–45; 15% under 6 months, 40% 1/2–1 year, 25% 1–2 years, 15% 2–3 years, 5% over 3 years
STUDIOS:	7
CLASS CARD:	Yes, allowing 2 free lessons, valid 6 months
BIOGRAPHY:	MR. JERALD is an accomplished musician who has been a voice student for 12 years, specializing in jazz, pop, and rock. He has written songs for Billy Davis and Marilyn McCoo as well as other artists. MS. GORDON received her M.A., Ph.D., and M.I.S. in music from the University of California at Los Angeles, incorporating research at Ox-

ford University, England. While working within the California State University system, Diane arranged concerts and performed musically and developed a professional chamber music series. She has been instructor in music with UCLA's Extension Division. She has lectured internationally, including at the Chinese University in Hong Kong, and is conversant with folk songs around the world and folklore in both modern English opera and twentieth-century American opera.

VALENTINA OUMANSKY
DRAMATIC DANCE WORKSHOP

Valentina Oumansky, Director
3433 Caheunga Boulevard
West Los Angeles, CA 90028
(213) 850–9487

PROGRAM:	Modern
ESTABLISHED:	1966
REGISTRATION FEE:	None
CLASS FEE:	$6 per class
SCHEDULE:	6 1½-hour sessions per week, ongoing
AUDITING:	Not permitted
ENTRANCE REQUIREMENTS:	Interview, all ages from 5 up
CANCELLATION POLICIES:	No refunds, make-ups
SCHOLARSHIPS:	One-year full work-scholarship for student taking minimum of 3 classes per week
REQUIRED MATERIALS:	Leotard, tights, bare feet/shoes
NUMBER OF STUDENTS PER CLASS:	10
TOTAL STUDIO ENROLLMENT:	40
STUDENT BREAKDOWN:	90% female, 10% male; 50% under 18, 25% 18–25, 25% 26–35, 0% over 35; 50% under 6 months, 0% ½–2 years, 25% 2–3 years, 25% over 3 years
VIDEO EQUIPMENT:	Yes
VIDEO CASSETTES:	Students may purchase video cassettes.
STUDIOS:	2
DRESSING ROOMS:	2
SHOWERS:	1
FLOOR:	Wood

ACCOMPANYING
   INSTRUMENT: Tape and/or record
CLASS CARD: Not available
WAITING AREA: Yes
BIOGRAPHY: MS. OUMANSKY, artistic director and choreographer, expanded her early ballet background as a member of the Ballet International to study and perform dramatic dancing. This personal investigation enabled Ms. Oumansky to define a method of choreography and movement education for aspiring students wishing to prepare for the performing arts. MR. TALAVERA, artistic director of the Los Angeles-based Spanish and Flamenco Dance Spectacular, is a specialist and master teacher in charge of the ethnic department. He is currently on staff as flamenco dance instructor.

CLASS: Based on a method of 12 dramatic dance études, Ms. Oumansky has sought to give the learner an understanding of characterization, dramatic movement gesture, and an artistic expression with which to communicate ideas, images, and emotions. A broad curriculum is offered at the Dramatic Dance Workshop which includes classical, ethnic, and contemporary dance, music, and drama correlating to dramatic dance theatre.

SUMMATION STATEMENT: "The aim of the Valentina Oumansky Workshop is to encourage students to develop choreographic skills for live concert and theatre, education, and the television market, as well as to prepare themselves for a career in the professional performing arts field. Music and dance videotapes are developed at the workshop in order to advance the learner's personal information as well as to document choreographic projects for future use, as an alternative type of arts programming on cable or PBS networks, with national distribution of the product subsequently brought about as broadcast quality is achieved."

GUY STOCKWELL ACTOR TRAINING

Guy Stockwell, Director
7420 Melrose Avenue
Los Angeles, CA 90046
(213) 658–6786/(818) 363–5704

PROGRAM:	Creativity Plus, Peak System, Cold Reading, Commercials, Voice and Movement, Showcase, Workout
ESTABLISHED:	1960
REGISTRATION FEE:	None
SCHEDULE:	1 4-hour class per week, 50 weeks per year, ongoing
AUDITING:	Not permitted
ENTRANCE REQUIREMENTS:	Adults may interview and audition.
CANCELLATION POLICIES:	Make-up sessions available
SCHOLARSHIPS:	Not available
NUMBER OF STUDENTS PER CLASS:	Limited to 12
STUDENT BREAKDOWN:	65% female, 35% male; 1% under 18, 75% 18–25, 20% 26–35, 4% 36–45, 0% over 45; 20% under 6 months, 60% ¹/₂–1 year, 0% 1–2 years, 20% 2–3 years, 0% over 3 years
VIDEO EQUIPMENT:	Yes
VIDEO CASSETTES:	Students are not permitted to purchase video cassettes.
CUE-CARD SYSTEM:	No
STUDIOS:	2
DRESSING ROOMS:	2
BIOGRAPHY:	MR. STOCKWELL has appeared in numerous theatrical and made-for-television films and television series, including "The Warlord," "Beau Geste," "Tobruk," "And Now Miguel," "Simon and Simon," "Magnum PI," "Return to Peyton Place," etc. He helped to create the Los Angeles Art Theatre, where he has performed in *Hamlet, Crime and Punishment, The Seagull.*
CLASSES:	Creativity Plus is a program custom-designed to meet the needs of each student. Overall goals are to increase the student's ability to solve problems creatively and to behave with confidence personally and socially. Peak System is a technical approach that enables the actor to make a choice that is clear and actable about any material, whether for film, stage, or audition. It differs from

the classic "method" in that it is much faster and more precise.

JOE TREMAINE DANCE CENTER

Joe Tremaine, Director
10960 Ventura Boulevard
North Hollywood, CA 91604
(213) 980–3336

PROGRAM:	Jazz
INSTRUCTORS:	Joe Tremaine, Fred Walton, Karin Kelly, Doug Caldwell
ESTABLISHED:	1974
REGISTRATION FEE:	None
CLASS FEE:	$6 per class
SCHEDULE:	7 1-to-1½-hour classes per week, ongoing
AUDITING:	Permitted
AUDITING FEE:	None
ENTRANCE REQUIREMENTS:	Minimum age 16
SCHOLARSHIPS:	Work-exchange scholarships available
NUMBER OF STUDENTS PER CLASS:	12–40, unlimited
TOTAL STUDIO ENROLLMENT:	1,500
STUDENT BREAKDOWN:	80% female, 20% male; 25% under 18, 60% 18–25, 15% 26–35, 0% over 35
VIDEO EQUIPMENT:	Yes
STUDIOS:	5
DRESSING ROOMS:	4
SHOWERS:	2
FLOOR:	Floating wood
ACCOMPANYING INSTRUMENT:	Records and/or tapes
CLASS CARD:	Not available
WAITING AREA:	Yes

REGIONAL
REGIONAL
REGIONAL
REGIONAL
REGIONAL
REGIONAL
REGIONAL
REGIONAL
REGIONAL
REGIONAL
REGIONAL

ALL DISCIPLINES
ALL DISCIPLINES
ALL DISCIPLINES
ALL DISCIPLINES
ALL DISCIPLINES
ALL DISCIPLINES
ALL DISCIPLINES
ALL DISCIPLINES
ALL DISCIPLINES
ALL DISCIPLINES
ALL DISCIPLINES
ALL DISCIPLINES
ALL DISCIPLINES
ALL DISCIPLINES
ALL DISCIPLINES
ALL DISCIPLINES
ALL DISCIPLINES
ALL DISCIPLINES
ALL DISCIPLINES
ALL DISCIPLINES
ALL DISCIPLINES
ALL DISCIPLINES
ALL DISCIPLINES
ALL DISCIPLINES

ACADEMY THEATRE SCHOOL OF PERFORMING ARTS

Margaret Ferguson, Director
1137 Peachtree Street, NE
Atlanta, GA 30309
(404) 873-2518

PROGRAM:	Scene Study, Beginning and Advanced Acting, Improvisation and Theatre Games, Voice Development, Creative Dramatics for Children I–II, Acting for Teens, Scene Study for Teens
INSTRUCTORS:	Acting—Brenda Bynum, Jean Marie Collins, Chris Kayser, Judith Shotwell; Voice—Holly Stevenson; Creative Dramatics—Betsy Gilmer
ESTABLISHED:	1956
REGISTRATION FEE:	None
CLASS FEES:	Acting—$90–$100 per term; Creative Dramatics, Teen Acting—$75–$90
SCHEDULE:	Acting—1 1½-to-2½-hour session per week, 8 weeks; Teen Acting/Play Production—1 4-hour session per week, 12 weeks; Creative Dramatics—1 2-hour session per week, 12 weeks
AUDITING:	Not permitted
ENTRANCE REQUIREMENTS:	Application; Creative Dramatics for children 6–12
CANCELLATION POLICIES:	No refunds; credit toward next quarter available
SCHOLARSHIPS:	Partial and full work-scholarships available
NUMBER OF STUDENTS PER CLASS:	Acting 12–15; Voice 7
STUDENT BREAKDOWN:	Acting—60% female, 40% male; 15% under 18, 45% 18–25, 35% 26–35, 5% 36–45, 0% over 45; 50% under 6 months, 50% ½–1 year, 0% over 1 year. Voice—60% female, 40% male; 0% under 26, 20% 26–35, 80% 36–45, 0% over 45; 50% under 6 months, 50% ½–1 year, 0% over 1 year. Creative Dramatics—90% female, 10% male; 100% under 18; 50% under 6 months, 50% ½–1 year, 0% over 1 year
STUDIOS:	4
DRESSING ROOMS:	4
SHOWERS:	2
BIOGRAPHY:	MS. BYNUM is currently an Academy Theatre mainstage company member, a visiting professor of theatre at Mercer University and Emory University; president of the Atlanta New Play Project, vice

president and treasurer of T.H.E. Theatre Ltd., and cofounder of the Southern Poets Theatre. MS. COLLINS received her training from Mercer University and the Drama Studio, London, England. It was in London that she was active in a Viola Spolin group under the direction of Andy Hasmon. Ms. Collins moved to Atlanta in 1981 where she became an actress and teacher with the Academy Theatre. MR. KAYSER holds a B.A. from Georgia State University and is in his third year with the Academy Theatre as a member of the professional resident company. He recently played the title role in the Academy's world premiere production of DLUA, by artistic director Frank Wittow. He has taught classes and workshops throughout the Northeast. MS. SHOTWELL has been a member of the Academy Theatre Company since 1979, and received her B.A. from Harvard University. She is an actress, director, teacher, and playwright. MS. STEVENSON has a B.F.A. in theatre and has studied singing for 7 years. She has taught several voice workshops and has studied speech privately in Atlanta. She is currently an actress, teacher, and director with the Academy Theatre in Atlanta. MS. GILMER has a B.A. in English, and has studied for 3 years as an apprentice, precompany member, and as a First Stage company member. She has directed 3 children's plays in the last 2 years.

CLASSES: Beginning Acting is an introduction to basic exercises, games, warm-ups, and concepts which prepare the actor for the performing experience. Relaxation, concentration, physical and vocal flexibility and variety, creative use of the imagination, and the freeing of emotional resources basic to the development of character are all covered. Advanced Acting includes physical and vocal warm-ups; character development through abstract and naturalistic technique; exploration of emotions and free expression of them; scripted scene work. Improvisation begins with warm-ups, followed by a series of theatre games structured to give focus on fellow players, relationship with space, when to give and take, and working toward obtaining the ultimate goal, an ensemble environment. The class does not work with scripts or rehearsed scenes. Scene study pairs students off 3 times, each time with someone different, with one assigned scene, one classical scene, one scene of students' choosing. Class involves outside rehearsal time, then in-class performance and critique. Voice is concerned with vocal clarity and stage projection, and is conducted in a very relaxed fashion, as relaxation plays a large part in overall technique of vocal control. Class begins with some stretches, relaxation, and breathing exercises, and articulation; this is followed with frequent use of scripted material, vocal improvisations, and theatre games which stress vocal flexibility. Creative Dramatics—Focus is on the child's natural ability to play as the foundation of everything. Once a child is exhibilarated and caught up in the rhythms of various theatre games and/or improvised skits, you can then begin to help him or her sharpen technical skills in the area of voice, movement, and characterization. A nonjudgmental environment is necessary for students to feel safe in taking risks and breaking down inhibitions. Children, like adults, are often afraid of looking silly and being laughed at, so instructor enters into "play" with students, as a full participant.

SUMMATION STATEMENT: "The School of Peforming Arts is distinguished from other theatre training programs in the Southeast by the interdependence with exists between the professional resident company and the school. Classes are taught by professional actor-instructors from the Academy's own companies, and by guest artists from other major American theatres."

ALLEY THEATRE

615 Texas Avenue
Houston, TX 77002

PROGRAM:	Young Company Members (Equity Membership Candidates)
CLASS FEE:	YCMs receive a stipend of $100–$150 per week
SCHEDULE:	September–May, with a 16-week stipulation clause
ENTRANCE REQUIREMENTS:	Audition, application, picture, and resume; all candidates must have completed their university training.

CLASS: YCMs are apprentices of the company, selected primarily because of their acting potential, but they may be assigned, at times, to work in children's shows, workshops, or major productions, depending upon casting needs. Young company members also serve on running crews, as rehearsal assistants; they work all strikes and supplement the production staff when necessary. Time and scheduling does not permit any part-time work outside of the theatre.

BROADCAST TALENT WORKSHOPS

Peg Avery, Director
1655 Peachtree Street, Suite 1003
Atlanta, GA 30309
(404) 876–1264

PROGRAM:	Commercials
INSTRUCTORS:	Peg Avery, Marlys Moxley
ESTABLISHED:	1981
REGISTRATION FEE:	None
CLASS FEE:	$175
SCHEDULE:	2 2-hour sessions per week, ongoing
ENTRANCE REQUIREMENTS:	Interview
CANCELLATION POLICIES:	Make-up sessions available
SCHOLARSHIPS:	Not available
NUMBER OF STUDENTS PER CLASS:	6
STUDENT BREAKDOWN:	50% female, 50% male; 30% under 18, 0% 18–25, 30% 26–35, 30% 36–45, 10% over 45; 50% under 6 months, 50% ½–1 year, 0% over 1 year
VIDEO EQUIPMENT:	Yes
VIDEO CASSETTES:	Students may purchase their video tapes.
CUE CARD SYSTEM:	Yes
STUDIOS:	1
BIOGRAPHY:	MS. AVERY has appeared in many radio and television commercials, including national radio. MS. MOXLEY is an actress specializing in the International Phonic Alphabet.
CLASS:	The class offers practical, professional instruction, using videotape recording studio facilities. International Phonic Alphabet is covered.

SUMMATION STATEMENT: "We are a workshop. We also help with demo tapes. We are not a talent agency, nor are we producers or directors. Our students are slowly making their way in their fields of endeavor."

CLASSICAL BALLET
CAMBRIDGE, INC.

Carol Jordan, Director
11 Garden Street
Cambridge, MA 02138
(617) 491–2893

PROGRAM:	Classical Ballet, Young People
INSTRUCTOR:	Carol Jordan
ESTABLISHED:	1980
REGISTRATION FEE:	$5
CLASS FEE:	$100–$450
SCHEDULE:	2 to 5 1-to-1½-hour sessions per week, 43 weeks
AUDITING:	Permitted
AUDITING FEE:	$6
ENTRANCE REQUIREMENTS:	Applicant must take a placement class.
CANCELLATION POLICIES:	No refunds after term has begun
SCHOLARSHIPS:	Partial and full to students of 1 year or more according to financial need
REQUIRED MATERIALS:	Pink tights, slippers, black leotard. Any color leotard for advanced students
NUMBER OF STUDENTS PER CLASS:	Limited to 15–20
TOTAL STUDIO ENROLLMENT:	80
STUDENT BREAKDOWN:	99% female, 1% male; 100% under 18; 15% under 6 months, 20% ½–1 year, 15% 1–2 years, 35% 2–3 years, 15% over 3 years
STUDIOS:	1
DRESSING ROOMS:	2
SHOWERS:	None
FLOOR:	Lonstage
ACCOMPANYING INSTRUMENT:	Piano
CLASS CARD:	No
WAITING AREA:	Yes
BIOGRAPHY:	MS. JORDAN was born in London and trained at the Royal Academy of Dance. The major influences on her career have been Dame Marie Ram-

bert and Eileen Ward. In New York she studied at the American Ballet Theatre, Joffrey's American Ballet Centre, Ballet Russe. She has performed with the New York City Opera Ballet and Les Grands Ballets Canadiens. She was the Artistic Director of the Cambridge School of Ballet from 1971–1979.

CLASS: The class adheres to a traditional ballet class structure. Program of five levels of study from beginners to advanced. Intermediate and advanced levels include pointe work.

SUMMATION STATEMENT: "Our philosophy stresses an understanding of body placement in order to achieve control of the body and freedom of movement."

DANCESPACE

Rosemary Doolas, Director
410 South Michigan Street, Suite 833
Chicago, IL 60605
(312) 939–0181

PROGRAM:	Ballet, Modern
INSTRUCTORS:	Ballet—Rosemary Doolas, James Java, Mary Marzec; Modern—Nana Salbrig, Fred DeVare
ESTABLISHED:	1978
REGISTRATION FEE:	None
CLASS FEE:	Single class $6; $40 per term
SCHEDULE:	1 1½-hour class per week, 8 weeks (reduced rates for students taking several classes per week)
AUDITING:	Permitted
AUDITING FEE:	No fee
ENTRANCE REQUIREMENTS:	Application
CANCELLATION POLICIES:	Make-up sessions available
SCHOLARSHIPS:	Full work-exchange scholarships available
NUMBER OF STUDENTS PER CLASS:	Limited to 10
TOTAL STUDIO ENROLLMENT:	140
STUDENT BREAKDOWN:	75% female, 25% male; 25% under 18, 35% 18–25, 30% 26–35, 10% 36–45; 25% under 6 months, 25% ½–1 year, 20% 1–2 years, 20% 2–3 years, 10% over 3 years
STUDIOS:	1
DRESSING ROOMS:	2

SHOWERS:	None
FLOOR:	1600 square feet; air-suspended maple
ACCOMPANYING INSTRUMENT:	Piano
CLASS CARD:	8 and unlimited classes, valid 8 weeks
BIOGRAPHY:	MS. DOOLAS had her early classical training in Chicago at the Stone-Camryn School of Ballet. She continued her training in ballet and modern dance while attending the Julliard School of Music, where she studied with Margaret Craske, Antony Tudor, and Jose Limon. She has performed with the Southern Pacific Ballet Company, the Wurzburg Opera Ballet (in Germany), and the Phyllis Sabold Dance Company. She has taught dance at Barat College and at the Carol Walker School. Ms. Doolas also teaches ballet at the Latin School of Chicago. MS. SALBRIG directs the Chicago Moving Company.
CLASSES:	Ms. Doolas teaches a unique blend of classical ballet and contemporary dance. She stresses body placement, control, musicality, and energy flow, combined with the discipline and science that make dance a creative process.
SUMMATION STATEMENT:	"Dancespace is the school of the Chicago Dance Medium."

THE NATIONAL THEATRE SCHOOL OF CANADA

5030 Saint-Denis Street
Montreal, Quebec, Canada H2J-2L8

PROGRAM:	Full-Time Programs in Acting, Design, Playwriting
INSTRUCTORS:	Jean Louis Roux, Jean Pol Britte, Joel Miller, Francois Barbeau, Perry Schneiderman, Michael Mawson, Freddie Grimwood, Penny Ritco, Peter Wylde, Robert Chapline, Therese Petit
ESTABLISHED:	1960
REGISTRATION FEE:	$35 application fee; $75 registration fee
CLASS FEE:	Annual tuition: $900
SCHEDULE:	2 16-week semesters, August–May; Acting and Playwriting 3 years; Technical and Design 2 years
ENTRANCE REQUIREMENTS:	Acting students must be between 18 and 25 years of age, Technical and Design 18–30; no maximum

age for Playwriting. Actors must interview and audition.

CANCELLATION POLICIES: $100 nonrefundable; registration fee nonrefundable

SCHOLARSHIPS: Emergency loan fund available

TOTAL STUDIO ENROLLMENT: 83

STUDIOS: 2 theatres, gymnasium, sound and recording studio, 2 dance studios, 2 voice studios, 6 rehearsal rooms, 2 makeup rooms, 15 classrooms, store, recreation room, lounge, library, reading room, cafe

DRESSING ROOMS: 2

SHOWERS: Yes

CLASSES: Acting—The school places special emphasis on the development of the students' physical means of expression—flexibility, strength, and expressiveness of body and voice. This is accomplished through movement, dance, gymnastics, aikido, fencing, voice, and singing courses. First-year focus is on laying a foundation in recognition and use of impulse, playing and living off each other, understanding the nature of action, etc. Second-year focus is on the sharpening of craft with attention to period style. Third-year focus is on public performance. Playwriting—Students who have already reached a certain level of skill are accepted and provided with the opportunity to learn about theatre, and to learn the dramaturgical skills necessary to apply their writing talents to the requirements of the theatrical profession. Technical study teaches the student architecture, drawing, costume, theatre history, development of styles through the ages. First year focuses on acquiring the techniques of design; second year in applying those techniques to practical projects. Technical provides courses in production management, technical direction, stage management, and lighting. First year acquaints students with basic theatre techniques, principles of stage management, and production organization; second-year students are assigned to positions on various student projects.

THE SPEECH IMPROVEMENT CO., INC.

Paula Borkum Becker, Director
1614 Beacon Street
Brookline, MA 02146
(617) 739–3330

PROGRAM:	Voice and Articulation
INSTRUCTORS:	Paula Borkum Becker, Tom Glauner
ESTABLISHED:	1964
REGISTRATION FEE:	None
CLASS FEE:	$60 (private instruction available at $40 per hour)
SCHEDULE:	1 1-hour session per week, six weeks
AUDITING:	Not permitted
ENTRANCE REQUIREMENTS:	Open
CANCELLATION POLICIES:	No refunds past registration for first class
SCHOLARSHIPS:	Not available
NUMBER OF STUDENTS PER CLASS:	Limited to 12
TOTAL STUDIO ENROLLMENT:	12
STUDENT BREAKDOWN:	40% female, 60% male; 10% under 18, 60% 18–25, 20% 26–35, 5% 36–45, 5% over 45; 90% under 6 months, 0% $1/2$–1 year, 10% 1–2 years, 0% over 2 years
VIDEO EQUIPMENT:	Yes
VIDEO CASSETTES:	Students may purchase video cassettes.
STUDIOS:	1
DRESSING ROOMS:	Yes
VOCAL CASSETTES:	Students are permitted to record exercises at class.
WAITING AREA:	Yes
BIOGRAPHY:	MS. BECKER has had over 20 years of experience in the field of voice and speech, and has helped thousands of individuals from all walks of life with accents, regionalisms, voice coaching, and therapy. A graduate of Emerson College and Antioch College, her special techniques and informal work-style make her a much sought after resouce. MR. GLAUNER has worked in all areas of theatre performance, and has coached voice, drama, and interpretation at Bradley University in Illinois, and Emerson College in Boston. As an instructor for Speech Improvement Co., he has worked with hundreds of individuals in all areas of voice and speech.

CLASSES:

The work-style of the classes is informal, informative, and always interactive. Cooperating consultation with professional theatres, doctors, and counselors can also be arranged. Work is spent on developing a strong, lasting voice, and correct articulation, pronunciation, vocal variety, subtext, and expression through exercises, critiques, readings, and lectures. Methods of vocal warm-up are explored, along with dynamics, expression, and articulation

SUMMATION STATEMENT:

"Through the many years of helping people with the care and development of their speech and voice, the Speech Improvement Co. has developed this unique service for performers of all kinds. Trained staff and certified pathologists, who have worked in the theatre as performers themselves and are aware of the difficulties facing performers, work in classes and in private or semiprivate sessions."

TERPSICHORE DANCE EXPRESSIONS

Patricia Bromley, Director
1843 Cheshire Bridge Road
Atlanta, GA 30324
(404) 874–8755

PROGRAM:	Dance
INSTRUCTORS:	Gary Harrison, Patsy Bromley, guest teachers
ESTABLISHED:	1980
REGISTRATION FEE:	$6
CLASS FEE:	$6
SCHEDULE:	1½-hour sessions, 7 days per week, ongoing
AUDITING:	Permitted
AUDITING FEE:	None
CANCELLATION POLICIES:	Make-up sessions available
SCHOLARSHIPS:	Work-exchange scholarships available
NUMBER OF STUDENTS PER CLASS:	15
TOTAL STUDIO ENROLLMENT:	200
STUDENT BREAKDOWN:	60% female, 40% male; 20% under 18, 20% 18–25, 60% 26–35, 0% over 35; 10% under 6

months, 40% 1/2–1 year, 20% 1–2 years, 20% 2–3 years, 10% over 3 years

VIDEO EQUIPMENT:	Yes
VIDEO CASSETTES:	Students may purchase video cassettes.
STUDIOS:	2
DRESSING ROOMS:	2
SHOWERS:	1
FLOOR:	Marley
ACCOMPANYING INSTRUMENT:	Piano
CLASS CARD:	Yes, 20 classes per card, valid September–May, June–August
WAITING AREA:	Yes
BIOGRAPHY:	MS. BROMLEY was trained at the School of American Ballet, where she performed until she was forced to leave due to a foot injury. She moved back to her hometown and opened Terpsichore.
CLASS:	The structure of the class is designed around a central step or movement, allowing the dancer to begin with it from the barre and following it throughout the class—i.e., adagio, allegro, etc.
SUMMATION STATEMENT:	"The training of both school and company shall key on the concept of discipline. Discipline in itself shall allow for a speedier advancement within the field while translating directly into every aspect of human life-style development. We concentrate specifically on training young talented dancers in order to develop them into fine artists."

TRANSFORMATION THEATRE

Omega Arts Center
P.O. Box 1227
Jamaica Plain, MA 02130
(617) 522–8300/522–4181

PROGRAM:	Transformation Theatre
INSTRUCTORS:	Saphira Linden-Bair, Daena Giardella-Grant
REGISTRATION FEE:	None
CLASS FEE:	$105
SCHEDULE:	3-day workshop
ENTRANCE REQUIREMENTS:	Open
SCHOLARSHIPS:	Not available
BIOGRAPHY:	MS. LINDEN-BAIR is the artistic director of The-

atre Workshop Boston and of the Omega Arts Center. She has also been a leader of the Boston Sufi Order Center for Esoteric Arts and Sciences for 10 years. She has developed many training programs for theatre artists, therapists, educators, and managers in the use of theatre and meditation disciplines. Currently, she has a private counseling practice and is writing a book entitled *Transformational Theatre: In Art, In Life.* MS. GIARDELLA-GRANT works professionally as an actress and director in the Boston area, where she has been involved in numerous productions in theatre, television, and radio. She is production director of Theatre Workshop Boston. Currently, she teaches movement and acting at Emerson College. Daena is cofounder of TheraVision, a video/theatre process for training therapists, and she has a private counseling practice. She is also a leader of the Sufi Order Center for Esoteric Arts and Sciences.

CLASS:

In this workshop, participants experience the integration of a wide variety of theatre disciplines and meditation practices. Breath, voice, and body movement, character development, ensemble acting, storytelling, improvisation, and other theatre skills are introduced as tools to explore the relationship between the transpersonal and artistic realms. Sufi meditation practices and esoteric arts are taught as a means of centering and "channeling," and visualization techniques are given as ways of receiving inspiration. Also included are explorations of our image life, dreams, and fantasies as we create tales of transformation.

INDEX
INDEX
INDEX
INDEX
INDEX
INDEX
INDEX
INDEX
INDEX
INDEX
INDEX
INDEX
INDEX
INDEX
INDEX
INDEX
INDEX
INDEX
INDEX
INDEX
INDEX
INDEX
INDEX
INDEX

A

Aberkalns, Sandra 75, 76
Abernathy, R. 194
Academy Theatre School of
  Performing Arts 232
Act for Fun 4
Actors and Directors
  Lab 5, 58, 100, 120, 166
Actors Information Project 6
Actors Institute 7, 194
Actors Training and Acting Therapy
  Center of America 8
Adler, Stella, Conservatory of
  Acting 9, 194
Aesthetic Realism Foundation,
  Inc. 10, 59, 101, 121, 194
Ailey, Alvin, American Dance
  Center 60, 195
Alberini Vocal Studio 122
Alberini, Ellen 122
Alderson, William 42
Alexander, Susan 69
All, Harriet 83
Allan, Rasa 179
Alleckson, Lowell 123
Alley Theatre 234
American Academy of Dramatic
  Arts 11
American Ballet Theatre School 60
American Conservatory
  Theatre 208
American Dance Machine Training
  Facility 61
American Mime Theatre 167
American Musical and Dramatic
  Academy 11
American Renaissance Theatre 12,
  124
Amos, Wendy 60
Anderson, Pamela 91
Andrews, Nancy 54
Andrisano, Gui 83
Andros, Dick 89
Anthony, Mary, Dance Studio 62

Appet, Hugh 89
Applebaum, Neil 89
Archer, Sandra 209, 210
Aspen Music School 124
Assante, Claude 72
Avery, Peg 235
Axiltree, George 148

B

Bachmann, Sarah 151, 152
Baker, Word 148
Ballet Academy East 62,196
Ballet Hispanico School of
  Dance 63, 196
Barak, Ari 218
Barak, Ofra 89
Barbeau, Francois 238
Bardakh, Stan 175, 187
Barentyne, Ross 125
Barnes, Ruth 69
Barnett, Gina 24, 25
Barr, Tony 215
Barracuda, Karen 75, 76
Barry, B.H. 16
Bassat, Shirley 89
Beck, Jill 75
Becker, Bruce 91
Becker, Paula Borkum 240
Beckett, Michael 34
Beeler, Eric 84
Benjamin, Theo 91
Bennett, Fran 208, 209
Benthien, Simone 94
Berghof, Herbert 34, 179
Berkeley, Edward 16
Berl, Kathe 179
Bernard, Andrea 22
Black, Phil 64
Black, Phil, Dance Studio 64
Black, Robin 64
Blake, Leslie Hoban 13, 101, 102
Blitz, Rusty 189
Blumenfeld, Bob 102

Bogden, John 54
Bond Street Theatre Coalition 14, 168
Borough, Beverly 65
Bostic, Ron 85
Bousard, Joe 148
Bowe, Florence 11
Brendel, Jane 71
Brick, James 31
Bridgman, Art 89
British-American Acting Academy 15
Britte, Jean Pol 238
Broadcast Talent Workshops 235
Bromley, Patsy 241, 242
Brookes, Jacqueline 16
Brooks, Dick 182, 183
Brown, Beverly 66
Brown, Beverly, Dancenter 66
Brown, Bill 84
Brown, Deloras 60
Brown, Marc 54
Brown, Tony 169, 170
Broyles, Douglas 103
Burchill, Emily 126
Burmann, Wilhem 82
Burns, Linda Amiel 160
Bynum, Brenda 232

C

Caldwell, Doug 227
Calzada, Alba 64
Cameron, Sandra 89
Canner, Barbara 89
Caplan, Roberta 89
Carmel, Lisa 19, 170, 171
Carlberg, Norman 11
Carleton, Paul 218, 219
Carpenter, Margot 59
Carr, Kate 54
Carter, Brian 15
Cartwright, Hilary 82

Cavalier, Janice 127
Center for Speech and Theatre Arts 103
Cesbron, Virginia 63
Chapline, Robert 238
Charisse, Nenette 61
Chelsi, Lawrence 129
Chismar, Nancy 61
Christopher, Robert 60
Christopher, Russell 130
Circle in the Square Theatre School 16
Clark, Barbara 22
Clarke, Shirley 190
Classical Ballet Cambridge, Inc. 236
Classical Voice Training 130
Clement, Nansi 60
Cohen, David 38
Colby, Rita, Ballet School 67
Cole, Barbara 42, 60
Collier, Bob 18
Collier, Bob, Success Seminars 18
Collins, Jean Marie 232, 233
Colton, Barbara 16
Comedy Performers Studio 19, 170
Confrontations on Casting 20
Conway, Carol 68, 69
Conway, Carol School of Dance 68
Cook, Ray 75, 76
Cornfield, Ellen 69
Cornish, Theresa 84
Corvino, Alfredo 72
Corvino, Andra 72
Corvino, Ernesta 72
Cotton, Anne 131
Cottrell, Jacqueline 93
Cowan, Gary 85
Coyle, Jerry 54
Critelli, Pamela 62
Cultice, Thomas 132
Cumeezi Center 172
Cunningham, Merce 69, 70
Cunningham, Merce, Studio 69
Currie, Dan 218, 219

Currier, Ruth 71
Currier, Ruth Dance Studio 71
Curtis, Paul J 167, 168
Cwikowski, Bill 24, 25

D

Daly, Joseph 42, 179
Damestoy, Sima 93
Damien, Alex 133
Dance Circle 72
Dance Classes for Children 197
Dance-June Lewis & Company 73,
   197
Dance Movement 74
Dance Notation Bureau 75
Dance Theatre of Harlem 77
Dancespace 237
Danielian, Leon 60
Darius, Laura 103
David, Clifford 46
Davis, Joan 11
De Boer, Karlyn 93
DeBlas, John 11
del Pozo, Cal 77, 78
Dell 'Arte School of Mime &
   Comedy 209
Dempster, Curt 24, 25, 173, 174
Dennehy, Dennis 64
Dennis, Rhett 85
Dennis, Sandy 34
Dennis, Sharon 100
Derra, Candace 5
DeVare, Fred 237
Dhimos, Christine 60
Dietrich, Dorothy 182, 183
Dilello, Ed 75, 76
Dillon, Elizabeth 34
Dlugoszewski, Lucia 81
Doeden, Janet 46, 114
Doolas, Rosemary 237, 238
Dorff, Dorothy 34
Doris, Virginia 75, 76
Douglas, Jan Eric 134

Drake, Jessica 21, 104, 105, 211
Drama Studio London at Berkeley,
   The 213
Drama Tree Inc. 22, 106, 134, 198
Dubno, Julia R. 62, 63
Dubsky, Dora 89
Duke, Mark 218
Duncan, Stephanie 135

E

Edmund, Jeff 85
Elmer, Todd 166
Elston, Robert 12, 124
Emmons, Shirley 135, 136
Emzig, Ken 184
English, Dennis 136
Ensemble Studio Theatre 24, 173
Ensley, Barbara 70
Ericson, Richard 16
Esper, William, Studio Inc. 26, 107,
   137
Estes, Barrie 83
Eubanks Conservatory of Music and
   Arts 214
Exercise Exchange, The 78
Expressions 27

F

Fauci, Dan 7
Fedine, Vicki 77
Feinsinger, Mary 138
Fencing Center, The 175
Ferguson, Jeff 60
Fernandez, Laura 184
Ferron, Ed 54
Fey, Jonathen 139
Fielding, Anne 10, 101, 194, 195
Fields, Michael 209, 210
Fights Are Us 176
Film Actors Workshop 215
Finch, June 70

Find Your Real Voice 139
First Amendment Comedy Theatre,
    The 177
Fischer, Kristina 107
Fischer, Ken 46, 47
Flaherty, Karen C. 178
Flanigan, Maggie 26, 27
Flomine, Debra 89
Focus Is You: Auditioning and
    Performing Workshop 29
Fond, Miriam 30
Forbes, Barbara 84
Forbes, Sam 108
Forrest, Donald 209, 210
Forsythe, Anne Marie 60
Foster, Richard 140
Fox, Ilene 75, 76
Frank, Diane 70
Frank, Penny 60
Frankel, Aaron 34, 148, 179
Frankel, Gene 31, 179
Frankel, Gene Theatre Workshop
    Inc. 31, 141, 179, 198
Frankel, Kenneth 16
Freidenberg, Carol 216

G

Gabor, Nancy 46, 47
Gal, Hillary 89
Gamson, Annabelle 90
Garcia, Mariano 93
Gardner, Clark, Studio 142
Gardner, Rita 148
Garfein, Jack 5, 166
Garner, Jerri 79
Garner's, Jerri, Dance for
    Singer-Actors Only 79
Gartenburg, Max, Studio 33
Garth, Charles 75, 76
Gates, Linda 17
Gawryn, Myrna 218, 219
Gebbia, Carmen 42

Geiwitz, Coralie 203
Gendell, Gary 42
Geraci, Frank 34
Geyer Gottlieb, Elizabeth 95, 96
Giardano, Jean 64
Giardella-Grant, Jaena 242, 243
Gillis, Margie 90
Gilmer, Betsy 232, 233
Glauner, Tom 240
Gleason, Laura 54
Godreau, Miguel 60
Goldman, Phyllis 60
Gondek, Julie 143
Goodman, Erika 58
Goodman, Gerry 32
Gordon, Diane 223
Gordon, Richard 11
Gough, Trent 20
Grabina, Susan 108, 109
Grace Notes Studio 144
Gradkowski, Richard 188
Graham, Martha, School of
    Contemporary Dance 80, 199
Greas, Christine 89
Green, Nancy 145, 146
Grimwood, Freddie 238
Grubb, Thomas 146
Guilet, Helene 11
Gullmartin, Ken 153
Gushee, Phillip 42
Gustafson, Karen 11
Guthrie, Ian 62
Guzman, Paschal 93

H

Hagan, Uta 34
Hall, Carol 148
Hall, Ralph 209, 210
Hanvik, Jan 75
Hardee, Lewis 147
Harman, Eden 218, 219
Harman, Estelle 218

Harman, Estelle, Actors
  Workshop 217
Harman, Samuel 218
Harpaz, Leah 89
Harper, Meg 70
Harrell, Rya Evans 153
Harris, Susan 218, 219
Harrison, Gary 241
Hauser, Emmy 130, 131
Hawkins, Erick 81
Hawkins, Erick, School of Dance 81
Hayden, Melissa 82
Hayden, Melissa Inc. 82
Hayden, Therese 16
Hayman-Chaffey, Susana 69
HB Studio 34, 83, 109, 148, 179,
  199
Hedwall, Deborah 24
Heefner, David Kerry 35, 36
Heinz, Judy 218
Heller, Patricia 100
Henry, Mary Pat 89
Hermes, Alice 109
Hickey, William 34
Hill, Larry 148
Hinkson, Mary 77
Hodes, Elizabeth 148
Hoffman, Jane 24
Hogan, Dan 89
Holden, Hal 34
Holdstein, Dan 93
Holmes, Prudence 110
Horde, Ellen 190
Hormann, Howard 72
Howard, Rand 81
Hudson Guild Theatre School 35
Hull, Loraine 220

I

Inglis, Ann 89
Irwin, Holly 89

Ivcich, Steve 51, 52

J

Jacker, Corrine 190
Jacobi, Henry N. 134, 149
Jacoby, Gordon A. 111, 114, 116
Java, James 237
Jefferson, Denise 60
Jerald, Gralin 223
Jhung, Finis 84
Jhung, Finis, Studio 84
Jordan, Carol 236
Jung, Audrey 5

K

Kachadurian, Gail 74
Kagen, David 7
Kahn, Hannah 90
Kahn, Michael 16
Kanter, Shauna 114
Kaplan, Genette 150
Kastendieck, Carol 11
Kayser, Chris 232, 233
Keenan, Kevin 42
Kelly, Karin 227
Kennon, Skip 42
Khindy, Stephen 175
Kipnis, Claude, Mime School 181
Kisor, Dennis 150, 151
Kline, Eric 215, 216
Knapp, Jacqueline 46, 47
Komar, Chris 70
Kominsky, Jane 91
Kostura, Annamarie 54
Kovens, Ed 44, 45
Kramer, Jim 54
Krasner, David 112
Kravitz, Barbara 93
Krieger, Mitchell 151
Krell Music Studio 223

Rodiger, Ann 75, 76
Roof, Mary 148
Rooks, Joel 26, 27
Rosen, David 6
Rosenfeld, Carol 34
Rosens, Bunny 75
Ross, Bertram 63
Ross, Carmel 46, 47
Ross, Dylan 48
Ross, Dylan, Acting Academy 48
Rotman, Leslie 75, 76
Roux, Jean Louis 238
Rowe, Dee Etta 11
Rubin, Joseph 158
Rubin, Lucille 17
Rutherford, Virginia 68, 69

S

St. James, David 11
Salbrig, Nana 237, 238
Salle Bardakh 187
Saltus Fencing Club 188
Satin, Alyssa 73
Schirle, Joan 209, 210
Schlamme, Martha 17, 148
Schneiderman, Perry 238
Schons, Alain 209, 210
School for Creative Movement 91
School of Ballet de Puerto Rico 93, 202
School of the Riverside
   Shakespeare Company 189
Schulman, Michael 15
Sciarratta, Patrick 14
Scott, Joseph K. 120
Seidman, Cliff, Studio 115
Seidman, Clifford E. 48, 115, 159
Semer, Neil 159, 160
Sergava, Katherine 34
Seto, Judith 198
Sherman, Joanna 168
Shetler, Ron 42
Shook, Karel 77

Shotwell, Judith 232, 233
Siegel, Abbie 90
Silliman, Sally 84
Silver, Fred 31, 141
Simon, Victoria 77
Simone's Jazz Classes 94
Singer, Lynn 100
Singing Experience, The 160
Slater, MaryJo 54
Smith, Christopher 53
Smith, Geddeth 106
Smith-Durham, Beryl 11
Somers, Melodie 24, 25
Sommer, Kathy 161
Speech Improvement Co., Inc.,
   The 240
Spencer, Frank 54
Spencer, Stuart 173, 174
Starck, Sue 11, 162
Stenborg, James 11
Stephenson, Albert 17
Stevenson, Holly 232, 233
Stix, John 5
Stockwell, Guy 226
Stockwell, Guy, Actor Training 226
Storefront Blitz 189
Story, June Eve 83
Strasberg, Anna 48
Strasberg, Lee, Theatre
   Institute 48, 202
Strimpell, Stephen 34
Strober, Joan 103
Studio EGG 95
Suddeth, J. Allen 176
Sumner, Carol 77
Swymer, Gayle 148

T

Talavera, Juan 225
Taliaferro, Clay 71
Taylor, Vivian 54
Terpsichore Dance
   Expressions 241

Terry, Cori 81
Testani, Grace 144, 145
Theodore, Lee 61
Third Street Music School
  Settlement 203
Thomas, Richard 89
Thompson, Peter 16
Thornton-Sherwood, Madeline 7
Tischler, Audry 90
Tokunaga Dance Studio 96
Tokunaga, Emiko 96, 97
Tokunaga, Yasuko 96, 97
Tolle, Roger 66
Topaz, Muriel 75, 76
Total Artists Workshop 50
Tots to Teens Stagemom
  Workshop 203
Towson, Toby 64
Transformation Theatre 242
Tremaine, Joe 227
Tremaine, Joe, Dance Center 227
Trezlie, Helen 11
Trules, Eric 172
Tucci, Maria 17
Tushar, Jim 148

U

Udovicki, Ani 87, 88
Urman, Joyce 201

V

Val, Edwige 85
Vaughan, Steve 176
Vernon, Michael 60
Villamil, Jackie 90
Vinson, Clyde 51, 116
Vinson, Clyde, Studios 51, 116

W

Waldron, Martin 107
Wallace, Barbara 90

Walman, Jerome 8, 9
Walton, Fred 227
Wanich, Nancy 90
Ward, Cathy 81
Weiner, Hattie 91
Weiner, Jack 91
Weist, Dwight 54
Weist-Barron School of
  Television 54, 204
Welter, Bob 181
White, Vivian 73
Wideman, Beverly 42
Wilcox, Tamara 53
Wilde, Patricia 60
Williamson, Lloyd 34
Wilson, Carrie 121
Wilson, Randall 68, 69
Winder, Susan 163
Winn, B. 194
Wischner-Reder, Claudia 90
Witcover, Walt 34, 179
Women's Interart 190
Wong, Mel 90
Woolever, Harry 11
Wray, Suzanne 87, 88
Wyeth, Syms 100
Wylde, Peter 238

Y

Yakim, Mina 17, 184
Yakim, Moni 17, 184
Young, Arabella Hong 148
Youskevitch, Anna 85
Yusim, Marat 39

Z

Zinn, Randolyn 17
Zittel, Greg 42, 43
Zuckerman, Ira 43, 44
Zuckerman, Stephen 17